Cosmopolitani

STUDIES IN SOCIAL AND POLITICAL THOUGHT 15

STUDIES IN SOCIAL AND POLITICAL THOUGHT
Editor: Gerard Delanty, *University of Liverpool*

This series publishes peer-reviewed scholarly books on all aspects of social and political thought. It will be of interest to scholars and advanced students working in the areas of social theory and sociology, the history of ideas, philosophy, political and legal theory, anthropological and cultural theory. Works of individual scholarship will have preference for inclusion in the series, but appropriate co- or multi-authored works and edited volumes of outstanding quality or exceptional merit will also be included. The series will also consider English translations of major works in other languages.

Challenging and intellectually innovative books are particularly welcome on the history of social and political theory; modernity and the social and human sciences; major historical or contemporary thinkers; the philosophy of the social sciences; theoretical issues on the transformation of contemporary society; social change and European societies.

It is not series policy to publish textbooks, research reports, empirical case studies, conference proceedings or books of an essayist or polemical nature.

Cosmopolitanism and Europe

EDITED BY CHRIS RUMFORD

LIVERPOOL UNIVERSITY PRESS

First published 2007 by
Liverpool University Press
4 Cambridge Street
Liverpool
L69 7ZU

Copyright © 2007 Liverpool University Press

British Library Cataloguing-in-Publication Data
A British Library CIP Record is available

ISBN 978-1-84631-046-1 hardback
      978-1-84631-047-8 paperback

Typeset in Plantin by R. J. Footring Ltd, Derby
Printed and bound in the European Union by
Bell & Bain Ltd, Glasgow

Contents

Contents

Contributors

Daniele Archibugi is a Research Director at the Italian National Research Council in Rome, and Professor of Innovation, Governance and Public Policy at Birkbeck College, University of London, UK. His books include *Cosmopolitan Democracy: An Agenda for a New World Order* and *Reimagining Political Community* (both co-edited with David Held) and the edited collection *Debating Cosmopolitics*. In his forthcoming book *A World of Democracy* he reassesses the cosmopolitan challenge for the twenty-first century.

Barrie Axford is Professor of Politics at Oxford Brookes University, UK. His books include *The Global System: Politics Economics and Culture*; *Politics: An Introduction* (with Gary Browning, Richard Huggins and Ben Rosamond); and *New Media and Politics* (coedited with Richard Huggins). He is working currently on several new books: *Theories of Globalization*, the third edition of *Politics: An Introduction* and *Globalization in One Country*.

Ulrich Beck is Professor of Sociology at the University of Munich, Germany, and the British Journal of Sociology Visiting Centennial Professor at the London School of Economics and Political Science, UK. His books include *World Risk Society*; *Power in the Global Age*; *The Cosmopolitan Vision*; and *Cosmopolitan Europe* (with Edgar Grande). His books have been translated into thirty-five languages.

Vivienne Boon is a Duncan Norman Research Scholar at the University of Liverpool, UK. She is currently finishing her doctoral thesis provisionally entitled *On the Problem of Otherness in the Writings of Jürgen Habermas on Europe*. She has recently edited a special edition of the *European Journal of Social Theory* (with

Robert Fine), entitled *Cosmopolitanism: Between Past and Future*, and has written articles on issues of cosmopolitanism with Robert Fine and Gerard Delanty.

Gerard Delanty is Professor of Sociology, University of Liverpool, UK. He is editor of the *European Journal of Social Theory* and author of ten books and editor of five, including *Inventing Europe*; *Social Science*; *Social Theory in a Changing World*; *Citizenship in a Global Age*; *Community*; *Rethinking Europe: Social Theory and the Implications of Europeanization* (with Chris Rumford); *Handbook of Contemporary European Social Theory* and (with Krishan Kumar) *The Handbook of Nations and Nationalism*.

William Haller is an Assistant Professor in the Department of Sociology and Anthropology at Clemson University, South Carolina, USA. He has published articles in the *American Journal of Sociology*, *Ethnic and Racial Studies*, *American Sociological Review* and *Research in Stratification and Social Mobility*, and contributed to *The Handbook of Economic Sociology*.

Richard Huggins is Assistant Dean of Social Sciences and Law, Oxford Brookes University, UK. Recent publications include *Politics: An Introduction* (with Barrie Axford, Gary Browning and Ben Rosamond) and *New Media and Politics* (edited with Barrie Axford). He acted as consultant editor for *Encyclopedia of the City*, and has authored articles in *Innovations*; *Javnost*; *Telematics and Informatics*; *Drugs, Policy, Prevention and Education*; and *Parliamentary Brief*.

Paul Jones is Lecturer in Sociology at the University of Liverpool, UK. His research addresses the politicization of collective identities, with a focus on architecture, space and power. He has recently published articles in journals including *Sociology, European Journal of Social Theory* and *Local Economy*, and he is completing a book entitled *The Sociology of Architecture: Constructing Identities*.

Eleonore Kofman is Professor of Gender, Migration and Citizenship at Middlesex University, UK. Her books include the coauthored *Gender and International Migration in Europe*, the coedited *Globalization: Theory and Practice*, and *Mapping Women Making Politics*. She is preparing a coedited book entitled *Branding Cities and Cultural Borders: Cosmopolitanism, Parochialism and Social Change*.

Daniel Levy is Associate Professor in the Department of Sociology at the State University of New York – Stony Brook, USA. His books include *The Holocaust and Memory in the Global Age* (with Natan Sznaider), *Challenging Ethnic Citizenship:*

German and Israeli Perspectives on Immigration (coedited with Yfaat Weiss) and *Old Europe, New Europe, Core Europe: Transatlantic Relations After the Iraq War* (coedited with Max Pensky and John Torpey).

Kate Nash is Senior Lecturer in Political Sociology at Goldsmiths College, University of London, UK. She is the author of *Contemporary Political Sociology*, editor of *Readings in Contemporary Political Sociology* and coeditor (with Alan Scott) of *The Blackwell Companion to Political Sociology*. She is currently writing *The Cultural Politics of Global Human Rights*.

Maurice Roche is Reader in Sociology at the University of Sheffield, UK. His books include *Rethinking Citizenship: Welfare, Ideology and Change in Modern Society*; *European Citizenship and Social Exclusion* (coedited with Rik van Berkel); and *Mega-Events and Modernity: Olympics and Expos in the Growth of Global Culture*. He is currently working on a book on the sociology of the European Union.

Victor Roudometof is Assistant Professor in the Department of Social and Political Sciences at the University of Cyprus. He is the author of *Nationalism, Globalization and Orthodoxy* and *Collective Memory, National Identity and Ethnic Conflict*. His latest volume is *Eastern Orthodoxy in a Global Age*, coedited with Alexander Agadjanian and Jerry Pankhurst. Currently he is editing a volume on the Orthodox Church of Greece.

Maria Rovisco is a Postdoctoral Research Fellow at the Department of Sociology, ISCTE – University of Lisbon. She has published articles on the tradition of European films of voyage, cosmopolitanism and questions of migration, boundaries and collective identity formation. She is currently coediting the book *Cosmopolitanism in Practice*.

Chris Rumford is Senior Lecturer in Political Sociology at Royal Holloway, University of London. His books include *Rethinking Europe: Social Theory and the Implications of Europeanization* (with Gerard Delanty), *The European Union: A Political Sociology* and *European Cohesion? Contradictions in EU Integration*. He is currently editing *The Sage Handbook of European Studies* and completing a book entitled *Cosmopolitan Spaces: Europe, Globalization, Theory*.

Nick Stevenson is Reader in Cultural Sociology at the University of Nottingham, UK. His publications include *Understanding Media Cultures, Cultural Citizenship*, and *David Bowie: Fame, Sound and Vision*. He is currently working on questions of education and cultural citizenship.

List of Contributors

Natan Sznaider is Professor of Sociology at the School of Behavioral Sciences at the Academic College of Tel-Aviv-Yaffo, Israel. His books include *The Compassionate Temperament: Care and Cruelty in Modern Society* and *The Holocaust and Memory in the Global Age* (with Daniel Levy). He is coeditor *Global America: The Cultural Consequences of Globalization* (with Ulrich Beck and Rainer Winter).

F. Peter Wagner currently teaches in the School of Public and International Affairs, North Carolina State University, USA. His books include a monograph on Rudolf Hilferding and a coedited volume on *fin-de-siècle* Vienna. He has also published on south-eastern Europe, and the European and international transformation after 1989/1991. He is presently editing a book on Romania in the European Union.

Editor's acknowledgements

I would like to thank all those who attended the 'Cosmopolitanism and Europe' conference held in the Department of Politics and International Relations at Royal Holloway, University of London, in April 2004, the event which provided the starting point for this volume. Thanks also to Gerard Delanty, Ray Lee and Ralph Footring for their help during the preparation of this book, and to Anthony Cond at Liverpool University Press.

CHAPTER 1

Introduction: Cosmopolitanism and Europe

Chris Rumford

Cosmopolitanism is again a key theme in the social sciences, although this is not to say that there exists much consensus on what constitutes cosmopolitanism, who can be described as cosmopolitan or where cosmopolitanism is to be found. The recent revival of interest in cosmopolitanism has deeply divided opinion in the social sciences.[1] Viewed by some as an idea whose time has come and a welcome antidote to the nationalism that pervades the political and sociological imagination, it has received a more ambivalent response from those who see it either as an attempt to legitimize individualism or as the latest attempt to rescue a faltering theory inspired by 'the cultural turn' or to breathe new life into globalization studies. Cosmopolitanism is criticized by some for its utopianism, idealism or elitism, and is taken to task for its supposed association with neo-liberalism and the values associated with 'good governance'; by others, it is commended for its critique of nationalism, its subversion of the territorialist assumptions of much contemporary social and political thought, and its potential inclusivity and embrace of 'otherness'. Cosmopolitanism, it may be concluded, can be all things to all people. Is this the secret of its resurgence: an infinitely flexible mission statement for politics in the global age; a badge of identity politics, deference to difference and the high value placed on plurality?

Cosmopolitanism (re)enters the scene at a time when social scientists are coming to terms with an ever-expanding number of 'theories of the present' (Shields 2006): late capitalism, reflexive modernity, second modernity, global age,

---

1 The growing interest in cosmopolitanism can be gauged from the increasing number of publications dealing with the topic, and also by the number of journals devoting special issues to this theme. See for example: *British Journal of Sociology*, 57(1) (2006); *Innovation: European Journal of Social Science Research*, 18(1) (2005); *Theory, Culture and Society*, 19(1–2) (2002); *Public Culture*, 12(3) (2000); and *Global Society*, 14(4) (2000).

network society and world risk society have been added to earlier designations such as post-Fordism, post-industrial society, postmodernity and knowledge society. In this sense the rise to popularity of cosmopolitanism may be viewed as an unwelcome addition to an already overcrowded field and as making it more difficult for social scientists to gain purchase on the vexed question of how best to characterize the times in which we live. In addition, cosmopolitanism is often associated with a group of terms which are interlinked and sometimes used interchangeably: globalization, trans-nationalism, post-nationalism, multiculturalism. A key question, then, would be: what is distinctive about cosmopolitanism? Furthermore, to what extent can it help us to make sense of developments in contemporary Europe and the place of Europe in the world?

To make matters more complicated, there is not just one version of cosmopolitanism. As such, it is preferable to talk of cosmopolitanisms, in the plural. Moreover, the various cosmopolitanisms are not necessarily compatible: they do not all advocate forms of world citizenship or global justice, or even share a common political, philosophical or social foundation. It is not even the case that they share a concern with global consciousness or belonging. A couple of decades of thinking about globalization has both provided new ways of conceiving the globe and undermined the universalist presumptions of early forms of cosmopolitanism. The recent wave of cosmopolitan theorizing has revealed a variety of positions, ranging from Daniele Archibugi and David Held's neo-Kantian 'cosmopolitan democracy' thesis to Ulrich Beck's ideas on 'cosmopolitanization', and encompasses a host of interpretations, which focus on mobilities, multiple belongings, individual identity, global justice and post-national community, for example. The cosmopolitan kaleidoscope is made more vivid by a further series of debates on whether cosmopolitanism should be understood as a political philosophy, an individual orientation to the world, a societal condition, a political project or a pejorative designation (see Vertovec and Cohen 2002). Cosmopolitanism thus has the potential to confuse and fragment. Is there any value in a concept which can mean so many different things, and can be used in different ways, and to different ends? Clearly, in a book entitled *Cosmopolitanism and Europe* the answer has to be a resounding 'yes', but the grounds for such an optimistic position have to be established at the outset. What, then, is the value of cosmopolitanism?

Cosmopolitanism draws attention to new relationships between the individual, the community and the world – and to the fact that these relationships are fluid and evolving. In other words, cosmopolitanism highlights both that social transformation is occurring and also that there is an increasing awareness that we are caught up in a transformative process (or processes). Moreover, cosmopolitanism signals that there are now many models for imagining the world, and the place of the individual in it, and that these models coexist and may be conflictual. In other words, cosmopolitanism implies a recognition that the world is being transformed and that the direction this transformation takes is open and contingent. Cosmopolitanism thus requires us all to negotiate our relationships to the communities we live in (or live in proximity to), their relationship to others, how they are bordered and bounded, and how we move between them. Cosmopolitanism requires us to recognize that we are all positioned simultaneously as outsiders and insiders, as individuals and group members, as self and the other, as local and global. Cosmopolitanism is about relativizing our place within the global frame, positioning ourselves in relation to communities, crossing and recrossing territorial and community borders. It is also about reconciling increasing self-autonomy with a multiplicity of governance regimes and about electing to live in some communities while at the same time negotiating with others that may make claims on our allegiances.

It has to be acknowledged that there are potential problems associated with making definitive statements about how cosmopolitanism should be understood. One might be that cosmopolitanism as understood here is but one more variation on the theme, and that yet another contribution to an already crowded field is not necessary. This objection can be countered by pointing out that the approach outlined here does not preclude others. It was stated above that cosmopolitanism recognizes that there will exist a multiplicity of interpretative approaches and we should no longer all expect to view the world from the same vantage point. A second problem may well be more relevant to the current project, that is, an edited volume comprising essays from a number of contributors. It could be objected that the definition of cosmopolitanism offered above may not square with the approaches adopted by the various authors collected here. In response to this, I can only say that the benefits of outlining a productive framework of understanding outweigh the costs of disagreement with individual authors. Inevitably, not everybody would agree with the approach advanced here, nor would I wish them to. I do believe, however, that, through the lens of cosmopolitanism adopted in this Introduction, it is possible to better contextualize all the contributions to the book.

The European context

In addition to an interest in cosmopolitanism in general, there has been a marked interest in cosmopolitanism specifically in the European context (Delanty 2005; Delanty and Rumford 2005; Entrikin 2003; Eriksen 2005). Moreover, there is a growing literature on the cosmopolitan credentials of the European Union (EU), especially in relation to its emerging role as an actor in global governance, but also in relation to its supranational regulatory powers and its institutionalization

3

of European citizenship, for example. This interest is not surprising, as the EU does exhibit some cosmopolitan qualities. According to Daniele Archibugi, 'the first international model which begins to resemble the cosmopolitan model is the European Union' (Archibugi 1998: 219). At the same time, we must bear in mind that the EU does not see itself as a cosmopolitan project. Indeed, the absence of a cosmopolitan dimension to the EU's self-image is striking: EU policy-makers almost never refer to cosmopolitanism (see below); EU politicians tend not to allude to Europeans as cosmopolitans; and reports and other publications of the EU eschew the language of cosmopolitanism. The absence of a cosmopolitan discourse emanating from the EU is even more surprising given that the European Commission has spent more than a decade attempting to give substance to the idea of European citizenship, to invigorate the idea of European civil society and to export the 'European model of society' to its near abroad and beyond.

There are, of course, exceptions to this rule, though they are few. One is the report entitled *The Spiritual and Cultural Dimension of Europe* (Biedenkopf *et al.* 2004), which is dealt with in detail by Maria Rovisco in Chapter 12. Another example is to be found in the speeches of former Commissioner (for Trade) Pascal Lamy, who talks occasionally of 'cosmopolitics'. For example, in a lecture delivered at the London School of Economics in 2001 entitled 'Harnessing globalization, do we need cosmopolitics?' (Lamy 2001), Lamy voices his dissatisfaction with the term 'governance', which 'sounds a little too much like control', but at the same time acknowledges that conventional notions of politics 'do not capture the essence' of governance. He invokes a new term, 'cosmopolitics', to fill this conceptual gap. But his idea of 'cosmopolitics' is more than a substitute for the familiar terms in which the politics of governance are inscribed. It does have a strong cosmopolitan connotation, in that it signifies an orientation to:

> world politics, itself the product of the weakening of 'identity' that in turn has resulted from globalization itself. In part, the notion of cosmopolitics describes a new world that is coming into being. But in part, cosmopolitics is needed in this new world to organize and mediate between different interests. (Lamy 2001)

So Lamy's cosmopolitics is an attempt to capture both the polycentric and diffuse nature of global governance and the need to incorporate multiple perspectives in any world view. In sum, 'cosmopolitics may simply be about thinking globally, and acting locally' and in Lamy's assessment the EU should adopt this *Weltordungspolitik*.

These exceptions apart, there appears to be a curious mismatch between the perceived cosmopolitanism of the EU in social science accounts of the dynamics of contemporary Europe and the declared intentions of the EU itself. This is a theme that is investigated by several of the contributors to this volume. However, it is necessary to say something about it at this point, as it appears to be a major issue for any account of cosmopolitanism and Europe. The relationship between cosmopolitanism and Europe is certainly made more confusing by the lack of consensus on what cosmopolitanism is (although this by itself does not explain its absence from EU discourse). There are two plausible explanations for the mismatch between the EU's self-image and the idea that it represents 'actually existing' cosmopolitanism.

The first explanation is that while the EU displays cosmopolitan qualities (its role in funding humanitarian efforts, institutionalization of post-national citizenship, advocacy of global environmental regimes, etc.) the fact that this equates to cosmopolitanism is not recognized for what it is by EU representatives and officials. In other words, the EU may act in a way that can be described as cosmopolitan but this is not the interpretation or designation favoured by EU institutions, which may prefer the terms 'humanitarian' or 'globally aware', for instance. A good example of this is contained in the report produced by a former French finance minister, Dominique Strauss-Kahn, who was commissioned in January 2003 by the then Commission President, Romano Prodi, to establish a round table to investigate the viability of a 'European model of development'. He writes that the European social model should defend the 'dignity of all human beings, not just of Europeans' (Strauss-Khan 2004) but, significantly, he does not label this perspective 'cosmopolitan' (Delanty and Rumford 2005).

A second explanation for the EU not acknowledging its incipient cosmopolitanism is that, for some reason, it is wary of the term. It could be that the EU does not want to promote a cosmopolitan identity, or want Europeans to feel themselves to be cosmopolitan, for fear that this will lessen their already weak attachment to the European project. After all, there is no reason why trans-national solidarities have to cease at the external borders of the EU. Cosmopolitanism cannot be domesticated and delimited to a European sphere of operation. Furthermore, it is possible that the EU sees a difficulty in 'selling' the idea of further integration to member states if European citizens perceive the EU as working on behalf of all humanity rather than promoting the interests of Europeans. It is also possible that the EU feels that it would be more difficult to secure Europe's borders and thereby block the flow of terrorists, drug traffickers and illegal immigrants if it were to advocate citizenship of the world.

All of this is speculation on a topic which presents European studies with a conundrum: to what extent is the EU cosmopolitan, and what is at stake if it is to become more of a cosmopolitan project? To begin to address this issue we would need to ask additional questions. Is a cosmopolitan Europe desirable? What form would a cosmopolitan Europe take?

Three recent accounts of cosmopolitanism and Europe

In order to explore these issues more thoroughly, I will examine three examples of recent attempts to portray Europe (or the future of Europe) as cosmopolitan. All three examples are newspaper articles by leading commentators on European affairs and each presents a case for a cosmopolitan Europe. The three pieces are by Ulrich Beck and Anthony Giddens ('Nationalism has now become the enemy of Europe's nations', published in *The Guardian* on 4 October 2005), Jeremy Rifkin ('This is the first attempt to create a global consciousness', also published in *The Guardian*, on 16 November 2004) and Jürgen Habermas and Jacques Derrida ('February 15, or, what binds Europeans together', published in both *Frankfurter Allgemeine Zeitung* and *La Liberation* on 31 May 2003). It is interesting to note that the idea of a cosmopolitan Europe has registered strongly in popular discourse and that there is clearly felt to be some resonance between cosmopolitanism and Europe (some would go further and see cosmopolitanism and Europe as natural bedfellows) at a time when the EU still eschews a cosmopolitan identity.

The puzzle of the EU's reluctance to embrace cosmopolitanism is perhaps less perplexing if one takes the view that the EU actually works to shore up European nation states rather than overwhelm them (Meyer 2001; Milward 1993). On this reading, from the EU's perspective a more cosmopolitan orientation would not serve the interests of its member states and therefore is not an attractive prospect. Yet this line of thinking is skewed towards an intergovernmental interpretation of the EU and ignores recent attempts by the European Commission to downgrade the role of the member states in a new vision of multi-agency European governance (Armstrong 2002; European Commission 2001). In other words, there is enough evidence to suggest that the European Commission is happy to act as 'policy entrepreneur' for ideas which promote supranationality over member states' interests. Why, then, has the Commission not taken up cosmopolitanism as a stick with which to beat the member states?

The answer to this question may reside in the fact that contemporary interpretations of the nature and dynamics of the EU are rooted in ways of thinking which see the nation state as the baseline of all political analysis. The questions asked of the EU typically include the following: What type of state does the EU represent? How can its state-like qualities best be understood? Is the EU building a supra- or super-state? The EU is conceived as becoming more like a state or as departing in a major way from the norms of the nation state – either way, it is the nation state which forms the point of reference for understanding the EU (Delanty and Rumford 2005). This statist imaginary leaves little room for cosmopolitanism, especially when it is conceived as a challenge to the autonomy of the nation state.

In their newspaper article Beck and Giddens turn this logic around and argue that the EU works to advance the interests of member states. Membership of the EU involves exchanging national sovereignty for 'real power' and economic success: 'the EU is better placed to advance national interests than nations could possibly do acting alone' (Beck and Giddens 2005). We need to start to see the EU as a new kind of cosmopolitan project, they argue, not one which is rooted in the belief that the future of the EU requires it to undermine a Europe of nations, nor one which sees the EU as an incomplete federal entity (neither one thing nor the other). In other words, they argue against the incompatibility of the idea of a Europe of nation states and a vision of a cosmopolitan Europe.

Beck and Giddens advance a novel position. The context within which European cosmopolitanism is emerging is a Europe where the global role of the EU is still very much in formation, and nationalism is seen less and less as a solution to the domestic social and economic problems faced by European countries. An embrace of cosmopolitanism could emerge through the EU's orientation towards the rest of the world. This, however, remains a potential only: 'the European Union can be a, if not the, major influence on the global scene in the current century' (Beck and Giddens 2005). The realization of this potential depends very much on the future enlargement of the EU and its openness to ideas emanating from the rest of the world. Beck and Giddens believe that European countries realize that nationalism is no longer a safe haven (even if they do not flaunt this rationality). It is the EU that provides security for European nation states: 'nationalist or isolationist thinking can be the worst enemy of the nation and its interests' (Beck and Giddens 2005). On this view, Europe is fertile ground for the development of cosmopolitanism. A cosmopolitan Europe can be constructed upon the foundations of a Europe of national differences coupled with a new sense of global mission rooted in a concern to promote peace, democracy and open markets. A cosmopolitan Europe turns its national diversity to its own advantage, allowing for the survival of the nation state at the same time as advancing a Europe-wide model of social justice. This requires the EU to be more open, flexible and reflexive, and much less introspective, defensive and solipsistic.

This idea of the EU also appeals to Rifkin. His interpretation of Europe's cosmopolitanism is rooted in the Kantian tradition. He is particularly taken with the EU's concern with the wider world and how this concern is framed within the (now stillborn) constitutional treaty. Rifkin's claims may be exaggerated – the 'European Dream' as a 'fully articulated vision of global consciousness' and a 'watershed in human thought' – but the global concerns and outward projection of European values are portrayed accurately enough. In Rifkin's view, the EU has successfully transcended the territorial restrictions inherent in nationally ordered politics. The aims of the European constitution are much more cosmopolitan: to 'respect human diversity, promote inclusivity, foster quality of life, pursue sustainable development, and build a perpetual peace' (Rifkin 2004b). It is in this sense that the 'European Dream' articulates a vision of global consciousness. Rifkin's newspaper article is interesting not least because it highlights the EU's transcendence of territorial governance and signals the growing cosmopolitan commitments of the EU without actually using the 'c' word, although it does use suggestive Kantian imagery. The article draws upon the arguments developed more fully in Rifkin's book *The European Dream* (Rifkin 2004a), in which he roots the post-war European order in a Kantian framework of cooperation rather than conflict, laying the ground for a 'cosmopolitan order' based on 'mutual respect, empathy, and a recognition of "the other"' (Rifkin 2004a: 298).

The interventions by both Beck and Giddens and Rifkin can be read as cosmopolitan contributions to two of the debates which have come to define the study of Europe in the post-Cold War period. These are: the impulse to define European identity; and the puzzle of exactly what kind of 'state' the EU is becoming. However, since the terrorist attacks in the US of 11 September 2001 it is possible to identify an emerging third key theme, which these recent cosmopolitan interventions also highlight very well: that is, the need to define Europe in distinction from the US. For Rifkin, the 'European Dream' is displacing its US counterpart and it is Europe that offers the more compelling role model for the twenty-first century. For Beck and Giddens, Europe has responded to the threat of globalization by seeking to overcome its nation state fragmentation by accommodating difference. As Andrew Moravcsik points out in his review of Rifkin's book, whereas the Europeans have sought a trans-national solution to globalization, the Americans have responded by 'reasserting international legal autonomy' and have chosen unilateralism over multilateralism (Moravcsik 2004). The most celebrated and widely read attempt to combine cosmopolitanism with alternatives to Americanism (or with naked anti-Americanism on some interpretations) is the intervention by Jürgen Habermas and Jacques Derrida published shortly after the US-led invasion of Iraq in 2003.

The need to crystallize a European identity and endow the EU with state-like qualities in order that it can formulate a common foreign policy in opposition to that of the US is at the heart of Habermas and Derrida's call for a 'core' European response to the war in Iraq. The article, entitled 'February 15, or, what binds European together', which was written by Habermas but also signed by Derrida, identifies the need for a 'core' Europe constructed upon shared Enlightenment values to act as a European vanguard which could forge an EU capable of acting as a global player and of opposing US aggression in Iraq. In its attempt to promote a common European identity, the article prioritizes Europe-building over cosmopolitanism. The Habermas–Derrida article (raised to the status of a 'manifesto' by their supporters) proceeds from rather shaky foundations. It assumes that Europe has an identity crisis because it does not have a singular identity. It further assumes that Europe has a 'core', comprising France, Germany and a few others, and that these countries can draw upon a shared set of cultural values. The idea is that 'core' Europe should act as a locomotive of integration, and a group of 'followers' (the rest of Europe) will eventually take their cue from this lead. In formulating this idea, Habermas and Derrida reproduce US attempts to polarize 'old' and 'new' Europe, and in framing the issue of European identity in these terms Habermas and Derrida fall into a rather obvious trap. The impulse to search for an elusive European identity is hamstrung by an inability to think of the EU in terms other than that of a state. More than this, they advance the idea that the EU *should* become more state like. It is hard to imagine Europeans, other than the political elites in France and Germany perhaps, agreeing that the 'big idea' the EU is searching for in order to create a meaningful political community is Europe as a super-state. Promoting a narrowly defined and exclusionary sense of identity coupled with old-style state-building as solutions to the EU's current problems, particularly its inability to become an effective actor in global politics, is more conservative than cosmopolitan.

According to Habermas and Derrida, in terms of a common political identity, 'core' Europe can cite secularization, trust in the state coupled with scepticism towards markets, sensitivity to 'the paradoxes of progress' (a wonderful phrase which celebrates the pluralism of European political party systems), preference for forms of social solidarity represented by the welfare state, and desire for a multilateral world order based on international law. Habermas and Derrida are correct to assert that these are values that many Europeans can identify with. However, they are also values that half the world can identify with: secular, Enlightenment and social democratic traditions are rooted in many modern societies. Equally important, they are not values which mark off 'core' Europe from the rest. The line of argument pursued by Habermas and Derrida is that all Europeans can associate with these values. The point that needs making is not so much that New Zealanders and Canadians share them too (Garton Ash and Dahrendorf 2005) but that European countries can share these values and yet *still want to act in a different way*. Sharing an Enlightenment heritage does automatically lead to a common foreign policy.

There is a heavy dose of Euro-nationalism in the Habermas–Derrida position and the argument, from Enlightenment values all the way down, points to the absence of a European super-state as the solution to understanding the EU's foreign policy failures. Again, possession of 'core' European values is seen to be the key: 'only the core European nations are ready to endow the EU with certain qualities of a state' (Habermas and Derrida 2003). So, not only do Spain, the UK and other members of 'new Europe' align themselves with the US in its intervention in Iraq, thereby precluding a common European response, but they are also holding back the development of a state-like EU.

The preoccupation with state-building resonates with Habermas and Derrida's interpretation of the anti-war demonstrations of 15 February 2003 as signalling the birth of a European public sphere. In the hands of other commentators, notably Strauss-Kahn, this rhetoric can be cranked up a further notch and signs of a nascent European public sphere can be mistaken for the wonders of nation-building: 'On Saturday, February 15, 2003, a nation was born in the streets. This nation is the European nation' (quoted in Levy *et al.* 2005: xvi). Habermas and Derrida (and Strauss-Kahn) are happy to ignore the fact that those demonstrations took place in many cities across the world. In reality, the European credentials of this public sphere are called into question by the fact that demonstrations took place in Tokyo, Sydney, Sao Paulo, Moscow and many other places. According to one critic of Habermas and Derrida, the anti-war protests 'may signal the emergence of a *global* public, of which European publics are wings, but whose heart may lie in the Southern Hemisphere' (Young 2005: 154). Ignoring the global nature of this protest does not square with the 'new European political responsibilities beyond any Eurocentrism' claimed by Habermas and Derrida.

Their rather conservative views on European identity and state-building notwithstanding, the most significant aspect of the Habermas–Derrida rallying call to Europe is its muted cosmopolitanism. The idea that Europe's identity could ever embrace cosmopolitanism, while hinted at, is never formulated with any conviction. Moreover, cosmopolitanism, when it does appear timidly from behind the idea of EU as a putative global actor, is 'cosmo-lite' – applying to Europeans but not reaching out to the rest of the world. European identity is here conceived as a 'consciousness of a shared political fate, and the prospect of a common future', with the emphasis very much on a *European* political fate and a common *European* future. According to Habermas and Derrida this will allow 'the citizens of one nation' to 'regard the citizens of another nation as fundamentally "one of us"'. However, as we have seen, the cosmopolitan dimension to the 'manifesto' struggles to engage with the wider world. In its 'cosmo-lite' variety, cosmopolitanism becomes a badge of common European identity and an alternative to a Europe of nation states. In other words, a cosmopolitan Europe is an inward-looking Europe: 'cosmo-lite' produces a Europe which celebrates its internal diversity, its history of conflict (class struggle, church versus state, urban/rural) and its institutionalization of differences. However, cosmopolitanism as a means of identifying with the wider world is virtually non-existent, amounting to no more than a passing reference to the Kantian tradition and a suggestion that Europe could work to 'defend and promote a cosmopolitan order on the basis of international law'.

The cosmopolitan credentials of the Habermas–Derrida 'manifesto' are queried by Iris Marion Young, who asks 'just how cosmopolitan is the stance taken?' (Young 2005: 153). She suggests that to observers in the rest of the world 'the philosophers' appeal may look more like a re-centring of Europe than the invocation of an inclusive global democracy' (Young 2005: 153). She also makes the pertinent point that invoking a European identity may inhibit solidarity with those far away. The more exclusively European the identity, the less cosmopolitan is its potential. The difficulty for Habermas and Derrida is that in attempting to give form to a European political identity which could lead to a common foreign policy, they have erred too far on the side of nationalist caution. By drawing so heavily on the imagery of state-building, they 'may reinscribe the logic of the nation-state for Europe, rather than transcend it', as Young rightly argues (Young 2005: 156). This is not a vision of Europe as a post-national constellation: it is a Europe which is as self-regarding and lacking in global vision as the much criticized US.

In the run-up to the invasion of Iraq the governments of eight European countries supported the US initiative. In addition to the UK, a more consistent supporter of US foreign policy, Spain, Portugal, Poland, Hungary, the Czech Republic, Italy and Denmark signed the 'letter of the eight' pledging support to the US, of 30 January 2003. Many of these countries are at the heart of European affairs and, even if their citizens were broadly opposed to the invasion (as manifested by the demonstrations of 15 February), taken together they represent a significant body of international support for the US. By comparison, France and Germany appeared rather isolated and impotent. In this context it is worth noting that it was Turkey which offered the most meaningful European opposition to the US war effort, by refusing US troops access to its territory for the purpose of launching a land invasion. Interestingly, this did not lead to Turkey being situated in 'core' Europe by France and Germany.

Turkey aside, governmental support for the invasion of Iraq across Europe was seized upon by the US in an attempt to isolate France and Germany still further, and resulted in a recasting of the idea of Europe: 'the centre of gravity is shifting to the east', remarked Donald Rumsfeld (as reported in the media on 23 January 2003), 'if you look at vast numbers of other countries in Europe, they're not with France and Germany ... they're with the US'. Habermas and Derrida in their 'manifesto' seek to identify cosmopolitan mechanisms for endowing the EU with a state-like sense of identity and purpose which ties citizens, civil society and foreign policy to a particular of vision of Europeanness. However, cosmopolitanism cannot be advanced by creating two Europes, old and new, the 'core' and the rest. By framing the problem in this way the Habermas–Derrida 'manifesto' risks being remembered only as a footnote to Donald Rumsfeld's too easily dismissed idea that Germany and France represent 'old Europe'.

Some concluding comments: towards a cosmopolitanism agenda for Europe

The interventions of Beck and Giddens, Rifkin, and Habermas and Derrida have made cosmopolitanism much more visible and have added a valuable dimension to public debate on European identity and the role of the EU in the world. In the public sphere, if not in the institutions of the EU itself, cosmopolitanism is gaining a purchase on European affairs. The EU has been largely unsuccessful in endowing Europe with an identity in the post-Cold War period (and has also found it difficult to overcome the East–West division which is the enduring legacy of communism). European identity, to the extent that it is conceptualized by the EU, revolves around an increasingly contested notion of the social model, which, just as it is being touted as a governance model ready to be exported around the world, is beginning to creak under the weight of economic competitiveness, to which it is subsumed (Delanty and Rumford 2005).

Despite a shift towards a cosmopolitan register, the problem of European identity is never going to be resolved in the way outlined by Habermas and Derrida. For a start, the EU has shown no interest in recasting Europe in cosmopolitan terms. Secondly, the idea of a 'core' Europe stands at odds with an avowed cosmopolitanism. Thirdly, Habermas and Derrida's 'cosmo-lite' Europe may be attractive to some European intellectuals but to be genuinely cosmopolitan Europe has to engage with and open up to the rest of the world. There are other worrying tendencies to emerge from the recent debate on Europe and cosmopolitanism, for example the idea that Europe is (potentially) more cosmopolitan than anywhere else, which often goes together with the idea that cosmopolitanism has a distinctly European provenance.

Cosmopolitanism has not yet staked out a distinctive position vis-à-vis the study of Europe, partly as a result of the plurality of cosmopolitanisms that can be brought to bear and partly as a result of the recent preference for interpreting Europe's 'cosmopolitan moment' rather narrowly. As cosmopolitan approaches were just beginning to influence debate on Europe's identity and role in the world, a rather restricted version of cosmopolitanism has risen to the fore. But anti-Americanism is only one of the pitfalls social scientists must avoid if a productive cosmopolitan research agenda is to be established. The study of cosmopolitanism in Europe must also avoid both becoming conflated with the search for European civil society and being equated with a self-congratulatory humanitarianism, or what Stjepan Mestrovic (1997) would refer to as 'postemotional tolerance'. Having already dealt with the popularity of anti-Americanism we must give some thought to these other two problem areas, which are in fact closely related.

The European dimensions of global civil society have been more discernable in recent years, especially as a consequence of the anti-war movements of 2003 and the debates on European identity (including those inspired by Habermas and Derrida's intervention) to which they gave rise. The emergence of cosmopolitan perspectives on Europe has facilitated these debates, particularly where trans-national solidarities and communicative networks of Europeanization are evoked. This has led to the idea that Europe's nascent cosmopolitanism can be associated with the growing (grass-roots) criticism of the EU's preference for markets over citizens and welfare provision, as reflected in the slogan 'Not too much Europe; not enough social Europe' (an attitude thought to explain, in part at least, the Dutch and French electorates' rejection of the constitutional treaty).

The emergence of cosmopolitanism as a discourse of European belonging has been opportune for those who seek to establish the ground for civil society in Europe, as it has worked both to locate an 'alternative' Europe in civil society and to resist US hegemony. This trend is compounded by the desire to connect Europe to the rest of the world, through attempts to initiate institutions of global governance (Lamy and Laidi 2001), to export a humane social model (Strauss-Kahn 2004) or to adopt a compassionate foreign policy. As a result, cosmopolitanism can appear as little more than an effort to achieve 'a superficial intimacy with and response to everyone' (Riesman, quoted in Mestrovic 1997: 47). The result is a romanticized distortion of European identity: Europeans as Zapatistas – *Todo para todos, nada para nosotros*[2] – offering to work on behalf of the world through attempts to construct humanitarian coalitions (of anti-Americanism). This triple burden – giving Europe identity in distinction to the US, representing a nascent civil society and giving content to a humanitarian mission statement – weighs heavily on cosmopolitanism and works to distort its meanings and relevance to Europe.

This book attempts to establish the ground for a fruitful dialogue between various stands of cosmopolitanism. To achieve this, it is necessary not only to avoid the pitfalls outlined above but also to prevent debate on cosmopolitanism and Europe being reduced to questions of integration and institutionalization. A starting point is the recognition that cosmopolitanism and Europe will necess-arily remain in tension with each other. In other words, it is not possible to fix cosmopolitanism in some concrete, singular identity. If Europe is to become more cosmopolitan, it will be because it remains open to questions of identity and its

2 'Everything for everyone, nothing for ourselves.'

relation to the rest of the world, and because it recognizes the multiplicity of cosmopolitanisms that are possible, and also the plurality of Europes that this presupposes.

References

Archibugi, D. (1998) 'Principles of cosmopolitan democracy', in D. Archibugi, D. Held and M. Kohler (eds), *Re-imagining Political Community: Studies in Cosmopolitan Democracy*, Cambridge: Polity Press, pp. 198–228.

Armstrong, K. A. (2002) 'Rediscovering civil society: the European Union and the white paper on governance', *European Law Journal*, 8(1), 102–32.

Beck, U. and Giddens, A. (2005) 'Nationalism has now become the enemy of Europe's nations', *The Guardian*, 4 October.

Biedenkopf, K., Geremek, B. and Michalski, K. (2004) *The Spiritual and Cultural Dimension of Europe – Concluding Remarks*, Brussels: European Commission. Available at http://ec.europa.eu/archives/commission_1999_2004/prodi/pdf/michalski_281004_final_report_en.pdf (last accessed January 2007).

Delanty, G. (2005) 'What does it mean to be European?', *Innovation: The European Journal of Social Science Research*, 18(1), 11–22.

Delanty, G. and Rumford, C. (2005) *Rethinking Europe: Social Theory and the Implications of Europeanization*, London: Routledge.

Entrikin, N. (2003) 'Political community, identity and cosmopolitan place', in M. Berezin and M. Schain (eds), *Europe Without Borders: Remapping Territory, Citizenship and Identity in a Transnational Age*, Baltimore, MD: Johns Hopkins University Press, pp. 51–63.

Eriksen, E. O. (2005) 'Towards a cosmopolitan EU?', ARENA working paper no. 9, Oslo: Centre for European Studies, University of Oslo. Available at http://www.arena.uio.no (last accessed January 2007).

European Commission (2001) *European Governance: A White Paper*, COM(2001) 428 final, Brussels: European Commission. Available at http://ec.europa.eu/governance/white_paper/en.pdf (last accessed January 2007).

Garton Ash, T. and Dahrendorf, R. (2005) 'The renewal of Europe: response to Habermas', in D. Levy, M. Pensky and J. Torpey (eds), *Old Europe, New Europe, Core Europe: Transatlantic Relations After the Iraq War*, London: Verso, pp. 141–45.

Habermas, J. and Derrida, J. (2003) 'February 15, or, what binds European together', *Frankfurter Allgemeine Zeitung/Liberation*, 31 May.

Lamy, P. (2001) 'Harnessing globalization, do we need cosmopolitics?', lecture, 1 February, London School of Economics. Available at http://old.lse.ac.uk/collections/globalDimensions/lectures/harnessingGlobalisationDoWeNeedCosmopolitics/transcript.htm (last accessed January 2007).

Lamy, P. and Laidi, Z. (2001) 'Governance or making globalization meaningful'. Available at http://www.laidi.com/papiers/governance.pdf (last accessed January 2007).

Levy, D., Pensky, M. and Torpey, J. (2005) 'Editors' introduction', in D. Levy, M. Pensky and J. Torpey (eds), *Old Europe, New Europe, Core Europe: Transatlantic Relations After the Iraq War*, London: Verso, pp. xi–xxix.

Mestrovic, S. (1997) *Postemotional Society*, London: Sage.

Meyer, J. W. (2001) 'The European Union and the globalization of culture', in S. S. Andersen (ed.), *Institutional Approaches to the European Union*, ARENA report no. 3/2001, Oslo: Centre for European Studies, University of Oslo, pp. 227–45.

Milward, A. (1993) *The European Rescue of the Nation-State*, London: Routledge.

Moravcsik, A. (2004) 'Europe is the new role model for world', *Financial Times*, 6 October.

Rifkin, J. (2004a) *The European Dream: How Europe's Vision of the Future is Quietly Eclipsing the American Dream*, New York: Tarcher/Penguin.

Rifkin, J. (2004b) 'This is the first attempt to create a global consciousness', *The Guardian*, 16 November.

Shields, R. (2006) 'Boundary thinking in theories of the present: the virtuality of reflexive modernization', *European Journal of Social Theory*, 9(2), 223–38.

Strauss-Kahn, D. (2004) *Building a Political Europe: 50 Proposals for Tomorrow's Europe*, report by chairperson of the Round Table 'A sustainable project for tomorrow's Europe' formed on the initiative of the President of the European Commission. Available at http://ec.europa.eu/dgs/policy_advisers/archives/experts_groups/docs/rapport_europe_strauss_kahn_en.pdf (last accessed January 2007).

Vertovec, S. and Cohen, R. (eds) (2002) *Conceiving Cosmopolitanism: Theory, Context and Practice*, Oxford: Oxford University Press.

Young, I. M. (2005) 'De-centering the project of global democracy', in D. Levy, M. Pensky and J. Torpey (eds), *Old Europe, New Europe, Core Europe: Transatlantic Relations After the Iraq War*, London: Verso, pp. 153–59.

Part I
Cosmopolitan Europe: Theory and Politics

Cosmopolitanism and Europe: Historical Considerations and Contemporary Applications

Vivienne Boon and Gerard Delanty

Cosmopolitanism differs significantly from both a narrow patriotism or nationalism, on the one hand, and from internationalism, on the other. It points to something different, something which is particularly useful for examining the recent political, social and cultural developments of Europe, that is, a Europe which is both distinct from a Europe based on a conglomeration of nation states and a Europe perceived as a 'global Europe'. In order to explicate this, this chapter will trace the historical origins of cosmopolitanism in ancient Greek thought and Kantian philosophy. We will argue that universal legal cosmopolitanism, which resulted out of the Kantian model, lacked a political, cultural and social dimension, and consequently became indistinguishable from internationalism – which in fact fostered nationalism. When, after the fall of the Berlin Wall in 1989, this legal form of cosmopolitanism was radicalized into a political project, it was frequently presented as a more sensitive form of cosmopolitanism. However, at the heart of this politicized form of cosmopolitanism was the aim of overcoming particular and local identities in favour of a universalistic cosmopolitan affiliation. The upshot was that when cosmopolitanism was applied to Europe, it remained somewhat restricted by the conventional nationalist and internationalist framework, and so the complicated and ambiguous nature of cosmopolitanism in Europe was overlooked. By tracing the historical origins of cosmopolitanism and elaborating upon its varied applications to Europe, we will argue for a recognition of Europeanization as a particular expression of cosmopolitanism. Important to this application of cosmopolitanism is the interplay between the local and the global, a dynamic that gives rise to various kinds of societal transformation. This approach to cosmopolitanism is in line with post-universalistic notions of cosmopolitanism (see Delanty 2006).

Vivienne Boon & Gerard Delanty

The origins of cosmopolitan thought

Cosmopolitanism is rooted in Ancient Greek thought. When Diogenes the Cynic (*c.* 412–323 BC) uttered the words 'I am a citizen of the world', he articulated one of the first notions of cosmopolitanism as an act of individual freedom. By this statement, Diogenes repudiated the definition of himself as determined by his local origins and group affiliations and, rather, defined himself in terms of more universal aspirations and concerns (Nussbaum 1997: 5).

Despite the cosmopolitan outlook of the Cynics, it was not until the Stoics, at the end of the classical Athenian period (from around 300 BC), that cosmopolitanism became explicitly advocated as an idea and that the political tradition of cosmopolitanism that we now associate with the term became established. The Stoic idea of being a citizen of the world, *kosmou polités*, reflected a universalistic conception of human belonging, rather than an act of individual freedom as such. By asserting that we ought to 'measure the boundaries of our nation by the sun', cosmopolitanism in the Stoic sense radically challenged the narrow view of the Greek polis as the exclusive measure of human community. That is to say, the Stoics were critical of the tendency in Greek thought to reduce political community to a narrowly defined polis. Instead they declared that all human beings should be regarded as our fellow citizens, since we all live in the same universal order. It is in this light that the Stoic Zeno of Citium (333–264 BC) advocated an ideal cosmopolitan city based on membership of a wider human society and argued that political obligation derives from deep subjective feelings. The dangers of such a cosmopolis turning into a form of despotism have been well documented. Nevertheless, it is this idea of the citizen belonging to a universal order that gave the modern age a vision of human community extending beyond the community into which one is born or lives.

It was, furthermore, precisely this vision of a universal human unity extending beyond one's own particular surroundings and political borders that profoundly inspired the political writings of Immanuel Kant (1724–1804) (see Nussbaum 1997). Despite its classical origins, cosmopolitanism was characteristically a product of modernity and played only a marginal role in ancient thought. It did not play a significant role in medieval thought, which was dominated by Christian universalism. Kant's political writings are arguably the main sources of inspiration for contemporary cosmopolitan theory, and specifically so his *Idea for a Universal History with a Cosmopolitan Purpose* (1784) and his *Perpetual Peace* (1795). In these writings Kant offers us a profound defence of cosmopolitan values. In the former, Kant anchored the development of cosmopolitanism within a historical framework and claimed that history was leading to the creation of a republican order which would replace a world of national republican nations.

Thus a cosmopolitan republican order would emerge as a result of the unfolding of providence, of the fundamentally moral nature of humanity. However, Kant later realized that 'the positive idea of a world republic cannot be created' (Kant 1795: 105) so, in his later work, *Perpetual Peace*, he hinted that what was more likely to come about was a cosmopolitan law which would limit the actions of nation states. While strongly bemoaning the state of nature among sovereign states as nothing but a Hobbesian 'war of all against all' writ large, Kant proposed the idea of a cosmopolitan order constituted by both an external legal order and a universal civic society (Fine 2003). This external legal order, according to Kant, would arise when sovereign states voluntarily gave up their lawless freedom and submitted themselves to a pacific federation, which would not merely stop specific confrontations but, indeed, end all wars for good (Kant 1795: 104). Hence, just as the peoples within the territory of the nation state abandoned their lawless condition and entered into a social contract to end all their internal strife, so would nation states willingly limit their freedom and submit to a legal international order.[1]

This somewhat negative perception of cosmopolitanism – namely as the prevention of warfare – was combined with the idea of a universal civic community which transcends the boundaries of the nation state. At the heart of this idea of a universal civic community is, of course, Kant's conception of perpetual peace, which would amount to a situation in which standing armies were abolished, national debt was not contracted in connection to the costs of warfare, and the acts of hostility during times of war that 'would make mutual confidence impossible during a future time of peace' were no longer permitted (Kant 1795: 106). But most significant of all is Kant's argument that as long as foreigners behave in a peaceful manner, they have a right to hospitality when they arrive on someone else's territory, since 'all men are entitled to present themselves in the society of others by virtue of their right to common possession of the earth's surface' (Kant 1795: 106). Thus, essential to his notion of a civic community is the presupposition that 'the human community has entered in varying degrees into a universal community', which means that 'a violation of rights in one part of the world is felt everywhere' (Kant 1795: 107–8). Consequently, 'no-one originally has any greater right than anyone else to occupy any particular position of the earth' (Kant 1795: 106–8). Given this basic human commonality, it is not permissible for the 'civilised countries' to oppress the natives in the colonized countries,

---

1 As Habermas (1997) noted, this leads to something of a paradox in Kant's writings: it is unclear how a federation of states based on a purely voluntary principle is 'to be permanent, the feature upon which a civilised resolution of international conflict depends, without the binding character of law based on something analogous to a constitution' (Habermas 1997: 117).

since this leads only to 'widespread wars, famine, insurrection, treachery and the whole litany of evils which can afflict the human race' (Kant 1795: 106). Hence one could argue that Kant's legal cosmopolitan framework touches humanity as a whole, or, as Kant himself remarks, that 'cosmopolitan right is a necessary complement to the unwritten code of political and international right, transforming it into a universal right of humanity' (Kant 1795: 108).

However, one has to be careful not to overstate Kant's advocacy of the universal citizen, for Kant, it seems, wavers between a sovereign cosmopolitan order which recognizes individuals as citizens of the world and a federal order of sovereign nation states with strong civil societies. So, while Kant's model touches upon the rights of the citizens beyond the boundaries of their nation states and makes reference to laws of humanity, he chiefly focuses on laying the foundations of a theory of international law. That is to say, his cosmopolitan framework remains a form of internationalism which is primarily concerned with states, rather than citizens as such. In other words, one could safely suggest that Kant's cosmopolitan project is one which is predominantly based upon a legal rather than a political cosmopolitan project, and consists of a theory of law rather than a project of democratic governance. Arguably this lack of a political dimension meant that, in some respects, Kant's writings did not actually bring about a Copernican revolution in our political thinking, where we no longer perceive the world in terms of nation states or, indeed, bounded political entities. Rather, as Robert Fine remarks, 'when the Kantian approach seeks to universalise existing legal forms of justice beyond the nation state ... it remains fundamentally at the level of conceptual thinking' and has not been worked out in any great detail (Fine 2003: 464). Furthermore, because of the very formalistic nature of Kant's cosmopolitanism, it fails to take note of the point that every universal is in fact the universalization of a particular. Moreover, his cosmopolitanism was highly Eurocentric. One can therefore conclude that the legalist cosmopolitan project as initiated by Kant is in fact not capable of countering the xenophobic traits inherent in nationalism, since bounded political entities in the form of nation states remain intact. Accordingly, his legalistic cosmopolitanism may even turn out to foster nationalism as such.

Furthermore, after the writings of Kant, the importance of the civic and moral dimensions of cosmopolitanism significantly decreased, and instead increasing attention was paid to the debate on international society and internationalism. Notable examples of this are, of course, communism, pan-nationalism and federalism. Communism from the very start was a universal project preoccupied with the 'withering away of the state', whose aim it was to create an equal social order that was not to be bounded by the nation state. And the new ideas of federalism, which emerged at the close of the First World War, were specifically geared towards rebuilding the Europe which lay in shatters as a result of nationalism. Examples of these were proposals for a European federal state, for instance the pan-European movement founded by Richard Coudenhove-Kalergi in the 1920s, which was modelled on the US federal system. However, it soon became apparent that the Enlightenment's principle of self-determination was destined to become the universalism of the particular, as enunciated by Soviet leader Vladimir Lenin and US President Woodrow Wilson, who shaped the Versailles order. Under the Versailles agreement, the nation state became generally regarded as the best basis for a new Europe – a Europe ideally founded on peaceful relations between nation states. Thus, this upsurge of internationalism did nothing much to replace the nation state with a trans-national federation of states but, rather, subordinated the idea of a cosmopolitan citizenship to a state-centred world.

Contemporary cosmopolitanism and the question of Europe

Despite all of this, the works of Kant on cosmopolitanism have proven to be a great impetus for many contemporary cosmopolitan thinkers to develop a mode of political thought which goes beyond the boundaries of the nation state. In light of the catastrophes of the twentieth century, Kant's writings on cosmopolitan rights have a contemporary relevance, as many theorists point out (Bohman and Lutz-Bachmann 1997). They believe that whereas internationalism allowed nationalism to masquerade as universal, a more sensitive politicized cosmopolitan outlook will be genuinely universalistic, in that it 'recognises the point of view of humanity as a whole as well as the diversity of the human species' (Fine 2003: 461). Hence, by radicalizing the break from the nation state where it was incomplete and by taking into account the different social contexts, these theorists set out slowly but surely to transform Kant's legal cosmopolitanism into a distinct political project. This project affirms the possibility and desirability of overriding the nation state in the name of cosmopolitan justice (Fine 2003: 453).

There are three main avenues out of internationalism and into a more cosmopolitan spectrum: the first is a revival of moral cosmopolitanism; the second is cosmopolitan governance; and the third is what can be called cultural cosmopolitanism. The first two have a strong universalistic dimension, while the third suggests a post-universalistic cosmopolitanism.

On the universalistic end of this cosmopolitan spectrum, we find an influential essay by Martha Nussbaum. Heavily influenced by the writings of the Stoics and Kant, Nussbaum asserts that our allegiance should be to the worldwide community of human beings and not merely to that which is local, regional or national. She argues that it is only through this cosmopolitan allegiance to the whole of humanity that we are able to transcend the divisions created between human beings by nationalism and ethnocentrism. This loyalty to humanity has to be learned and practised through the vivid imagining of the different, which will enable us to recognize humanity in all its strange guises (Nussbaum 1996: 9). It is only through this exercise of looking through the lens of the other that we are able to 'conceive of the entire human world as a single body, its many people as so many limbs' (Nussbaum 1996: 10). It will allow us to see 'what is local and nonessential [and] what is more broadly or deeply shared' (Nussbaum 1996: 11). It will enable us to step outwards from our inner circle of local affiliations and identifications and towards the greatest circle of all – the whole of humanity. Evidently, the implication of this claim is that while we are not discouraged from loving our specific affiliations in the world, we are discouraged from identifying with them too excessively, since this could lead us to narrow our viewpoint and exclude others. The argument is clear: the more outward one's affiliations are, the better and more moral one's actions are.

While we shall return later in this chapter to the problems that Nussbaum's universalistic outlook raises, it is worth briefly noting the most fundamental objection, namely that 'our attachments start parochially and only then grow outward' (Barber 1996: 34). By pulling the whole of humanity towards the centre – as Nussbaum asserts we should do – we run the risk of bypassing these more parochial identifications in favour of an immediate cosmopolitanism. Consequently, we are in danger of '[ending] up nowhere – feeling at home neither at home nor in the world' (Barber 1996: 34). Nussbaum admits to this problem when she remarks that cosmopolitanism 'offers no ... refuge [but] only reason and the love of humanity, which may seem at times less colourful than other sources of belonging', but she brushes aside the full implications of this assertion (Nussbaum 1996: 13). One of the possible consequences, for example, is that, by short-circuiting our reflection on our concrete surroundings in the name of humanity at large, we are in danger of proclaiming that we know 'in advance the meaning to be assigned to the utterance of universality' (Butler 1996: 47). We thereby run the risk (albeit unintentionally) of doing precisely the kind of harm to others we wish to avoid. More important, however, is the fact that political deliberations often require a high degree of mobilization. This mobilization can often be accomplished only through a common identity (Taylor 1996: 120). Surpassing debates on particular identity formations therefore could easily result in political impotence and even a blind allegiance to authority.

The second kind of cosmopolitanism goes beyond Nussbaum's essentially moral conception and is associated with the notion of global governance. David Held and Daniele Archibugi are among the leading proponents of this kind of universalistic democratic cosmopolitanism (see Archibugi 1995; Held 1995).

According to Held, the nation state is unable to realize any of three key principles of democracy: individual autonomy, political legitimacy and democratic law. This is an argument for a strong kind of cosmopolitan governance, as represented by international non-governmental actors and trans-national organizations such as the United Nations. From the point of view of Europeanization, this approach has its limits, in that its main concern is with global governance and it is, moreover, highly normative (in the sense of prescriptive). One of the major drawbacks with it is that it does not fully appreciate that some of the main cosmopolitan developments have been within nation states.

It is possible to point to a third strand within contemporary cosmopolitanism, namely cultural cosmopolitanism. This is reflected in wide-ranging contributions on issues of identity and belonging (see Appiah 2005; Breckenridge *et al.* 2002; Cheah and Robbins 1998; Urry 2000). Two of the main characteristics of this turn in cosmopolitan thought are the local–global nexus and a general concern with diversity, solidarity and what has been called a 'cosmopolitanism from below' (Calhoun 2003; Kurasawa 2004). Pertinent examples of cultural cosmopolitanism derive from globalization and are in consumption, travel and multiculturalism. Where earlier kinds of cosmopolitanism were universalistic, the various approaches that can be described under this heading could be called post-universalistic and moreover have an application to different modernities (Gaonkar 2001). From this perspective, cosmopolitanism refers to multiple sites of social and cultural transformation arising out of local global encounters. The articulation of a universalistic morality or world polity is less central to this conception of cosmopolitanism. We cannot enter into a detailed consideration of cultural cosmopolitanism other than pointing out that many cultural approaches tend to suffer from limiting cosmopolitanism to a generalized condition of diversity. However, some of the more promising applications of cosmopolitanism are to be found in these approaches, especially where a certain confluence of cultural and political transformations is apparent.

On the basis of these considerations, what can be said about Europeanization and cosmopolitanism? Europeanization viewed from a cosmopolitan perspective could be seen in terms of political as well as socio-cultural transformation, for it is precisely the problematic relation between belonging, processes of identification and political deliberation that has been so central to recent debates on the idea of Europe. The European political community was initially founded in 1951 to prevent warfare among European nation states in light of the atrocities of the Second World War. It was primarily formed around a Western alliance against the Soviet East, based on economic cooperation, rather than political integration. This meant that – in the words of J. H. H. Weiler – what was to become the European Union (EU) was established according to a 'we will do, then we will hearken attitude' (Weiler 1999: 5). Whereas many politicians were eager to create a more economically integrated Europe, the political deliberative questions which necessarily accompanied this process of integration were largely left unanswered. The consequence of this has been that the EU more or less consists of 'a constitutional legal order the constitutional theory of which has not been worked out, its long term, transcendent values not sufficiently elaborated, its ontological elements misunderstood, its social rootedness and legitimacy highly contingent' (Weiler 1999: 8).

After the fall of the Berlin Wall in 1989 and the collapse of state socialism, these questions of what it means to be European and what constitutes Europe gained special resonance. We are now forced to reflect upon who should be included and who should be excluded from the EU, and on what basis these decisions should be made. Put differently, the question is raised of what Europeanness stands for. Moreover, the increasing pooling of sovereignty from the level of the nation states towards the EU raises the questions of what level of political deliberations should be formed, and how. It not only alters our relation to the European political process but also fundamentally modifies our relation to territoriality, which used to be bound up with our sense of self. Thus, the political questions that, as Weiler remarked, were neglected when the EU was founded have now come to the fore and can no longer be ignored. Hence Europe has proven much more than a mere economic process, for it raises questions which go straight to the heart of our political, social and cultural self-understanding. It is in this sense that we can speak of a process of Europeanization, since the progression of European integration in fact reaches far beyond a process of the integration of nation states or of economic (systemic) cooperation. Rather, Europeanization consists of a pervasive and ongoing cross-fertilization of identities and discourses to which can be related a new imaginary, or socio-cognitive cultural model, in which the idea of Europe itself becomes a reality.

Essential to this debate over a European imaginary is the discussion on the European constitution. A major contribution to this debate has been made by Jürgen Habermas, especially through his works on constitutional patriotism (Habermas 1992, 2001). In these writings Habermas proposes that a European constitution will both enable us to overcome the divisions of national interests and create a more viable democracy on a European level. In order to understand this assertion more fully, we should first of all note that Habermas argues – in a true cosmopolitan fashion – that in an era of globalization the nation state is slowly being rendered obsolete by internal and external forces. While the sovereignty of the state is increasingly undermined externally through the pressures of global capital, the cultural cohesion of the nation is being eroded internally through the increasing complexity of the social make-up. Habermas regards this not merely as a negative development but also as a further maturation of society, since it gives rise to an increasing rationalization of the life-world as we enter the post-conventional stage. That is, owing to the increasing complexity and plurality of the social make-up, we are now forced to look beyond that which is constituted as normatively right within our own frame of reference (the conventional stage) and widen our horizons to that which lies beyond our boundaries (the post-conventional stage) – thereby taking on the moral role of the generalized other (see Habermas 1979). So, one can clearly see that Habermas's theoretical insights have the cosmopolitan aim of raising humanity out of its immaturity through the widening of horizons.

However, the problem is that, with the deterioration of traditional world views, these outlooks are losing both their integrative force and their power to counteract the systemic pressures of market forces. Consequently, it becomes increasingly difficult to guarantee a level of social welfare and to counter the pathological effects of capitalism (see Habermas 2003). Thus, Habermas argues, we are in urgent need of a political closure to these global economic forces over and above the level of the nation state – that is, on the European level. This political closure should, however, not exist as a thick cultural prescription but, rather, ought to be based upon the cosmopolitan principles of tolerance and respect for diversity.

This, according to Habermas, can be achieved only when we turn to the medium of law as a saviour, for law provides us with a more abstract mode of social and political integration. It is through law and the allegiance to a constitution that we are enabled to produce a sense of collectivity on a European level, which would provide a political counterbalance (or closure) to global market forces (Habermas 2001). The formation of law, however, has to be rooted in discursive processes which are formed in autonomous, vibrant public spheres located at the periphery (see Habermas 1996), for it is through the procedural working out of all these divergent interests at the centre of the political apparatus that an allegiance to a common European constitution is born, that we regard ourselves and others as being part of the same (weak) political culture. Thus, overall, Habermas's position is one in which he argues for a democratic cosmopolitanism based on a legal system strengthened by a European constitution. It is only through such a democratic political order – based on a thin liberal political culture – that a cosmopolitan Europe can be founded which in principle is all-inclusive. As Habermas himself concludes, 'only a democratic citizenship that does not close itself off in a particularistic fashion can pave the way for a *world citizenship* which is already taking shape today in worldwide political communications' (Habermas 1996: 514, original emphasis).

While Habermas's aim of establishing a democratic cosmopolitan Europe is admirable, it does suffer from a number of shortcomings. Firstly, from a sociological point of view there is little evidence that people identify with the constitution to the extent that Habermas claims they do, as suggested by the rejection of the constitutional treaty in the Dutch and French referendums in 2005. Secondly, as Charles Turner (2004) has noted, Habermas's idea of constitutional patriotism may not reflect a genuinely European consciousness but, rather, one that is largely based on a specifically German learning curve – namely the overcoming of the painful memories of the Second World War. It is therefore not obvious that all European countries have renounced their national past in favour of a post-national identity. Thirdly, when Habermas institutionalizes his conception of an all-inclusive cosmopolitan Europe, it turns out that he is in fact more exclusive than he is perhaps willing to admit. For example, Habermas writes that:

> Any political community that wants to understand itself as a democracy must at least distinguish between members and non-members. The self-referential concept of collective self-determination demarcates a logical space for democratically united citizens who are members of a particular community. Even if such a community is grounded in the universalistic principles of a democratic constitutional state, it still forms a collective identity, in the sense that it interprets and realizes these principles in light of its own history and in the context of its own particular form of life. This ethical–political self-understanding of citizens of a particular democratic life is missing in the inclusive community of world citizens. (Habermas 2001: 107)

In this passage, Habermas admits that democratic legitimacy is not possible for a political body which embraces everyone, since it does not provide a particular foundation for collective identity or civic solidarity (Fine and Smith 2003: 474). Thus, Habermas's post-national model in reality requires some sort of substantive foundation, which thereby raises the question of how one distinguishes between self and other, members and non-members, European and non-European. Or, rather, it raises the question of what it is exactly that constitutes 'Europeanness'. Perhaps it is because of this implicit reliance upon some sort of a substantive foundation that Habermas's vision of a post-national Europe is in fact based upon a somewhat limited conception of a 'core' Europe that will lead the way to democracy (Habermas and Derrida 2003). This core Europe is a synonym for 'old Europe', for France and Germany (Habermas 2004). Thus, the tension between the universal and the particular does not seem to be resolved in Habermas's work.

Having said all this, the idea of a Europe based on discursive interactions and a vibrant civil society is a very powerful one. Hence it is not surprising that several other theorists have looked to civil society as a model for Europeanization. This civil society approach can more or less be divided into two theoretical strands, consisting of, on the one hand, a trans-nationalist outlook based on human rights and legal citizenship – which we could term civic cosmopolitanism – and, on the other hand, the idea of Europe as a network society. Before turning to the former, we shall pay some attention to the latter.

This latter position has primarily been advocated by Manuel Castells, who argues that Europe is a multilevel polity based on a horizontally connected network society (Castells 1998). The network is typical of our modern information society, since it is fundamentally based around various nodes of power of different shapes and forms, rather than a particular central structure. That is to say, it consists of a polycentric structure in which information flows in various directions, simultaneously linking different centres of power. Consequently, Castells argues that, as the local, regional and global are now capable of being connected horizontally, nation states have become less significant. In relation to Europe, this implies that the local and the regional can be connected with the EU directly. It is in this sense that one could say that Europe has its own inner globalization, and hence Castells' claim that 'European integration is, at the same time, a reaction to the process of globalization and its most advanced expression' (Castells 1998: 348).

Leaving aside any criticisms of his somewhat technocratic conception of information flows, the main problem with his account is that Europeanization is predominantly seen as a process resisting globalization and one that is essentially reduced to mobilities. To regard Europeanization as a development separate from the rest of the world, rather than interacting with the global, is to dismiss the transformative dimension of the interactive encounter. For even though Castells' writings do touch upon the transformation of identities through cross-fertilization, they remain fundamentally tied to the political and economic integration process rooted in the institutions of the EU. Thus, again, little attention is paid to the wider context of social and cultural transformations, which Beck and Grande (2004) have drawn attention to (see also Delanty and Rumford 2005).

This critique could in fact be applied to Habermas's post-national conception of Europe as well (Habermas 2001), for Habermas's model of Europe also fails to relate to the global level, and thereby remains limited by a national frame of reference. Habermas's framework is abstracted from the national level, on the one side, and, on the other, is seen as distinct from the wider global context. Cultural issues are excluded and the assumption appears to be that there is an underlying shared 'European humanity'. Habermas thus fails to see that, in fact, cosmopolitan currents are evident within national identities and as a result he reduces Europeanization to a supranational process. So all in all, while these contributions are extremely valuable, it appears that, over 200 years after Kant's writings, we still have not witnessed a true Copernican revolution in our political thought.

We now turn to the other position we briefly mentioned earlier, namely civic cosmopolitanism, which is promoted by theorists such as Etienne Balibar, Klaus Eder and Ulrich Beck.[2] This approach advances the idea that in an increasingly multicultural and diversified Europe we witness the intensification of a European civil society, which is based upon a form of trans-national citizenship. Balibar (2004), for example, argues that the idea of citizenship has undergone profound changes through the uncoupling of rights and identity, for rights that were once defined by nationality have become increasingly universal and codified at the European as opposed to national level (see also Soysal 1994). A major impetus to this process is the codification of universal human rights, which ascribe rights to the individual person, rather than to nation states. It is becoming increasingly apparent that national courts are activating trans-national human rights conventions as the basis of their decisions. Or, rather, international concepts of human rights have now been incorporated into national law, which no longer distinguishes between inside and outside. The cultivation of universal human rights in combination with the increased mobility and multiplicity of political allegiances and social belongings has resulted in a blurring of the boundaries between foreigners and nationals. We can therefore speak of a new form of post-national belonging in Europe, where social processes are cutting across the boundaries of individual nation states. This form of post-national belonging is fluid and open ended, and it empowers migrant, ethnic and other minority groups, who are no longer constrained by national codifications of citizenship. Not surprisingly, therefore, many theorists have regarded this new form of post-national belonging as the foundation for a new kind of European society (see Balibar 2004; Delanty 2000, 2005; Eder and Giesen 2001), one that is based upon a progressive reinvention of Europe according to the cosmopolitan principles of tolerance, diversity and respect for otherness.

Now, our previous objection to the theoretical undertakings of Habermas and Castells could, of course, also be applied to this conception of Europe as a trans-national entity based on post-national belonging – for again, the tendency is to regard Europeanization as a process separate from the rest of the world. But more important perhaps is the objection that this strand of thought makes too large a case for citizenship as the central animus of Europeanization. The reality of citizenship is that there are various different traditions (see Bellamy *et al.* 2004): there is no common European model and it is unlikely that the EU will be able create one. Despite these limitations, however, civic cosmopolitanism does mark a shift away from perceiving Europeanization in purely political and legal terms and towards something much more cultural. By drawing our attention to

---

2 The term 'civic cosmopolitanism' was proposed by Delanty (2000).

the increasing ambiguity between inside and outside, to the social formations that cross national boundaries, it raises our awareness of the socio-cognitive transformations which are taking place within Europe at the moment.

Europeanization between the national and the global

Rather than perceiving Europe in either nationalist or globalist terms, where an international Europe led by the EU institutions would pave the way forward, the thesis of this chapter is that Europeanization is something much more multi-levelled and polycentric, namely, a form of mediation between the national and the global which enables the emergence of a new social reality. This new social reality is by no means a purely normative idea based on various abstract ideals but is, rather, empirically situated in the here and now – while making reference to that which is beyond the local, national or even European level. That is to say, it is existent *both within and beyond* the boundaries of the nation state. It relates to the local and the global simultaneously, and in so doing consists of an interplay between these elements.

This newly emerging social reality above all consists of a pervasive and ongoing cross-fertilization of identities and discourses that gives rise to various socio-cognitive transformations. These socio-cognitive transformations, in our opinion, highlight the fact that Europeanization is both much more than merely a political process, since it involves a cultural logic of self-transformation, and much less, in that it does not necessarily lead to the erosion of the nation state. Europe is neither simply a trans-nationalization of nation states nor a process of integration of European societies, but consists of constantly changing relations. It is not merely a question of increasing hybridity, mobility, interconnectivity or, indeed, consumerism but, rather, is a self-reflexive development of one's social, cultural and political subjectivity as a result of these changing relations. It can perhaps best be described as a learning process, one which involves a playing out of various contested claims and outlooks. So, it is through the interplay between the local and the global that the idea of Europe unfolds as a reality (Delanty and Rumford 2005).

Europeanization entails horizontal links between European societies, vertical links between European societies and the EU, and transversal links between European societies and the global, as well as between the EU and the global. The resulting cosmopolitanism is more than the coexistence of difference. Rather than simply coexistence of the various levels as the outcome, what in fact is occurring is the co-evolution of societal levels, which might be reflected in a transformation in self-understanding. From a macro-societal perspective, what are also significant are changing core–periphery relations, with the core having to redefine itself from the perspective of the periphery. This point has a more general application to cosmopolitanism as a condition that concerns the formation of an emergent reality (see Delanty and Rumford 2005).

We should note that, while this unfolding of Europe may bare resemblances to Hegel's dialectical method – by which he attempted to bridge the gap between the universal and the actual – our conception of Europe is much more ambiguous. Europeanization by no means occurs in a dialectical fashion, resulting in a synthesis, and neither does it consist of a historical unfolding, leading to a universalizable outcome. It operates much more ambiguously and contradictorily, and most of all consists of a process that has no particular end nor aim. All it consists of is a process of a transformation of loyalties and identities, which are not stable but are constantly being altered. Thus the newly emergent social reality in Europe is not based upon a particular substantive cultural or political subjectivity, since it is much more ambivalent than that. It is more a process of self-reflexivity than a sense of uniformity or cohesion. It comprises a decentred, distant form of self which is more rooted in discursive actions and based on the principles of recognition than in a specific cultural or political essence. Put differently, it is more about the form (in the sense of an organizing process) than the content – yet the form is nevertheless shaped by the particular contexts in which it unfolds.

It is for this reason that we should realize there is not just one universal form of cosmopolitanism based on an abstract idea of universal humanity, but that there are various 'actually existing' cosmopolitanisms, which develop within particular cultural contexts and exist simultaneously and contradictorily (Robbins 1998). That is, they are located within a particular framework or situation. Cosmopolitanism, therefore, involves a constant process of reattachment, multiple attachments and, indeed, attachments from a distance, rather than a process of detachment as Nussbaum asserted (Robbins 1998: 3). As we have seen, cosmopolitanism in the universal perception of Nussbaum entails an *overcoming* of our local affiliations and identity formations, which are regarded as parochial and 'morally irrelevant'. Particular affiliations, according to Nussbaum, only blur the link between the most inner circle – the self – and the most outer and most moral circle – humanity, for identity formations, as a result of their particularity, are by definition hierarchical and exclusionary.

This conviction that identity formations are conflicting is ambiguous to say the least. We have only to refer to the writings of Georg Simmel to appreciate this point. Simmel argues that all individuals are unique in their affiliation to social circles, and that belonging to various groups enhances the integration of one's individual traits (Simmel 1955: 142). That is to say, by belonging to various groups (or identities) we find ourselves standing at the intersection of social circles – which initiates the development of an individual personality. Thus, for Simmel, there is no zero-sum competition between various references for identifications, and there may not even be a hierarchical relationship between them that is in need of overcoming. Our identities are not solid but, rather, are shifting constantly as we alter our involvements. Just as Simmel argued that belonging to various groups simultaneously encourages the development of an individual personality, so we would argue it also enables the emergence of a new social reality on a broader (European) level. Thus there is no need to overcome our various affiliations, as they encourage the realization of the idea of Europe. It is through the cross-fertilization of various affiliations and discursive actions that a new imaginary – or socio-cognitive model – emerges in which Europe itself becomes a reality.

Essential to this process of Europeanization is the creative tension between the inside and outside of our affiliations. It is precisely this theme that Beck and Grande elaborate upon in their recent writings on Europe and cosmopolitanism. Beck and Grande argue that the establishment of a democracy alone will not serve as a guarantor for cosmopolitanism. Instead, what is essential is the inter-play between inside and outside – or, rather, a form of cosmopolitan integration that works in two directions simultaneously: internally and externally. So, for example, Beck and Grande see a creative tension between integration within Europe and between Europe and the outside – or between integration and expansion. This form of cosmopolitanism in no way entails the renunciation of local or national attachments. Rather, it is the dynamic interaction between the national and the European level which will give rise to a European cosmopolitanism. These assertions, of course, are informed by Beck's project of a 'rooted cosmopolitanism', which does not oppose the national to the cosmopolitan level (Beck and Grande 2004: 32). They evidently also form part of Beck's development of a 'methodological cosmopolitanism', which regards cosmopolitanism in a positive light and as a challenge to 'methodological nationalism'. Overall, the most important insight from Beck and Grande's work is the perception of cosmopolitanism as the transformation of cultural and political subjectivities in the context of the encounter of the local or national with the global. Cosmopolitanism captures the existence of a level of reality that is being constituted by Europeanization, whereby cultural models are emerging in which new visions of social order are crystallizing in different forms and discourses, at different speeds and via different agencies.

These empirical manifestations naturally require a critical and anti-reductionist approach which perceives the social world as an emergent reality and which has transformative capacities. Such an approach can be found in critical cosmopolitanism, or what Walter Mignolo terms 'border thinking'. Border thinking mostly entails 'the recognition and transformation of hegemonic imaginary from the perspectives of people in subaltern positions' (Mignolo 2002: 174). This form of cosmopolitanism is distinct from Kant's universalist cosmopolitanism, but also differs from, for example, the radical socialist critique as offered by Marxism. While these projects were firmly rooted within a particular mode of modernity, border thinking attempts to open up a space for different discursive formations, which are not necessarily rooted within modernity but, rather, emerge from the exteriority of modernity (as in coloniality) (Mignolo 2002: 160). In doing so, border thinking raises our awareness that every universal is a universal of a particular, and that this universalization often results in the attempt to silence (rather than encourage) alternative voices. So, cosmopolitanism should 'no longer be articulated from one point of view, within a single logic, a mono-logic' (Mignolo 2002: 179) but should, rather, be built on a principle of diversality. Diversality comprises a polyvocality which emerges as a consequence of the interplay between global designs and local history that has to deal with these global developments. It mostly entails a relentless practice of critical and dialogical cosmopolitanism which is open ended, rather than a blueprint of a future ideal society projected from a single point of view (Mignolo 2002: 182).

In the context of Europe, border thinking (or the upsurge of polyvocality) amounts to an increasing awareness of the vacillation of borders – of the vaporization of old established certainties. By this we not only mean the vaporization of the material borders which demarcated one sovereign nation state from another – for this could quite easily result in the simple redrawing of boundaries. Rather, it implies the realization that, as a result of the interaction with the global level, every internal (or spiritual) border is continuously reshaped, and hence in essence uncertain (see Balibar 1998: 226). This, of course, truly affects our own mode of being, for we become increasingly aware of ourselves as a border – in that we are not quite this nor quite that. So, in the age of complexity, border thinking does not necessarily merely apply only to the people on the margins or the outskirts of Europe but, rather, takes place within all of us. This loss of certainty is not a negative development for, as we asserted earlier, it leads to a growing emphasis on a more communicative logic, one which is underpinned by new discursive spaces. This enables us to gain a reflexive distance on ourselves, and allows us to engage in a process of self-understanding – which leads to the emergence of a new social reality. After all, we are engaged in a continuous process of self-transformation – a dialogue between particular life-worlds and the global. The point is, though, that this new social reality is by no means uniquely European, however much it is a feature of the current situation. That is to say, while Europe may be becoming more and more cosmopolitan, this form of cosmopolitanism is not unique to Europe, for inside and outside, self and other, can no longer be easily demarcated. It is in this sense that we can speak of a cosmopolitan Europe but not of a European cosmopolitanism.

Conclusion

In this chapter we have traced cosmopolitanism back to its roots in Ancient Greek thought, with the Cynics and the Stoics. We then noted how the Stoic tradition formed a source of inspiration for the works of Immanuel Kant – who is regarded by many as the founding father of cosmopolitanism as a political project. However, while Kant's writings marked the first steps towards a form of cosmopolitanism which would have serious political implications, Kant's writings remained rather legalistic, as they focused on nation states as subjects, rather than on individual human beings. Consequently, Kant's legalist cosmopolitanism lacked a political dimension and in fact was indistinguishable from internationalism, which often fostered nationalism. Since the fall of the Berlin Wall, we can perceive the upsurge of a more politicized cosmopolitanism. On the universalist end of the spectrum we explored the writings of Nussbaum, who argued for an overcoming of particular affiliations and the discovery of that which was essential – namely the universal core of humanity. This idea of overcoming localized affiliations was explored within the context of a post-national Europe through the writings of Jürgen Habermas on constitutional patriotism. The allegiance to a European constitution and the establishment of a cosmopolitan (proceduralized) democracy would enable us to overcome the aporias of nationalism and create a European political system that would counter the pathological aspects of global capitalism. The problem is that there remains something like a specific common European humanity at the core of his post-nationalist framework. We also found this problem in the writings of Castells and in civic cosmopolitanism, which regarded Europe in terms distinguishable from the global. So, while in Castells' perception Europe could be seen as a network society with various nodes of power that relate directly to the institutions of Brussels, in the writings of civic cosmopolitanism Europe is a mere trans-nationalization of various national societies. This transnationalization did, however, lead to the uncoupling of territory and rights, and thereby pointed in the direction where we would perceive Europeanization in terms of socio-cognitive transformations.

It is this latter aspect of socio-cognitive transformations as a consequence of a newly emergent social reality that we emphasized. Europeanization, we argued, should not be seen in terms of *overcoming* national or parochial identifications, as the writings of Nussbaum and Habermas seem to imply but, rather, is a continuous process of *becoming*. This process of becoming, moreover, unfolds through the discursive interplay between various local affiliations and the wider global context.

Hence it inevitably involves a critical questioning of the categories 'inside' and 'outside', 'self' and 'other' – and consequently entails the loss of old certainties. This we perceive in a positive light, since it allows us to engage in a self-reflexive process of questioning and dialogue. It is through an open-ended encounter between the various life-worlds and the global that Europeanization takes place, as a mediation. Thus, there is no reason to believe that cosmopolitanism has to imply that we give up our local affiliations and identity formations in favour of a larger – more moral – cosmopolitanism. It is in fact through the interaction of these various affiliations that we engage in a process whereby Europe becomes a reality. This naturally complicates matters somewhat, for it is no longer clear what is European and non-European, what is self and other, for Europeanization entails nothing but the process of self-transformation. Accordingly, we can speak of a cosmopolitan Europe but not of a particular European cosmopolitanism.

References

Appiah, K. A. (2005) *The Ethics of Identity*, Princeton, MA: Princeton University Press.

Archibugi, D. (1995) *Cosmopolitan Democracy: An Agenda for a New World Order*, Cambridge: Polity Press.

Balibar, E. (1998) 'The borders of Europe', in P. Cheah and B. Robbins (eds), *Cosmopolitics: Thinking and Feeling Beyond the Nation*, Minneapolis, MN: University of Minnesota Press, pp. 216–32.

Balibar, E. (2004) *We, the People of Europe: Reflections on Transnational Citizenship*, Princeton, MA: Princeton University Press.

Barber, B. J. (1996) 'Constitutional faith', in J. Cohen (ed.), *For Love of Country: Debating the Limits of Cosmopolitanism*, Boston, MA: Beacon Press, pp. 30–37.

Beck, U. and Grande, E. (2004) *Das Kosmopolitische Europa*, Frankfurt: Suhrkamp.

Bellamy, R., Castiglione, D. and Santoro E. (eds) (2004) *Lineages of European Citizenship: Rights, Belonging and Participation in Eleven Nation-States*, London: Palgrave.

Bohman, J. and Lutz-Bachmann, M. (eds) (1997) *Perpetual Peace: Essays on Kant's Cosmopolitan Ideal*, Cambridge, MA: MIT Press.

Breckenridge, C. A., Pollock, S., Bhabha, H. K. and Chakrabarty, D. (eds) (2002) *Cosmopolitanism*, Durham, NC: Duke University Press (special issue of *Public Culture*, 12(3)).

Butler, J. (1996) 'Universality in culture', in J. Cohen (ed.), *For Love of Country: Debating the Limits of Cosmopolitanism*, Boston, MA: Beacon Press, pp. 45–52.

Calhoun, C. (2003) '"Belonging" in the cosmopolitan imaginary', *Ethnicities*, 3(4), 531–53.

Castells, M. (1998) 'The unification of Europe: globalization, identity, and the network state', in M. Castells, *End of the Millenium, Volume 3: The Information Age*, Oxford: Blackwell, pp. 338–65.

Cheah, P. and Robbins, B. (eds) (1998) *Cosmopolitics: Thinking and Feeling Beyond the Nation*, Minneapolis, MN: University of Minnesota Press.

Delanty, G. (2000) *Citizenship in a Global Age*, Buckingham: Open University Press.

Delanty, G. (2005) 'The idea of a cosmopolitan Europe: on the cultural significance of Europeanization', *International Review of Sociology*, 15(3), 405–21.

Delanty, G. (2006) 'The cosmopolitan imagination: critical cosmopolitanism and social theory', *British Journal of Sociology*, 57(1), 25–47.

Delanty, G. and Rumford, C. (2005) *Rethinking Europe: Social Theory and the Implications of Europeanization*, London: Routledge.

Eder, K. and Giesen, B. (eds) (2001) *European Citizenship Between National Legacies and Postnational Projects*, Oxford: Oxford University Press.

Fine, R. (2003) 'Taking the ism out of cosmopolitanism', *European Journal of Social Theory*, 6(4), 451–70.

Fine, R. and Smith, W. (2003) 'Jürgen Habermas' theory of cosmopolitanism', *Constellations*, 10(4), 469–87.

Gaonkar, D. P. (ed.) (2001) *Alternative Modernities*, Durham, NC: Duke University Press.

Habermas, J. (1979) *Communication and the Evolution of Society*, translated and introduced by T. McCarthy, London: Heinemann.

Habermas, J. (1992) 'Citizenship and national identity: some reflections on the future of Europe', *Praxis International*, 12(1), 1–19.

Habermas, J. (1996) *Between Facts and Norms: Contributions to a Discourse Theory of Law and Democracy*, translated by W. Rehg, Cambridge, MA: MIT Press.

Habermas, J. (1997) 'Kant's idea of perpetual peace, with the benefit of two hundred years' hindsight', in J. Bohman and M. Lutz-Backmann (eds), *Perpetual Peace: Essays on Kant's Cosmopolitanism*, Cambridge: Polity Press.

Habermas, J. (2001) *The Postnational Constellation*, translated, edited and introduced by M. Pensky, Cambridge: Polity Press.

Habermas, J. (2003) 'Towards a cosmopolitan Europe', *Journal of Democracy*, 14(4), 86–100.

Habermas, J. (2004) 'America and the world: a conversation with Eduardo Mendieta', *Logos*, 3(3).

Habermas, J. and Derrida, J. (2003) 'February 15, or, what binds Europeans together: a plea for a common foreign policy, beginning in the core of Europe', *Constellations*, 10(3), 291–97.

Held, D. (1995) *Democracy and the Global Order*, Cambridge: Polity Press.

Kant, I. (1784) *Idea for a Universal History with a Cosmopolitan Purpose*, in H. S. Reiss (ed.) (1991) *Kant: Political Writings* (2nd edition), Cambridge: Cambridge University Press, pp. 41–53.

Kant, I. (1795) *Perpetual Peace: A Philosophical Sketch*, in H. S. Reiss (ed.) (1991) *Kant: Political Writings* (2nd edition), Cambridge: Cambridge University Press, pp. 93–130.

Kurasawa, F. (2004) 'Cosmopolitanism from below: alternative globalization and the creation of a solidarity without bounds', *European Journal of Sociology*, 45(2), 233–55.

Mignolo, W. D. (2002) 'The many faces of cosmo-polis: border thinking and critical cosmopolitanism', in C. A. Breckenridge, S. Pollock, H. K. Bhabha and D. Chakrabarty (eds), *Cosmopolitanism*, Durham, NC: Duke University Press, pp. 721–48 (special issue of *Public Culture*, 12(3)).

Nussbaum, M. (1996) 'Patriotism and cosmopolitanism', in J. Cohen (ed.), *For Love of Country: Debating the Limits of Cosmopolitanism*, Boston, MA: Beacon Press, pp. 2–17.

Nussbaum, M. (1997) 'Kant and Stoic cosmopolitanism', *Journal of Political Philosophy*, 5(1), 1–25.

Robbins, B. (1998) 'Actually existing cosmopolitanism', in B. Robbins and P. Cheah (eds), *Cosmopolitics: Thinking and Feeling Beyond the Nation*, Minneapolis, MN: University of Minnesota Press, pp. 1–19.

Simmel, G. (1955) *Conflict: The Web of Group-Affiliations*, foreword by E. C. Hughes, translated by R. Bendix, Glencoe, IL: Free Press.

Soysal, Y. (1994) *The Limits of Citizenship*, Chicago, IL: University of Chicago Press.

Taylor, C. (1996) 'Why democracy needs patriotism', in J. Cohen (ed.), *For Love of Country: Debating the Limits of Cosmopolitanism*, Boston, MA: Beacon Press, pp. 119–21.

Turner, C. (2004) 'Jürgen Habermas: European or German?', *European Journal of Political Theory*, 3(3), 293–314.

Urry, J. (2000) *Sociology Beyond Society*, London: Sage.

Weiler, J. H. H. (1999) *The Constitution of Europe*, Cambridge: Cambridge University Press.

CHAPTER 3

Reinventing Europe – A Cosmopolitan Vision

Ulrich Beck

Europe can become neither a state nor a nation. Hence it cannot be thought of in terms of the nation state. The path to the unification of Europe leads not through uniformity but, rather, through acknowledgement of its national particularities. Diversity is the very source of Europe's potential creativity. The paradox is that nationalist thinking can be the worst enemy of the nation. The European Union (EU) is better placed to advance national interests than nations could possibly do acting alone.

More than two centuries ago, Immanuel Kant wrote that we live 'side by side', so 'violations of the law at one place of the earth are felt everywhere' (Kant 1795). Some 150 years ago, Friedrich Nietzsche declared:

> Europe would have to make up its mind ... so that the long spun-out comedy of its petty-statism, and its dynastic as well as its democratic many-willed-ness, might finally be brought to a close. The time for petty politics is past; the next century will bring the struggle for the dominion of the world – the *compulsion* to great politics. (Nietzsche 1966, original emphasis)

Karl Marx predicted that it would be globalizing capital, not the politics of states, that would break through national political axiomatics and open the game of great politics:

> In place of the old global and national seclusion and self-sufficiency, we have intercourse in every direction, universal interdependence of nations. And as in material, so also in intellectual production. The intellectual creations become common property. National one-sidedness and narrow-mindedness become more and more impossible, and from the numerous national and local literatures, there arises a world literature. (Marx and Engels 1848)

Lastly, Max Weber drew the conclusions for the historical sciences:

> But at some point the color changes. The meaning of the unthinkingly espoused views becomes uncertain, the path gets lost in the twilight. The light of the great cultural problems has moved on. At that point science, too, prepares to change its position and conceptual equipment and to look from the heights of thought down to the flow of events. (Weber 2002)

What Kant, Nietzsche, Marx and Weber prophesied is our present: a new cosmopolitanism is in the air!

What is enlightenment in the early years of the twenty-first century? Surely it includes the courage to make use of one's 'cosmopolitan vision' – to avow one's diverse identities, to take ways of life stemming from language, skin colour, nationality or religion and join them with the awareness that, in the world's radical uncertainty, all are equal and each is different (Beck 2006a). Applied to Europe, the cosmopolitan outlook acknowledges that Europe still suffers not only from its 'many-willed-ness' but even more from its national ontology of politics and society, which undervalues its historical uniqueness and causes political impasses. The paradox that one must fathom is that thinking of Europe as a great nation kindles the primordial national fears of the Europeans. It is either Europe or the European nations: a third alternative is out of the question. In the end, this national self-misunderstanding makes Europe and its member countries archrivals, threatening each other's existence. Misconceived in this manner, Europeanization becomes a diabolical zero-sum game in which Europe and its nations ultimately all lose.

The other side of the paradox is the need to part with the national mind-set of society and politics, to rethink Europe in cosmopolitan terms in order to relieve the member states of the fears that accepting the European constitution means committing cultural suicide. A cosmopolitan Europe is, first and foremost, a Europe of difference, of acknowledged national particularities. From the cosmopolitan viewpoint, this diversity – whether of languages, economic systems, political cultures or forms of democracy – appears primarily as an inexhaustible source, perhaps the source of Europe's cosmopolitan self-concept and not, as the national perspective would have it, as an obstacle to integration.

Europe, however, is still perceived in national terms as an 'unfinished nation', an 'incomplete federal state', as though it ought to become both a nation and a state. Europe's actual distress consists not least in precisely this inability to grasp and understand the historically new kind of reality that Europeanization represents. That lack of comprehension is also a major reason why the institutions of the EU come across as unapproachable, unreal and often menacing to the citizens they are intended to serve.

Even advanced research on Europe has scarcely dared venture beyond the conventional basic pattern of nation state thinking. The EU is considered in terms of territoriality, sovereignty, jurisdictions and demarcation. Even at higher levels of complexity, when speaking of 'governance' or a 'multilevel system', the legal and academic parlance of research on Europe remains biased towards organizational and regulatory systems designed to conceive of and cast the EU in the image of the nation state.

Sociology's failure with regard to Europe is particularly conspicuous. The discipline developed its instruments in the waning nineteenth century from the analysis of national societies. Because those instruments are ill suited to analysing contemporary European society, the conclusion in sociology is that, obviously, there exists no European society at all worth mentioning. This opinion has many causes, but one in particular deserves criticism: the concept of society is the crystallization point of sociology's methodological nationalism. In sociological analysis, Europe must therefore be understood as a plural – as societ*ies*; it must be understood in additive or, at best, comparative terms. In other words, the society of Europe overlaps Europe's national societies. This methodological nationalism practised by social science is becoming historically fallacious, because it filters out Europe's complex realities and space for interaction. In a nutshell, it is blind to Europe and blinds us to Europe. A similar thought pattern stems from the statement that there is no European demos, or populace. What populace is meant – that of the ancient Greek city states, the Swiss cantons or the nation states? What about the present-day societies of our intertwined countries? Do the nation states themselves still even have a homogeneous populace or citizenry?

The nation state is everywhere the tacit conceptual measuring stick that makes the realities of Europeanization appear deficient: no populace, no people, no state, no democracy, no public. In addition to disinterest in and sheer lack of understanding of the debates of other member states, there is a steadily increasing number of trans-national communication processes about common challenges, such as the responses to the 2003 war in Iraq, to the democratic revolt in Ukraine and to European anti-Semitism. Instead of making stereotyped assertions that there is no European public, people should expand the concept of 'public' beyond its fixation on the nation state and open it up to a cosmopolitan understanding that realistically accommodates the dynamics from which the trans-boundary forms of the European public sphere are developing.

What is 'European' in this sense are co-national forms of identity, ways of life, means of production and types of interaction that pass right through the walls of states. It is about forms and movements of ceaseless border-crossing. Horizontal Europeanization is giving rise to new shadow realities, which are lived in the blind spots of the aliens' registration office: multilingualism, multinational networks, binational marriages, multiple residences, educational mobility, trans-national careers, and linkages between science and the economy. Both science and the economy are globalized and Europeanized at the same time, and it will be not easy to distinguish between the two. These spots are spreading and are being taken for granted by the upcoming generations. Contemplating these developments, I see five lines of thought.

The first is the issue of the dynamic of inequality affecting Europe as a whole. What impact does the dismantling of national borders in Europe have on the European dynamic of inequality? For one thing, the nation-based limits to people's perceptions of social inequality begin to dissolve as Europeanization moves forward. In response to the question of what legitimizes social inequality, there are at least two possible answers: the merit principle and the nation state principle. The first answer is a familiar, well rehearsed one and has already been the subject of critique. It is a perfectly logical consequence of the national per-spective and relates to domestic inequalities (i.e. internal to the state). The second answer provides an explanation for the 'legitimation' of global inequalities and makes it possible to identify the major blind spots and sources of error to which methodological nationalism exposes the sociology of inequality. Perceptions of inequality that are based on the national outlook are subject to a fundamental asymmetry, as far as both society and social science are concerned. The 'legitima-tory achievement' of the nation state lies in turning attention inwards, to the exclusion of all else, thereby banishing trans-national and global inequalities from the field of vision.

To put it another way, the nation state outlook offers an 'excuse' for not looking at the misery in the world. It works on the basis of a double exclusion: it excludes the excluded. It is astonishing to witness the degree of stability with which the large inequalities suffered by humanity are 'legitimated' in tacit complicity between state authority and state-fixated sociology, by means of organized non-perception. What construct is it that enables this to happen?

The history of inequality presupposes the history of *equality*, that is, the institutionalization of norms of equality: without equality there can be no comparability and therefore no politically relevant inequality. The distinction between global and national inequalities is based on the fact that within different national arenas there are powerful norms of inequality at work – relating, for example, to civil, political and social rights, and pre-political national identities. It is these norms of inequality that establish both the comparability of inequali-ties within the national arena as well as the incomparability of inequalities between different national arenas.

This is the prerequisite for the political legitimation of socio-political activities within the nation state and passivity towards others 'outside' it. If inequality itself were the key political criterion, it would be extremely difficult to justify why prosperous European societies make such huge efforts to organize financial transfer systems within their own nation states on the basis of national criteria of poverty and neediness while a large proportion of the world's population is threatened daily with starvation.

The methodological nationalism that underpins the sociology of inequality unreflexively makes equality bounded by the nation state both a presupposition and a constant. This in turn obscures the fact that it is the nation state principle itself that generates the increasingly scarce resource of *legitimation through incomparability* – scarce on account of the dramatic growth and growing consciousness of global inequalities. To put it another way, the nation state principle *institutionalizes the act of looking the other way*. What does this mean when applied to Europeanization? As the barriers of interstate incomparability between inequalities fall away (for example through a growing European self-awareness or through the institutionalization of equality and self-observation), the EU can be expected to enter a period of turbulence – even given constant relations of inequality.

The issue can be illustrated with the help of a simple example. The slogan 'equal pay for equal work' was and still is a key demand of the workers' movement. However, the trade union struggle for equality has come up against a 'natural' boundary, namely that of the nation state. As natural as it is within Germany to struggle to maintain national agreements on pay and conditions and to fight for wage parity between East and West Germany after German unification, for a long time it was just as natural to ignore wage differentials in comparison with other European countries. Looked at through national spectacles, differences in wage levels between Bavaria and East Berlin are considered illegitimate, while the same differences between Bavaria and Belgium are seen as legitimate. But what happens when these same differences are viewed and judged through European spectacles? Aren't differences in wage levels between European countries illegitimate in that context? Shouldn't European trade unions be demanding 'equal pay for equal work' for every European worker? Or must this principle be discarded?

That these are far from being merely academic questions became abundantly clear in January 2004, when a great deal of heated polemical debate was conducted in different national public arenas over the move initiated by some members of the European Parliament to strengthen the institution's identity by standardizing Members' parliamentary allowances. Huge inequalities exist there with regard to levels of payment for the same work. An Italian Member of the European Parliament receives €11,000 a month before tax, a German party colleague is paid about €7,000, their Spanish neighbour has to make do with €3,000, while their new colleagues from the Central European countries get no more than €1,000.

No immediate plans exist to reduce these extreme inequalities, as the EU foreign ministers succumbed to public pressure and quashed the initiative.

Neo-liberalism has appropriated the old motto of the workers' movement in a new form: equal pay for equal work – as long as it is equal *low* pay! The unions seem to be faced with two equally unacceptable options as a result of this. One is to resist this move and demand equal pay for equal work – as long as it is equal high pay! This was the route taken after German unification, although it is generally agreed to be economically fatal and politically utopian. The second option is no less appealing, where the unions find themselves in the perverse position of taking up the slogan of their enemies and demanding *different* wages for the *same* work – in other words, defending existing wage differentials between European countries. This forces the unions into a neo-national position.

This example shows that, far from reducing the explosive potential of inequalities within Europe, the dismantling of borders actually makes it more likely to come to the fore. This is because the barriers blocking people's perceptions of international incomparability are also being dismantled, so that inequalities are starting to be judged in equal terms across country borders and calls for parity are becoming louder. This constellation contains the seeds of enormous political conflict. It could be exploited by post-communist parties just as much as by right-wing neo-nationalist movements. Even social democratic parties are not immune to this neo-nationalist temptation.

The second line of thought is that Europeanization is initiating a historically new positive-sum game: joint solutions serve the national interest. Europe's crisis is a mental one. National governments are struggling with seemingly national problems in a national setting and are trying to solve them by going their own national ways – and are failing. The export of jobs is an example, as is the attempt to control the taxation of corporate profits. Mobile business organizations operating within global networks are able to play individual states against each other and thereby weaken them. The more the national perspective predominates in the thinking and action of people and governments, the more these businesses succeed at expanding their own power. That is the paradox that must be understood. The national frame of reference violates national interests. The EU is an arena where formal sovereignty can be exchanged for real power, national cultures nurtured and economic success achieved. The EU is better placed to solve national problems than nations could possibly do acting alone (Beck 2006b).

No matter where one looks in Europe, it is the same situation. The ratio of old people to the total population is rising to uncomfortable levels and pension systems no longer function, but the necessary reforms are thwarted by the organized resistance of the groups affected. To escape this trap, the connection between decline in population growth, the ageing of societies, necessary reforms of social security systems, selective migration policy, the export of jobs and the taxation of corporate profits could be defined and cooperatively worked on as a European problem. This approach would benefit all governments currently contenting themselves with sham solutions in the dead end of the nation state.

However, Germany's left-of-centre federal coalition between the Greens and the Social Democratic Party (SPD) in its latter years headed again down the 'German path' to that dead end. The then head of the SPD, Franz Müntefering, was reported as saying that he did 'not want any more cheap eastern European labour in Germany's slaughterhouses', so the government was considering increasing the minimum wage. The message that Europe creates the evil neo-liberals and Berlin provides for the weak members of society was (and is) a disastrous lie. Tens of thousands of German jobs exist solely because the new Eastern EU countries import far more goods from Germany than they export to it. The national mind-set, whether partial to the right or the left, be it in favour of capitalism or critical of it, is always blind to the gains in domestic prosperity and the losses of welfare in poorer areas abroad.

Worse yet, perhaps, is that the German job protectors harm the country's national interest and torpedo the meaning of the EU constitution, the very document that brings the new logic of cosmopolitan realism to bear. It stresses that joint solutions go further than independent national approaches. The urgent national problems are especially those whose solutions require cooperation across boundaries. The national problem for Germans – for example 'wage dumping' – can be tackled only by Europe as a whole, through European-wide minimum wages. Lasting cooperation between states increases rather than constricts their ability to act. Paradoxically, surrendering sovereignty enhances sovereignty. That is the secret of success for the EU.

Looking at everything from the national perspective jeopardizes national prosperity and democratic freedom. Ensuring the health of the nation and the economy, effectively coping with unemployment and promoting a lively democracy all require the cosmopolitan viewpoint. Transcending national and post-national sympathies, cosmopolitan Europe does not threaten the nation state but, rather, prepares, facilitates, modernizes, changes and opens it for the global age.

The third line of thought is that Europeanization requires a memory culture that spans borders. In the words Thomas Mann wrote in anguish about the First World War, 'Alas, Europe', by which he meant the calamity of the Western world: 2,500 years shredded by war and bled to death. At the centre of every village in Europe stands a large monument engraved with the names of those killed in action in that conflict. On the wall of a nearby church, one then finds three more names from the same family on a stone tablet listing the casualties of the Second World War. That *was* Europe.

How long has it been? Not very. Until the late 1980s the peoples of this belligerent Europe were faced off in a nuclear stalemate. The policy of drawing East and West closer together seemed possible only through recognition of the seemingly eternal division of Europe. And today? A European miracle has taken place: enemies have become neighbours! That wonder is historically unique, actually even inconceivable. At precisely the most wanton moment in the history of states, a political invention comes along that makes possible what is almost unimaginable – states themselves transform their monopoly on power into a taboo on violence. The threat of violence as a political option, whether between member states or against supranational institutions, has been banished once and for all from the horizon of the possible in Europe.

That change became possible because Europe has experienced the advent of something qualitatively new – national horror at the murder of European Jews. The national wars and expulsions are no longer remembered only within a national compass; the national space for commemoration is bound to broaden to a European scope. A Europeanization of perspectives is occurring (or at least the first signs of it are – see Levy and Sznaider 2005).

Such cosmopolitanism in the opening of communication, in the acceptance of interdependence through inclusion of the stranger for the sake of common interests, and in the historical exchange of perspectives between perpetrators and victims in post-war Europe is something other than multiculturalism or postmodern non-commitment. Although this cosmopolitanism is intended to rest upon cohesive and reciprocally binding norms that can help prevent a slide into postmodern particularism, it is not simply universal. For an entity like Europe, interacting with the range of cultures, traditions and interests in the weave of national societies is a matter of survival. As Hannah Arendt argued, only the infinitely difficult forgiveness granted and received through remembrance creates the necessary trust in the relationship between states and nations, and empowers them.

The fourth line of thinking concerns the understanding of *European society as a regional world risk society*. The macro-sociology of Europeanization is in danger of repeating the same mistakes made by methodological nationalism, only at the European level – of getting caught up in what might be called a 'methodological Europeanism'. In order to counter this tendency, Europeanization should not be defined and analysed purely in endogenous terms, but also in exogenous terms, in relation to the frame of reference constituted by world society. Let me make just a few brief comments on this point.

The experience of modernity is one of risk, in the sense that, along with its successes, modernity has also conjured up the possibility of its self-destruction.

However, this insight of reflexive modernization needs to be opened up to the cosmopolitan point of view and thus to the question of whether the threats posed by modernization are perceived as the side-effects of one's 'own' decisions or of decisions made by 'others'. The dynamic of inequality that characterizes the 'world risk society' (Beck 1999) can thus be illuminated in terms of the distinction between self-induced threats and threats emanating from others. To put it in highly simplified terms, Europeanization refers to self-induced threats, while the ways in which modernity threatens to self-destruct in the Third World are perceived primarily as a threat emanating from others. Unlike the theory of dependency or the world system theory, the theory of reflexive modernization highlights the fact that the different regions of the world are affected unequally not only by the consequences of failed processes of modernization but also by the consequences of *successful* processes of modernization.

The major strands of conflict during the Cold War were politically open ended and acquired their explosive character on account of national and international security issues. By contrast, the geopolitical strands of conflict in the world risk society run between the different cultures of risk. In relation to risk perception, geopolitical conflicts are emerging between regions that bring highly divergent historical situations, experiences and expectations to the terrain of the world risk society. An outstanding example of this is the contrast between, on the one hand, the degree of urgency accorded by Europe to the dangers of climate change and by the US to international terrorism, on the other. Not only are cultural perceptions of global threats diverging more and more between Europe and the US, but, because this is so, Europeans and North Americans are effectively living in different worlds. The way it looks to the Americans, the Europeans are suffering from a form of hysteria in relation to the environment, while, to many Europeans, US Americans are paralysed by an exaggerated fear of terrorism. The danger is that the drifting apart of the transatlantic cultures of risk will lead to a cultural break between the US and Europe; to paraphrase Huntington, cultural *differences in perception are generating a clash of risk cultures* – either you believe in the existing climate disaster or else in the potential ubiquity of suicide terror attacks.

Let's not deceive ourselves: the choice between risks is not only about choosing between risks, it is also about choosing between two visions of the world. The issue is, who is guilty and who is innocent, who will get ahead and who will fall behind – the military or human rights, the logic of war or the logic of treaties?

The fifth, concluding line of thought is a question: How will a European empire of law and consensus become possible? In the final analysis, understanding the concept of cosmopolitanism in this way is also the key to understanding and shaping new forms of political authority that have emerged in Europe beyond the nation state. But globalization, specifically the problems with the flows and crises of global finance, and the neglected European dimension of current socio-political exigencies show that the opposite is now breaking over our heads. A nationally circumscribed labour market no longer exists. Even if we point the gun barrels at foreigners, well educated Indian or Chinese people can offer their services in Germany and the rest of Europe with a click of the mouse.

Reality is becoming cosmopolitan. The 'other' whom borders can no longer keep out is everywhere, but in a way that no cosmopolitan philosopher had anticipated and that no one willed – surreptitiously, unintentionally, without political decision or design. The real process of becoming cosmopolitan in this world is taking place through the back door of secondary effects; it is undesired, unseen and usually occurs by default.

How can anyone counter distortions of this sort? Through power? By means of the ability to shape sovereignty transferred to Europe? Do steps towards integration, like the European single currency, make it possible to parry the erratic fluctuations of international currency exchange and waves of speculation? Who has what leverage in Europe? And most important, what context of political rule is appropriate for it? Edgar Grande and I have proposed for it a redefinition of the term 'empire' (Beck and Grande 2004). Spoken in French, that word carries Napoleonic and colonial connotations and thus differs from the term when pronounced in English. The British empire was something other than the imperial US claims to be. The term 'European empire' attempts to place Europe on a par with the US empire. For all the similarities with the complex confederation or empire that emerged from the Middle Ages, the European empire of the early twenty-first century is built upon the existing nation states. To that extent, the analogy with the Middle Ages does not hold. The cosmopolitan empire of Europe is notable for its open and cooperative character at home and abroad, and therein clearly contrasts with the imperial predominance of the US. Europe's undeniably real power is not decipherable in terms of nation states. It lies instead in its character as a model of how Europe succeeded in transforming a belligerent past into a cooperative future, in how the European miracle of enemies becoming neighbours came about. It is this 'soft' world power that is developing a special radiance and attraction that is often as underestimated in the nation state mould of thinking about Europe as it is in the projections of power claimed by US neo-conservatives.

But what impact does that have on European integration? For a long time, that key concept consisted primarily in the abolition of national and local differences. This 'harmonization policy' confounded unity with uniformity or assumed that uniformity is required for unity. In this sense, uniformity became the supreme regulatory principle of modern Europe, transferring the principles of classical constitutional theory to institutions at the European level. The more successfully

EU policy operated under this primacy of uniformity, the more resistance grew and the more clearly the counterproductive effects surfaced.

By contrast, cosmopolitan integration is based on a paradigm shift in which diversity is not the problem but, rather, the solution. Europe's further integration must not be oriented to the traditional notions of uniformity inherent in a European 'federal state'. Integration must instead take Europe's irrevocable diversity as its starting point. That is the only way for Europeanization to link two demands that at first glance seem mutually exclusive: the call for the recognition of difference and the call for the integration of divergences.

Understood as a historically tested political model for a post-imperial empire of consensus and law – 'the European dream' (Rifkin 2004) of a soft world power – Europeanization is fascinating as an alternative to the US way, and not least to Americans critical of the US. Ultimately, it is about something completely new in human history, namely, the forward-looking vision of a state structure firmly based on recognition of the culturally different other.

So what is my cosmopolitan vision of Europe? We Europeans are, in Kant's words, crooked timber and pretty provincial. That aspect of us has endearing sides, too. Individual populations – the British and the French, for example – have the reputation of being cosmopolitan, but the attribution applies to them *as* French or British, less so as Europeans. Expansion can either cause the EU to roll up like a hedgehog or lead it to embrace cosmopolitanism and thus enhance the awareness of its responsibility in the world.

The national idea is unsuitable for unifying Europe. A large European superstate frightens people. I do not believe that Europe can issue from the ruins of the nation states. If there is an idea capable of uniting Europeans today, it is that of a cosmopolitan Europe, because it stills Europeans' fear of losing identity, makes a constitutional goal out of tolerant interaction among the many European nations, and opens new political spaces and options for action in a globalized world. The persistence of the nation is the condition of a cosmopolitan Europe; and today, for the reasons just given, the reverse is true too. The more secure and confirmed Europeans feel in their national dignity, the less they will shut themselves off in their nation states and the more resolutely they will stand up for European values in the world and take up the cause of others as their own. I would like to live in this kind of cosmopolitan Europe, one in which people have roots and wings.

References

Beck, U. (1999) *World Risk Society*, Cambridge: Polity Press.
Beck, U. (2006a) *Power in the Global Age*, Cambridge: Polity Press.
Beck, U. (2006b) *The Cosmopolitan Vision*, Cambridge: Polity Press.

Beck, U. and Grande, E. (2004) *Das kosmopolitische Europa*, Frankfurt a.M.: Suhrkamp Verlag.

Kant, I. (1795) *Zum Ewigen Frieden*, in *Dritter Definitionsartikel, Werke, Volume 11*, Frankfurt a.M.: Suhrkamp Verlag (1960).

Levy, D. and Sznaider, N. (2005) *The Holocaust and Memory in the Global Age*, Philadelphia, PA: Temple University Press.

Marx, K. and Engels, F. (1848) *Kommunistisches Manifest*, in *Studienhefte 4*, Munich: Fink Verlag (1969).

Nietzsche, F. (1996) *Werke, Volume 2*, Munich: Hanser Verlag.

Rifkin, J. (2004) *The European Dream: How Europe's Vision of the Future is Quietly Eclipsing the American Dream*, New York: Tarcher/Penguin.

Weber, M. (2002) 'Die Objecktivitat sozialwissenschaftlicher', in D. Kaesler (ed.), *Max Weber Schriften 1892–1922*, Stuttgart: Kroner Verlag.

CHAPTER 4

Cosmopolitan Europe, Post-colonialism and the Politics of Imperialism

Nick Stevenson

Teaching a class on citizenship in my first term at a new university, I tried to build up a picture of the way students view the contemporary globalized world. Over ten weeks the class discussed a range of contemporary issues, from global poverty to the environmental crisis and from the politics of security to multiculturalism and feminism. Despite the overtly 'global' nature of these issues I noticed how patriotic the students were, with politics mainly being defined in strictly national terms. Despite global communications, travel and multiculturalism, what really struck me was the Britishness of their views and perspectives. The most powerful narrative that would appear over the course of the following weeks was the need to preserve our British values and traditions and to guard them from the ways in which they were being eroded, sometimes by Americanization and at other times by foreigners and immigrants. Britain, it seemed, was a nation under siege, from the inside as well as the outside. What was lacking was any wider, cosmopolitan set of identifications. There was little interest in Britain's relationship with Europe and, despite a number of public campaigns on the inequality of global trade, very little awareness of their privileged position within a wider global society. Further, many found it difficult to consider how the host nation might look from the point of view of asylum seekers or other recently arrived immigrant populations. The dominant language most of the group had available to them, then, was overwhelmingly derived from national politics. This is why I think that cosmopolitanism and post-colonialism offer a uniquely intellectual challenge for our times. Even if the organization of our economy, politics and culture is increasingly global, for most of our citizens most of the time 'the nation' nonetheless remains their dominant point of reference.

The ability to be able to see the world from a position that is not completely determined by the rhetoric of our nation, clan or side is an urgent political concern.

This presses the need for a cosmopolitanism where we can think about 'us', but from the standpoint of the other. This, then, is not cosmopolitanism where we simply substitute warm talk of the nation for the idea of a shared European homeland. Here we need to construct an idea of a cosmopolitan Europe that has not only subverted nationalist rhetoric but also learned from its own imperialist past.

Post-colonial theory as part of the recent 'cultural turn' in the social sciences has much to contribute in terms of alerting us to the fact that there is no politics without cultural politics. If Europe has historically traded upon an internalist history (of capitalism, modernity and the Enlightenment), it also introduced the idea of historical development, which presumed these to be natural stages (Chakrabarty 2000). Historically this meant that liberal thinkers in the nineteenth century could argue that the colonies had to be civilized before they were deemed to be ready for self-development. The history of European liberal thought is riven with similar self-satisfied feelings of superiority that serve to legitimate rule over foreign peoples. Indeed, much sociology and political theory up until the arrival of post-colonialism was equally caught up with similarly Eurocentric forms of self-understanding. Immanuel Wallerstein (1997) has alerted us to the ways in which European definitions of history, universal thinking, civilization, Orientalism and progress have served to reinforce the West's sense of superiority. The development of post-colonial literature since the mid-1980s in Europe and North America has sought to ask a number of questions previously repressed within the sociological and political canon. Displacing previous research agendas that were concerned with exclusively national agendas, issues of rationalization or modernization, post-colonialism at its most radical has sought to remind us of a legacy that can be traced back to a period on the eve of the First World War when the 'West' dominated approximately 85 per cent of the world (Said 1993: 6). Despite the beginning of European decolonization with Indian independence in 1947, post-colonial studies have pointed to the continuation of the legacies of imperialism and colonialism in the politics and history of the present.

The world continues to live in the wake of the violent disruptions that can be traced in the multifarious histories of Western dominance, up to the present. The idea that the relations of dominance instigated by colonialism or imperialism can be 'swept under the carpet' is resisted by the argument that the global system of the twenty-first century continues to be dominated by the political, economic, military and cultural power of the West. Here post-colonialism for the most part continues to support a radical politics of liberation that offers critical solidarity with anti-colonial movements while deconstructing the role of political economy, knowledge and power in seeking to press the superiority of the 'West' over the 'rest' (Young 2001). Indeed, it is worth noting that processes of global interconnection have displaced rigid distinctions between Western and non-Western societies.

Increasingly, economic, political and cultural interconnections severely question the separation between the 'First' and 'Third' Worlds. In this respect, Robert Young (2001) argues that post-colonial criticism should not privilege the colonial, but rather seek to deconstruct specifically Western imaginaries in the light of complex histories of dominance and ongoing asymmetries of global power. Here post-colonial criticism is concerned with both the decolonization of the Western imagination and the creation of equal access to material, natural and technological resources. While there is an inevitable irony that most post-colonial work is at least in part a Western invention, this was necessarily so, given the extent to which anti-colonial movements have failed to establish the equal value of the cultures of decolonized nations. For Young (2001), the critique of Eurocentrism becomes key to the deconstruction of the ability of white, male and Western cultures to constitute the norm. Post-colonialism acts as a normative and political project, one which seeks to articulate a view of human futures that has broken with the dominance of the past to embrace a world of hybridity, difference and solidarity.

Here I wish to locate post-colonial critique and argument in the context of the liberal European project. Notably they both share a critique of nationalism and a desire to construct more genuinely inclusive post-national versions of citizenship. Further, we could argue that, owing to Europe's own imperial past, there is also a shared scepticism in respect of any attempt to resurrect an imperial politics from the past. However, my view is that the struggle for a genuinely cosmopolitan Europe has much to learn from post-colonial criticism. The development of a relatively pacified zone within Europe in the context of two world wars and the Holocaust is a considerable historical achievement. The fostering of the European Court of Human Rights and democratic forms of citizenship has helped create peaceful coexistence in place of warlike nationalism. However, the continuation of populist racism, particularly evident in the eruption of aggressive hostility towards asylum seekers, suggests that the shadow of Europe's imperial past continues to linger in the cultural and political sphere.

In this context, I return to Kant's (1795) essay *Perpetual Peace* as an important source of inspiration for a Europe governed by cosmopolitan law rather than war and violence. Here I seek to develop a post-colonial critique of Kant as a way of recovering his vision of a republican Europe, while also asking what his dream of a civilized world masks from view. Here my argumentative strategy is not to reject the idea of a cosmopolitan Europe, but to argue that such an intellectual mission would need to go beyond a return to Kantian ideals, to consider a more complex set of cultural entanglements. From this point, I seek to account for the legacy of European racism and imperialism, and argue that any European cosmopolitanism worthy of the name would need to deal with the persistence of ideologies and beliefs that continue to inscribe cultural forms of domination. A genuinely cosmopolitan Europe is not only a Europe that has 'internally' sought to pacify nationalist aggression but also one that has developed an alternative political imaginary that has reconfigured material and symbolic relations both 'inside' and 'outside' Europe. Here the cosmopolitan European project becomes redefined as the need both to develop internal forms of multiculturalism and to reconstitute geopolitical relations with the global South. Arguably such a project becomes possible only after we have established an intellectual debate between post-colonial criticism and some liberal understandings of the European project.

Cosmopolitanism and post-colonialism

The writing of the philosopher Immanuel Kant (1795) is often taken to be the starting point for cosmopolitan analysis in the European context. Here the law of nations becomes replaced by a possible future global order based upon cosmopolitan law. The 'perpetual peace' is created by states subordinating their right to go to war to an obligation to settle their differences in a court of law. The root of the problem of war lay with states coming into conflict with one another and with their capacity to mobilize standing armies. The overriding cosmopolitan principle was that 'no state shall forcibly interfere in the constitution and government of another state' (Kant 1795: 96). For its own security, each state should seek to establish a federation, whereby separate states are 'welded together as a unit' (Kant 1795: 102). Whereas 'savages' seek to protect their right to wage wars, Kant clearly believed that the granting of rights to citizens would both enhance the prospects of peace and bring to an end the hitherto lawlessness of nation states. Indeed, many have argued that the formation of the European Union on the principles of human rights and democracy is the realization of Kant's dream of peaceful coexistence. In this argument, the European Union (despite some of the claims of the Eurosceptics) is not a state but rather serves to 'preserve and secure the freedom of each state in itself' (Kant 1795: 104).

The republican view following Kant is that democratic rule requires an international order of democratic states. The development of genuinely civil societies requires not only internal pacification but also the rule of law governing the actions of states. This would change the foundation of citizenship that has existed in the majority of democratic states. In exchange for civil and political rights, citizens accept that they may become combatants during wars. However, after the 'total wars' of twentieth-century Europe, many have become aware that ideas of civil society need to find a more global expression (Kaldor 2003). The limitation of the idea of genuinely pacified civil societies to Western democratic states allowed colonial powers to participate in a politics of violent conquest. A genuinely international civil society requires an international system that is subject to the rule of law. If Europe is our current best expression of this ideal, many can perhaps be forgiven for thinking that the current polarizing rhetoric in respect of the 'war on terror' makes its wider adoption seem unlikely.

We should consider the view that such notions of cosmopolitan rule and civil society are intrinsically Eurocentric in nature. Before pursuing this argument I think we need to return to a debate about some of Kant's arguments in respect of the rule of law and civilization. David Harvey (2000) has argued that it is easy to detect a different Kant to that which is so loved by liberal cosmopolitanism. This is a Kant who is caught within the contradictions and evasions of Enlightenment thinking. As the cultural historian George L. Mosse (1978) has argued, racism is not an aberration of Enlightenment thinking but actually integral to its foundation. Many will undoubtedly find such a view uncomfortable; however, it is hard to comprehend the entirely shameful history of European scientific racism without coming to a similar conclusion. The Enlightenment passion for the categorization of 'man' in relation to 'nature' seemingly paved the way for numerous reflections on the racial hierarchy of peoples and cultures. Much of the work of eighteenth-century anthropologists sought to classify the white race in a way that stressed its correspondence with middle-class values of orderliness, ingenuity and being law-abiding. Even the most 'rational' of Enlightenment thinkers did not escape these formulations. For example, Kant argued that there were four main races: White, Negro, Mongol and Hindu. These races provided the basis for appearance, intelligence and potential human development. Notably these mutable ideas were followed by later generations of racial biologists and scientists, who linked questions of race to ideas of civilization and ultimately to notions of degeneration. Indeed, if for Kant the peoples of hot lands were timid, lazy and superstitious, we might question the extent to which universal principles actually operate as a form of discrimination rather than as a shared good (Harvey 2000). Does the Eurocentrism of Kant tell us less about a possible future civilized world and more about the need of European intellectuals to feel superior?

This is, indeed, what the post-colonial critic Gayatri Spivak (1999) has argued in relation to Kant. Spivak argues that, for Kant, civility is learnt through culture, which inevitably presents limited conditions of entry for non-European peoples. Indeed, it is the desire upon the part of Europeans to be global legislators that reproduces the binary opposition between master and native. Kant unknowingly reproduces 'the axiomatics of imperialism' (Spivak 1999: 37). Yet we might remind ourselves that Kant is by no means exceptional within the history of European philosophy in his attachment to the belief in the superiority of Western civilization (Wood 1999). Indeed, Bhikhu Parekh (1995) has similarly discovered that Western liberal writers such as Locke and Mill viewed non-Europeans with contempt. This is the point, he reasons, where liberalism can itself become illiberal. Such a view simply assumes that a European way of life is best and that there is nothing of value to be learnt from an intercultural dialogue with other traditions of thinking. Inevitably the division between the civilized and the primitive reproduces a racialized logic that seeks to uphold Western forms of superiority. Unlike Mill and Locke, Kant remained a critic of colonialism, even if he could not help but reproduce some of its basic assumptions. It should, however, make us pause to think how current cosmopolitan projects are being formulated. Here I would argue that we need to question the Kantian and Habermasian emphasis on history as a form of progress (Habermas 1997), whereby we emancipate ourselves, through the use of reason and public dialogue, from the domination of the past. In the context of the assumed superiority of European ways of life and living, such a dialogue is unlikely to offer much learning from a racially deformed 'other'.

Such views have led many to ditch universalistic thinking altogether. Here the argument is that universalistic Western values merely provide an ideological cover for the cultural dominance of the world's rich and powerful. Universal values – human rights, liberty, equality and the rest – seek to normalize the globe in the West's own interests. In truth, then, such a language acts as a kind of victor's justice. Engin Isin (2002) makes this point in a more sophisticated way. He argues that dominant political languages necessarily come to us from the powerful, who are then able to legitimate their rights and privileges through the discourses of citizenship. Indeed, instead of concentrating on the language of democracy and rights, we would be better disposed to look at how strangers and outsiders become constituted through the language of the political. In other words, white, male Europeans inevitably sought to naturalize their superiority and dominate aliens by representing themselves as the holders of civilized virtues. Within the rational kernel of the Enlightenment continue to lurk the nightmares of racism and imperialism. Here I want to consider two related questions: if this argument is followed, what are the implications for the ways in which Europeans constitute themselves, and what are the direct consequences of such legacies in respect of 'our' relations with the rest of the world?

Racism, Enlightenment and citizenship

Some recently published lectures of the late philosopher Michel Foucault (2003) serve to complicate this picture. As is well known, Foucault's (1977) main contribution to social and political theory has been the development of a radical view of disciplinary power. Liberal concerns with issues of rights and the need to set limits upon state power mask the development of the *carcéral* society. By focusing upon the techniques of power, Foucault points to the continuities between democracy and totalitarianism. Foucault re-reads the Enlightenment and argues that it reveals not so much the progress of reason but the regulation and normalization of the population. In Foucault's analysis there is a kinship between the normative arguments put forward by cosmopolitan liberals and the political rationality of totalitarianism and imperialism. In other words, in certain respects both totalitarianism and imperialism were the extension of a number of techniques that could be found within democratic societies. Further, along with disciplinary power emerged bio-power, which sought to regulate and manage the body. Bio-power was the attempt by various agencies, including the medical profession and the state, to sustain a healthy population (Foucault 1981). Yet the establishment of medical policing in the eighteenth and nineteenth century was influenced by racialized ideas of degeneracy. The need to categorize and regulate a 'healthy' population was driven by processes of normalization.

These arguments are developed further as Foucault (2003) charts the emergence of discourses of war, conquest and domination. Foucault seeks to analyse the historical emergence of the idea of a 'discourse of bitterness' – the idea that the history of mankind can be understood as a race war (Foucault 2003: 57). This discourse, argues Foucault, starts at the end of the sixteenth and the beginning of the seventeenth century in Europe, as a challenge to royal power, which then becomes connected to nationalism and European colonialism. Later, Foucault's genealogy traces the ways in which this discourse of domination erases its connection to racial conflict in order to define itself as class struggle. However, in Europe during the seventeenth century this discourse became a battle not between races but an attempt by a 'superior' race to defend itself against degeneracy (Foucault 2003: 60–62). The idea of race struggle therefore acted as a principle of exclusion and ultimately normalization. This discourse does not compete with ideas of sovereignty but moves beneath and within the law. From the point of view of this discourse, what appear to be the freedoms of liberal citizenship in respect of rights, laws and obligations are actually violence and extraction. The implication here is that the achievement of internally pacified civil societies acts to mask the continuation of this discourse through bio-power. The main function of racism in a society driven by the imperatives of bio-power is in making it possible for political power to kill. If power's basic objective is to foster life, then the idea of a hierarchy of races allows the state to eliminate the 'inferior'. The domestication of racism by the state also has a utopian function, in terms of the rooting out of the inferior and the abnormal. The state, then, requires racism in war and in peace as 'the pre-condition for exercising the right to kill' (Foucault 2003: 256).

In Foucault's argument, appeals to democracy and civil society serve to mask not only both the continuation and the normalization of racism, but also a range of disciplinary techniques that serve to normalize the body. Foucault's position famously questions an exclusively liberal concern with the limits of state power to investigate how different discourses and forms of disciplinary power are not necessarily inconsistent with the rule of law. However, this does not mean that Foucault simply dismisses the idea of human rights, democracy and civil society. If Kant defined European civilization through the ability to use 'reason' and to participate collectively in dialogue, Foucault's (1984) ethics seek to refuse the 'blackmail' of the Enlightenment that one is either for or against 'reason' and the rule of law. The Enlightenment is better viewed as an event located at a certain point in the development of European societies. In this respect, Foucault argues, we need historically to uncover the different ways in which we have become constituted by history. We need not define our essence as being 'rational' animals in the way that we are compelled to by the Enlightenment. Instead we are asked to experiment with the possibility of constituting ourselves in different ways. Hence, if the Enlightenment was not the discovery of our 'essence' but a historical invention among many others that were possible, the question becomes: how do we reinvent ourselves in a way that resists the imperatives of normalizing logic? In our terms, the question becomes less one of how Europe might convert the rest of humanity to the rational principles of democracy, but more one of how Europeanness might be redefined in the context of shared histories of racism and barbarism. In this respect, Europeanness would need to embrace languages of rights and democratic citizenship while being aware of the continuation of racial forms of domination.

Another way of putting this argument is that European universal thinking actually cuts two ways (Beck 2004). If the historical legacy of the Enlightenment can be connected to the demand that either the 'other' becomes like ourselves or is eliminated, it has also proclaimed human rights, as demanded by peoples the world over who have refused to accept their status as second-class citizens. Here we might admit, following Foucault, that these traditions are, indeed, 'inventions', but that they have an ambiguous trajectory. Problems occur when we can see only one side of the argument. In this view, human rights are only liberatory or colonizing, democracy is either a cover for capitalist domination or allows new forms of liberation, and so on. Arguably, in deciding how these discourses and practices actually operate, we need to become more contextual in our analysis. Here I want to investigate these historical features through an analysis of European imperialism and then to look at arguments in respect of the 'new' imperialism and recent political and media-led attempts to politicize global poverty.

European imperialism: a cosmopolitan legacy?

Having closed the previous section by arguing that a Foucauldian perspective has much to contribute to these debates, I now wish to add a word of caution. During an interview, Edward Said (2004) critically compared Frantz Fanon's

(1961) *Wretched of the Earth* and Michel Foucault's (1977) *Discipline and Punish*. He argued that whereas Fanon's book was the result of a collective struggle for human emancipation, Foucault's contribution emerged out of a more individualistic tradition. In other words, what is apparent in Fanon and absent in Foucault is a sense of active commitment to the values of solidarity and liberation.[1] Foucault's well documented ambivalence towards normative issues such as justice and truth ultimately leads to a political quietism. Fanon's work actively risks political commitment in a way that is largely absent from Foucault's legacy. By participating in an anti-colonial struggle Fanon was able to articulate a sense of solidarity with the oppressed without ever becoming a prisoner of that solidarity. We should note that these themes are also evident in Said's own writing, given his long-term commitment to the cause of Palestinian liberation, but never uncritically. In this respect, Said (1994: 24) summarized his own position as 'never solidarity before criticism'. However, Said also articulates what we might call the central ethics of post-colonial criticism, which is to speak up for those who have been ignored, repressed and forgotten by the powerful. The alliance between scholarly criticism and social struggle is a key theme in the seminal contributions of Frantz Fanon.

Frantz Fanon wrote his major works while practising as a psychoanalyst in French-occupied Algeria. Fanon, who had previously fought in the French army during the Second World War, was later to resign from his post at the Bilda-Joinville Hospital in 1956. The experience of practising psychiatry under colonial occupation had evidently been a transforming experience for Fanon. He would continue his work with the Algerian nationalist Front de Libération Nationale (FLN) and survived a number of assassination attempts by the French secret police before being forcibly expelled from Algeria. Fanon died at the age of thirty-six in a hospital bed in the US, having just completed his most famous book, *The Wretched of the Earth*. These details I think are important if we are to appreciate both Fanon's significance and his legacy, referring back to Said's remarks that his work was, indeed, produced in the context of intense struggle and contestation.

Fanon needs to be understood in the context of a national liberation struggle against colonial French occupation. The colonial context gives rise to a segregated world, where the natives are opposed to the colonists as if they are 'two different species' (Fanon 1961: 30). The brutal and violent rule by the French, argued Fanon, resulted in a certain kind of oppositional politics. This was not 'a rational confrontation of points of view' but was instead the confrontation of absolutes

---

1 That Foucault's politics have an individualistic bent has been noted by several scholars (Elliott 2001; Stevenson 2003). Indeed, such is Foucault's anti-normativity that it is difficult to imagine, within that frame of reference, how cosmopolitan forms of solidarity might become possible in our globalized world.

(Fanon 1961: 32). Colonial rule revealed the struggle for supremacy on the part of white Europeans over cultures they had deemed to be inferior. For Fanon, the native cannot help but laugh at the idea of Western values and violence. Colonial cultures are not places of reason and discussion, but of violence and oppression. Under colonialism, reason seemingly has no place and is over-determined by a context that can be transformed only where violence is 'confronted with greater violence' (Fanon 1961: 48). It was the violence of colonialism that actually allowed for the wellbeing of Europeans, whose economic prosperity is built upon the exploitation of the peoples of the underdeveloped world.

Despite the violence of this confrontation, the struggle for independence from colonial rule can easily turn into a curse. Fanon feared that the winning of national 'independence' would prove to be a Pyrrhic victory for colonized peoples, because of a withdrawal of economic resources. Indeed, he even went as far as to say that the contestation within colonial cultures might well prove to be historically of less significance than the global need to redistribute wealth (Fanon 1961: 77–78). In this respect, the defeat of European occupation was unlikely to be enough to repay the debt to the people that the Europeans colonized. At this point, Fanon explicitly acknowledged the connections between European fascism and colonialism. He argued that European capitalists behaved like 'war criminals' in utilizing deportations, massacres and forced labour in order to increase their wealth (Fanon 1961: 80). Given Fanon's personal history of fighting both with and against the French, the link between European totalitarianism and colonialism would have been apparent. Nazism in this context is understood as the attempt to colonize Europe from the 'inside'. National Socialism was literally an attempt to reduce Europe to the status of a colony.

Hannah Arendt (1958) also sought to outline the interconnections between imperialism and totalitarianism. In many respects imperialism paves the way for totalitarianism, in that they both undermine civilized politics and the rule of law, and in that European brutality under both allowed for the destruction of the other. For Arendt, all totalitarian rule can be described as evil, in that it seeks to eliminate classes or races who seemingly stand in the way of 'progress'. Yet whereas Arendt argued that the best defence against totalitarian rule was political institutions and democratic rights, Fanon was more inclined to look forward to a world that had eradicated racialized thinking. In place of ethnic absolutism, where civilizations and races confront each other, Fanon imagined a cosmopolitan culture, where Europeans had learned to take responsibility for their crimes. Previously colonized Third World societies have a legitimate demand for reparations from their capitalist occupiers. Indeed, Fanon's novel solution was that if the Cold War could be ended, then large investments and technical aid could be given to the globe's less developed regions. This would require a mutual transformation of the relationship between Europe and the Third World, from one of violence and oppression to one that aimed to 'rehabilitate mankind' (Fanon 1961: 84).

Given Fanon's concern to locate the struggle for independence in more global coordinates, he viewed the idea of 'national' struggle with a degree of ambivalence. The idea of a specifically 'national' route to liberation for colonized peoples was both a necessary transition as well as a potential trap. In particular, Fanon was concerned that the relative political inexperience of the colonized middle classes, coupled with the flight of capital, could lead only into a 'deplorable stagnation' (Fanon 1961: 121). For Fanon, questions of political economy were central to the liberation struggle, given the need both to forge new trading relations and to break relations of dependency with Europeans. Indeed, Fanon had a deeper concern, that without the politics of socialist transformation it was likely that the rising national bourgeoisie would merely 'replace the foreigner' (Fanon 1961: 127). By that, Fanon meant that, rather than securing justice, the resulting independence struggle could end by reinscribing similarly racist and tribal attitudes that had been developed during colonial domination. The national bourgeoisie would fail to provide a politics of transformation if they ended up mimicking the prejudices and feelings of superiority of the colonists. The problem that Fanon was wrestling with concerned how newly independent states emerging from colonialism could escape from a form of neo-colonialism likely to be imposed upon them by capitalist relations of development. Fanon, then, was not antinational but sought to connect anti-imperialism to internationalism based upon social forms of development.

Notably, however, the Fanon who has recently been so intensively discussed in post-colonial debates is not the theorist of national liberation struggle but the theorist of the colonialist condition (Lazarus 1999). Indeed, in a broadly post-structuralist re-reading of Fanon, Homi Bhabha (1994) and Stuart Hall (1996) focus on his earlier text, *Black Skin, White Masks* (Fanon 1952). Here the argument is that whereas Marxist interpretations tend to privilege 'Fanon the political activist', more recent 're-readings' of Fanon within cultural studies are more concerned with 'Fanon the theorist of cultural domination'. For Bhabha (1994) and Hall (1996), Fanon (1952) is primarily concerned with the ways in which a colonialist culture is able to fix certain stereotypes about black Africans and white Europeans. In this relationship the black African becomes the 'other' of European civilization. This not only elevates European cultures, but also leaves the colonized with a crippling sense of their own inferiority. As Fanon (1952: 79) writes:

I discovered my blackness, my ethnic characteristics; and I was battered down by tom-toms, cannibalism, intellectual deficiency, fetishism, racial defects, slave ships, and above all else, above all: 'Sho' good eatin'.

Indeed, it is not just that the other is stereotyped but also, as Hall (1996: 17) has argued, that the subject 'has no other self than – this *self – as –* Othered'. The colonial subject is not only economically exploited but is saddled with a deep sense of inferiority. Colonial racism produces two camps – 'the white' and 'the black' – where colonial subjects can relate to themselves only through a demeaning culture. This evidently raises an important set of questions avoided by an exclusive focus upon political economy. Centrally, the concern here becomes how it might become possible to reconstitute identities in a cultural context inscribed by relations of domination. Even in the colonial context, racism is not just something that the other does but also depends upon the agencies and struggles of the colonized.

Bhabha (1994) has taken these arguments further by suggesting that Fanon is not so much insisting that the colonized be granted liberal rights but that he is more investigating the way in which the colonial subject becomes determined through cultural practices that trade upon image and fantasy. Questions of madness, self-hatred and violence become cultural and psychic features poorly understood through civil discourses of rights. Indeed, by re-reading Fanon, Bhabha is able to draw out both colonialist fantasies of megalomania and persecution, and the internalized sense of inferiority of the colonized, which seems to suggest either 'turn white' or disappear.

It was the polarization of the political that led Fanon to believe that colonialist oppression could become transformed only through violent political struggle. This feature of Fanon's writing led Arendt (1970) to criticize Fanon for glorifying violence and propagating extremism. Arendt points out that Fanon does little to mediate the fantasies of blood and lust that reinscribe themselves in conditions of domination. More sympathetically, Bhabha (1994: 62) writes:

> Fanon must sometimes be reminded that the disavowal of the Other always exacerbates the edge of identification, reveals the dangerous place where identity and aggressivity are twinned.

Bhabha's more generous criticism opens the possibility of what he sometimes refers to as the hybrid moment of political change. This is a politics that refuses homogeneity (us versus them) but rather seeks translation, negotiation and above all difference. In other words, within Fanon's work we can detect both the continuation of a polarized politics that reinforces hatred and a concern to deconstruct the 'essentialized' categories of colonial culture. This means that, again something partially acknowledged by Fanon, political struggle is both a hegemonic war of position as well as 'the struggle of identifications' that ultimately need to be constructed (Bhabha 1994: 29). The problem is that Fanon's revolutionary politics partially reproduces the hatred of the colonial period through descriptions of colonists as 'flesh-eating animals, jackals and vultures which wallow in the people's blood' (Fanon 1961: 154).

However, before we leave the matter there, we should also remind ourselves of the more positive features of Fanon's cultural politics. Fanon is in no doubt that the bourgeoisie's proclamation of universal values is nothing more than a cover for racism, and that it seeks to impose its relations of dominance on all humanity. For Fanon, once humanity becomes free of colonialism and relations of dominance, a genuinely intercultural dialogue becomes possible (Bernasconi 1996). Despite the well founded concerns regarding Fanon's insistence upon the necessity of violence in the colonial context, it is the dream of a future where racialized categories have lost their capacity to fix identity that informs his politics of liberation.

In keeping with this argument, Paul Gilroy (2000) argues that Fanon's utopian legacy can still be located in contemporary black art forms, such as popular music, which continue to give voice to the desire for transcendence and escape from racism. However, if the desire for a future without racism – particularly for black Americans – was linked to the idea of a mythic return to Africa, today it is more likely to take refuge in a purely consumerist dream. What Gilroy (2000: 350) terms 'the quest for an uncontaminated place' no longer represents hope but escape from a racially segregated world. If the popular black American music of the 1960s and 1970s articulated a yearning for a better tomorrow, it has now given way to postmodern consumerism. An alternative black public sphere of hybrid musical culture has been colonized by a mostly visual culture that emphasizes the power and vitality of the black body. If Fanon's dream of 'starting a new history of Man' once found aesthetic expression in the utopian yearnings of popular music (Fanon 1961: 254), it now urgently needs to be given a more gritty political expression. In particular, Fanon, it will be remembered, advocates a new relationship between Europe and the Third World, one that has broken with shared histories and oppression. This is not a situation where European crimes are forgotten, but where new political and cultural relations are formed, to enable the mutual reinvention of collective and individual identities. These are crucial configurations. Arguably what is being opened up here is the view that questions of political economy and of culture need to find new ways of interrelating with one another to help make another world possible.

However, there are critics who have been pressing the case that post-colonial thinking has become overly concentrated upon culture, to the detriment of political economy. Arif Dirlik (1997, 2002), for example, argues that post-colonial criticism is more concerned with the deconstruction of Eurocentrism and cultural categories like the 'Third World' than it is with addressing contemporary capitalism. This has tended to mean that much post-colonial writing has little to offer in respect of an analysis of the present. Indeed, without capitalism it is likely that Eurocentrism would have remained an ethnocentrism.

Ultimately Dirlik takes his attack on cultural politics further than I would want to; I agree with Lisa Duggan (2003) that we should resist the either/or split that suggests we decide between political economy and cultural politics. Rather than viewing cultural politics as the 'other' of serious analysis we should remember that discourses of economics are also shot through with relations of race, class, gender and sexuality. As Fanon (1961: 255) fully recognized, for humanity to 'turn over a new leaf' involves the reconstitution of economic and cultural relations. Yet, as we shall now discover, if these ideas are to come to mean anything in the early twenty-first century they will need to be translated into political activity.

Neo-liberalism and civil society

The idea that European societies need to reinvent their relations with the global South has been the explicit focus of the campaign to 'Make Poverty History'. The appearance of a genuinely popular social movement at a time when about a third of the world's population live on less than US$1 a day is a significant development. Arguably this provides an opportunity for Europeans to rethink their cultural as well as their structural relations with their former colonies and with the global South more generally. Following on from the previous section, post-colonial critique is concerned to refigure cultural as well as economic and political relations between the West and the rest. What becomes crucial in this respect is an understanding of the context within which the predominately Western campaign sought to promote trade justice, cancel debt and promote more and better aid.

Indeed, there has been a considerable amount of debate recently as to whether the globe is currently going through a period that can be accurately described as a 'new imperialism', 'Empire' or 'neo-liberal globalization'. For example, Harvey (2003) has argued that, over the course of the twentieth century, the US has become an imperial power. This power has largely economic roots. Since the oil crisis of 1973 the US has aggressively sought to promote a global strategy of accumulation by dispossession. Through the World Bank, the International Monetary Fund and the World Trade Organization the US has sought to privatize public resources, commodify labour power and suppress alternative forms of production and consumption. Alternatively, Hardt and Negri (2000) have argued against the idea of a dominant, US-led imperialism and propose a notion of Empire that breaks with ideas of imperialism. The logic of Empire is different from that of imperialism in that it does not depend upon the expansion of state power; rather, it invokes a borderless world that fosters consumer subjectivities and the rule of postmodern global capitalism. Despite the different sides to this debate there does appear to be considerable agreement in respect of the dominance of neo-liberal economics. Pieterse (2004) has argued that there are, indeed, contrasts between neo-liberal globalization and the recent imperial turn evident in US foreign policy. The interconnection of neo-liberal measures of privatization and tax cuts with the expansion of military budgets is less the blind expression of the economy than it is a matter of politics. The Bush administration's withdrawal from a number of multilateral treaties and forceful promotion of neo-liberal economics is a matter of political policy. Further, that global inequality has increased sharply since the 1980s is itself a direct consequence of a systematic political campaign to provide neo-liberal forms of globalization by the West.

Despite the popular impact of the campaign to 'Make Poverty History' it is notable that it failed to politicize the dominance of neo-liberal policies on development or to question a number of assumptions that can be connected the culture of colonialism. The 'Make Poverty History' grouping is best thought of as broad coalition that includes Oxfam, Friends of the Earth, the World Development Movement as well as political parties like New Labour and well known celebrities like Bob Geldof and U2's lead singer Bono. During the summer of 2005 the coalition, in the lead-up to the G8 meeting in Gleneagles, ran a number of high-profile cultural events in order to raise awareness on questions of global poverty. This included Bob Geldof's appearance at the Glastonbury music festival and the Live 8 music festival (held in Tokyo, Berlin, London, Paris, Moscow, Barrie in Ontario, Rome, Philadelphia and Johannesburg).

In the run-up to these events Oxfam in the UK sought to promote the idea of global solidarity through a white wristband that read 'Make Poverty History'. The campaign actively encouraged ordinary people to buy the wristbands and to text, email or write to the government ahead of the G8 meeting urging action on global poverty. In the UK the media widely reported the plight of Africa. This was particularly evident on BBC television, where specially commissioned programmes carried the strap line 'Africa Lives on the BBC'. Despite notable exceptions, many of these programmes were both populist and reinforced stereotypes about Africa. For example, Bob Geldof presented a series of programmes on the African continent ('Geldof on Africa') where he was pictured in a white suit serving up tales of native superstition, political corruption and African irrationality.

The relatively small amount of research that has been done on representations of black Africans within contemporary media cultures suggests a remarkable degree of consistency (Stevenson 1999). Africa is overwhelmingly represented as intrinsically violent and anti-democratic, while constituted through tribal rule and the excessive use of force. These features are consistent with the ideologies of the colonial period, where underdevelopment was explained through anti-modern forms of superstition and cultural backwardness. The 'Make Poverty History' campaign singularly failed to interrogate these cultural meanings. In the lead-up to the Live 8 concerts, Geldof received a considerable amount of media criticism for failing to include any African artists in the original line-up, which had included mostly Western pop and rock acts such as Paul McCartney, Coldplay, U2 and Pink Floyd. Geldof responded to this criticism by arguing that he was simply seeking to attract as many people as possible to the event. Yet the fact that Live 8 and the 'Make Poverty History' campaign more generally lacked any cultural politics is best represented by Madonna's performance at Live 8. Before she entered the stage, Geldof came on and introduced an eighteen-year-old woman from Ethiopia (Birhan Woldu), whom he claimed 'we' had 'saved' with the money raised from the original Live Aid concerts. Madonna and Geldof were then pictured hugging the woman 'we' had 'saved' before she was ushered off the stage. *The Sun* newspaper (4 July 2005) pictured Geldof and Birhan Woldu under the headline 'Thank you world'.

Here my point is that the invisibility of African performers and the stereotypes of helpless Africans both depoliticized the event and turned the focus away from the plight of Africa into an explicit focus on the generosity of white Europeans. If 'they' are poor and needy, this is 'our' chance to play the role of generous providers. Despite well publicized claims that the day was about justice for Africa, the dominant discourse was one of charity. The lead-up to the G8 meeting, then, became 'our moment, the time for us to make history' (*The People*, 3 July 2005). Viewed in more Foucaldian terms, the images and identities that were reproduced through popular media cultures became less about an antagonistic politics and more a normalizing strategy that promoted feelings of superiority and cancelled any sense of critical engagement. Viewed culturally, the event did not so much signify the desire of Europeans to mourn the passing of imperial dominance but to celebrate our generosity. The carnivalesque possibilities evident in a large-scale music festival remained depressingly under-explored. As the Asian Dub Foundation (2000) put it in a different context, 'Union Jack and Union Jill, Back up and down the same hill'.

Many political commentators felt that the campaign suffered from being overly directed by New Labour. The construction of a 'Third Way' alliance of the progressive centre severely restricted the capacity of a number of social movements to press for a more radical political and cultural agenda. As Chantel Mouffe (2005) has argued, democratic politics is actually dependent upon passionate expression within an agonistic public sphere. The displacement of radical politics actively disallowed the emergence of a more openly contested public sphere, where different interests and positions could have been articulated and negotiated.

Cultural forms of democracy and citizenship require a more adversarial form of politics, one which could not find expression in the 'united' front presented by the 'Make Poverty History' campaign. That campaign represents a missed opportunity to develop a more contested form of cosmopolitanism. A genuinely cosmopolitan European social movement that aimed both to eradicate racism within Europe and to transform relations with the global South would need to emerge from below. As Gilroy (2004) has argued, such a movement would need to foster critical forms of estrangement from aggressive nationalism and colonialism while promoting cultures of solidarity with non-Europeans.

The 'Make Poverty History' campaign also utilized a number of dubious and misleading expectations and assumptions. A film that was continually replayed during the lead-up to the G8 meeting included a number of 'A list' celebrities, such as Richard Grant, Emma Thompson and George Clooney clicking their fingers to emphasize the fact that every three seconds a child dies of poverty. This in itself could have been a powerful message and yet it was hard to escape the impression that all the member countries of the G8 needed to do to make poverty disappear was to click their fingers. Indeed, Richard Curtis's film *The Girl in the Café*, which began the BBC's coverage, gave a similar impression. The film's narrative featured an 'ordinary' woman who became caught up at the high table of global politics only to insist to the globe's leaders that they take their responsibilities seriously. In the absence of any politics these images suggest that defeating global poverty is a matter of personal commitment and lifestyle choice, rather than political contestation.

Should we press these features too far, it is also worth remembering that it was estimated that two billion viewers watched Live 8 and that over 250,000 demonstrators gathered in Edinburgh to protest against global poverty. These cultural and political events were, not surprisingly, contested by many on the political right for not emphasizing Africa's own political corruption. This was an easy political point to make in a campaign where Africans were either rendered invisible or stereotyped. More positively, however, we could argue that we are witnessing the beginnings of a global cosmopolitan movement concerned about the global polarization of wealth. Indeed, 'Make Poverty History' is a broad coalition that includes a number of disparate voices and perspectives, and it has converted questions of global poverty into an ongoing public campaign and discussion. Despite some of the images traded upon by the campaign, it has played a crucial role in raising public awareness of the indebted and impoverished nature of African societies.

A critical social movement would need not only to engage in cultural politics but also to promote different understandings of neo-liberal economics. Yet part of the problem is the concentration on the theme of poverty, rather than inequality and neo-liberalism. Especially since the 1980s there has been a rapid increase in inequality both within and between global societies (Pieterse 2004). However, the focus upon poverty, rather than inequality, has avoided questions about the global influence of neo-liberalism. What was missing from the populism of 'Make Poverty History', then, was an appreciation of the way in which aid is connected to national strategic objectives (Pieterse 2004). Notably a more critical and contested politics is unlikely to make it felt through populist declarations that the G8 will save '10 million lives' (*The Sun*, 9 July 2005).

Here my argument is that Europeans have a unique opportunity and, returning to Fanon, responsibility both to develop a critical politics that shatters the colonialist assumptions of the past and to promote alternative forms of development to those fostered by neo-liberalism. In the European setting this would require the emergence of a critical alliance of social movements pressing for truly global solutions to global problems. Indeed, a more positive understanding of European history is required at this point. If Europe remains trapped within the legacy of imperialism it also developed a social model currently under threat by neo-liberal economics (Bourdieu 2003). The politics I am advocating here would require Europeans to defend a historical legacy that sought to 'civilize' capitalism but also to use this to suggest different models of development for the most impoverished societies on the planet. This pushes the argument beyond charity, but crucially asks Europeans to recognize their positive achievements while embracing more intercultural ways of living and talking.

We Europeans: a checklist for the future

The European cosmopolitan project needs to be reconstituted in terms of both the histories of European imperialism and global US hegemony. This can only be achieved along a number of intellectual fronts at once. Firstly, the European project requires that Europeans learn to view the neo-liberal project of privatization and commodification with scepticism and an increased sense of the importance of democratic engagement. The European Union has the scale both to contain the corrosive force of globalization and to articulate a different vision, one based upon social justice, sustainability and multiculturalism. Such a project needs to be deepened in opposition to those at the European level who are seeking its erosion. From its beginning, the European Union was intended to be more than a free-trade agreement and it will be its ability to offer social protection to its citizens that will determine its success. Given the relative historical success of the European social model and the legacy of histories of imperial rule, the continent is in the position of being able to promote its own interests as well as those of the world's poor. Yet Europe can do so only by including the critical voices of global civil society while refusing a narcissistic politics that becomes exclusively focused on mass consumption and our moral goodness.

Secondly, just as the neo-liberal project is a cultural project that works through the language of strategic advantage and privatization, so the European project needs to occupy this level. Here, learning from the imperialist and colonialist languages of the past, 'Europe' needs to become a project that reminds its citizens of the dangers of essentializing languages of civilization, racism and otherness. Post-colonialism continues to have a key role to play in subverting the continued imaginings of dominance that are repeated in both public and commercial cultures. The demand that we learn to live with 'difference' is a global rather than a national problem.

Thirdly, in the face of neo-liberal dominance, Europeans should seek to construct a new relationship with the global South. Returning to some of the arguments made earlier by Frantz Fanon, Europe could, given its historic burden in respect of imperialism and its own 'social' vision, play a key role in influencing the patterns of development that are deemed appropriate for the poorest human societies. This could suggest a different framework to the current neo-liberal model, which feeds the progressive economic and social polarization of our shared planetary society.

Finally, we Europeans, if I may use that phrase, need to reimagine and reconstitute ourselves less as consumers and more as citizens who are concerned to protect a relatively non-commodified public culture, one that develops the political sensibilities of critical citizens. This is not simply a republican call for enhanced political participation, but a call for the development of a post-national public sphere that is able to introduce alternative narratives of Europeanness, which reject the allure of imperial power in whatever version, and which seek a more concrete cosmopolitan imagination suitable for our age. European cosmo-politanism needs to look both inwards and outwards, joining with others to find solutions to global problems. These projections call for neither a hegemonic nor a diminished Europe, but mutual cultural and political projects that aim to construct an alternative politics to neo-liberalism.

References

Arendt, H. (1958) *The Origins of Totalitarianism* (2nd edition), London: Allen and Unwin.

Arendt, H. (1970) *On Violence*, New York: Harvest.

Asian Dub Foundation (2000) *Community Music*, London: London Records.

Beck, U. (2004) 'The truth of others: a cosmopolitan approach', *Common Knowledge*, 10(3), 430–49.

Bernasconi, R. (1996) 'Casting the slough: Fanon's new humanism for a new humanity', in L. R. Gordon, T. D. Sharpley-Whiting and R. T. White (eds), *Fanon: A Critical Reader*, Oxford: Blackwell, pp. 113–21.

Bhabha, H. (1994) *The Location of Culture*, London: Routledge.

Bourdieu, P. (2003) *Firing Back*, London: Verso.

Chakrabarty, D. (2000) *Provincialising Europe: Postcolonial Thought and Historical Difference*, Princeton, MA: Princeton University Press.

Dirlik, A. (1997) 'The postcolonial aura: Third World criticism in the age of global capitalism', in A. McClintock, A. Mufti and E. Shohat (eds), *Dangerous Liaison*, Minneapolis, MN: University of Minnesota Press.

Dirlik, A. (2002) 'Rethinking colonialism: globalisation, postcolonialism and the nation', *Interventions*, 4(3), 428–48.

Duggan, L. (2003) *The Twilight of Equality? Neoliberalism, Cultural Politics, and the Attack on Democracy*, Boston, MA: Beacon Press.

Elliott, A. (2001) *Concepts of the Self*, Cambridge: Polity Press.

Fanon, F. (1952) *Black Skin, White Masks*, translated by C. Lamb Markham (1972), London: Paladin.

Fanon, F. (1961) *The Wretched of the Earth*, translated by C. Farrington (2001), London: Penguin.

Foucault, M. (1977) *Discipline and Punish*, London: Penguin.

Foucault, M. (1981) *The History of Sexuality: An Introduction*, London: Pelican.

Foucault, M. (1984) 'What is Enlightenment?', in P. Rabinow (ed.), *The Foucault Reader*, London: Penguin, pp. 32–50.

Foucault, M. (2003) *Society Must Be Defended*, London: Penguin.

Gilroy, P. (2000) *Between Camps: Nations, Cultures and the Allure of Race*, London: Routledge.

Gilroy, P. (2004) *After Empire: Melancholia or Convivial Culture?*, London: Routledge.

Habermas, J. (1997) 'Kant's idea of perpetual peace, with the benefit of two hundred years' hindsight', in J. Bohman and M. Lutz-Bachmann (eds), *Essays on Kant's Cosmopolitan Ideal*, Cambridge, MA: MIT Press.

Hall, S. (1996) 'The after-life of Frantz Fanon: Why Fanon? Why now? Why *Black Skin, White Masks*?', in A. Read (ed.), *The Fact of Blackness*, London: Institute of Contemporary Arts.

Hardt, M. and Negri, A. (2000) *Empire*, Cambridge, MA: Harvard University Press.

Harvey, D. (2000) 'Cosmopolitanism and the banality of geographical evils', in J. Comfort and J. L. Camaroff (eds), *Millennial Capitalism and the Culture of Neoliberalism*, Durham, NC: Duke University Press, pp. 529–64 (special issue of *Public Culture*, 12(2)).

Harvey, D. (2003) *The New Imperialism*, Oxford: Oxford University Press.

Isin, E. F. (2002) *Being Political: Genealogies of Citizenship*, Minneapolis, MN: University of Minnesota Press.

Kaldor, M. (2003) *Global Civil Society: An Answer to War*, Cambridge: Polity Press.

Kant, I. (1795) *Perpetual Peace: A Philosophical Sketch*, in H. S. Reiss (ed.) (1970) *Kant: Political Writings* (1st edition), Cambridge: Cambridge University Press, pp. 43–130.

Lazarus, N. (1999) 'Disavowing decolonization: Fanon, nationalism, the question of representation in postcolonial theory', in A. C. Alessandrini (ed.), *Frantz Fanon: Critical Perspectives*, London: Routledge, pp. 69–98.

Mosse, G. L. (1978) *Toward the Final Solution: A History of European Racism*, London: J. M. Dent and Sons Ltd.

Mouffe, C. (2005) *On the Political*, London: Routledge.

Parekh, B. (1995) 'Liberalism and colonialism: a critique of Locke and Mill', in J. N. Pieterse and B. Parekh (eds), *The Decolonization of Imagination*, London: Zed Books, pp. 81–98.

Pieterse, J. N. (2004) *Globalization or Empire*, London: Routledge.

Said, E. (1993) *Culture and Imperialism*, London: Chatto and Windus.

Said, E. (1994) *Representations of the Intellectual*, London: Vintage.

Said, E. (2004) 'In the shadow of the West', in G. Viswanathan (ed.), *Power, Politics and Culture: Interviews with Edward Said*, London: Blackwell.

Spivak, G. S. (1999) *A Critique of Postcolonial Reason: Toward a History of the Vanishing Present*, Cambridge, MA: Harvard University Press.

Stevenson, N. (1999) *The Transformation of the Media*, London: Longman.

Stevenson, N. (2003) *Cultural Citizenship: Cosmopolitan Questions*, Maidenhead: Open University Press.

Wallerstein, I. (1997) 'Eurocentrism and its avatars: the dilemmas of social science', *New Left Review*, 226 (November–December), 93–107.

Wood, A. W. (1999) *Kant's Ethical Thought*, Cambridge: Cambridge University Press.

Young, R. C. (2001) *Postcolonialism: An Historical Introduction*, Oxford: Blackwell.

CHAPTER 5

Cosmopolitanism and Europe: Describing Elites or Challenging Inequalities?

Paul Jones

Given that cosmopolitanism is predicated on the transcendence of cultural and political boundaries, then the notion of a distinctly European cosmopolitanism seems something of a paradox. The extent to which Europe as a bounded – albeit ambivalently – community is being constructed in a suitably 'open' way so as to support the main tenets of cosmopolitan theories is a crucial question, with two related challenges: to construct a cosmopolitan model that guards against the essentialization of 'European' and other identity boundaries; and to move beyond descriptions of trans-national elites characterized by mobilities and other cultural competencies. This chapter argues that attempts to develop a particularized 'European cosmopolitanism' risk burdening the concept with undesirable elitist connotations, as well as with the sort of pseudo-national baggage that cosmopolitanism sets out to transcend. It is suggested that to move beyond this impasse, the European cosmopolitan project must actively address exclusionary identity discourses, both within and beyond the confines of the nation state, as situating such struggles at the heart of cosmopolitanism signals an attempt to move beyond the simple description of the elite realities of a highly mobile class of Europeans while also reinvigorating the concept with a critical dimension that is lacking in much contemporary discussion.

Challenging cosmopolitanism

Issues associated with conceptualizing society, politics and culture beyond the nation state – not to mention the vexed question of the definition of cosmopolitanism[1] – all

---

1 For a more thorough discussion of the origin and development of cosmopolitanism, see Zolo's *Cosmopolis* (1997).

contribute to cosmopolitanism's highly contested nature. Not least of the challenges facing the cosmopolitan project is the charge of elitism, which has long bedevilled this form of thinking. Many scholars have noted the exclusivity associated with the concept, with some going so far as to argue that in practice cosmopolitanism is little more than the description of a neo-liberal capitalist class, which serves primarily to reinforce the hegemony of this group (see for example Castells 1997; Mignolo 2002; Yeoh 2004). From this perspective cosmopolitanism is another way in which globally mobile, information-rich groups organize themselves trans-nationally; it is a strategy by which elites symbolically constitute 'their' societies via exclusive cultural codes that transcend particularized contexts. Manuel Castells (1996: 415) summarizes this limited understanding of cosmopolitanism by positing that 'elites are cosmopolitan, people are local'.

If cosmopolitanism is to give us any potential for understanding the politics and cultures associated with social transformations, it must be more than a simple description of the way in which such globally mobile elites organize and reconstitute themselves beyond the constraints of national boundaries. If cosmopolitanism is reducible to what is essentially a matter of comparable lifestyles – which are anyway most clearly evident in a highly mobile trans-national managerial class – this is solely an 'aesthetic cosmopolitanism' (Vertovec and Cohen 2002), a description of how elites 'find others who will interact with them in the terms of specialized but collectively held understandings' (Hannerz 1990: 244). We must also keep in mind that the consumption of space (Urry 2000) and the appropriation of a wide range of cultural experiences (Charlesworth 2000; Skeggs 2002) are still fundamental hallmarks of an elite who stand in stark contrast to a globally ever-expanding population of marginalized people. Accordingly, such partial understandings of cosmopolitanism undermine a crucial aspect of the concept; narrowly defined conceptual borders not only misrepresent a much broader emergent cosmopolitan reality but also serve to maintain exclusionary discourses of many kinds.[2]

However, there has recently been a renewed interest in more radical formations of cosmopolitanism, with some very notable attempts to redress the elitist tendency (Charlesworth 2000; Lamont 2000; Lamont and Aksartova 2002; Mignolo 2002;

---

2 Of course, this is not to say that the study of elites is not an important and valid research agenda. Isin and Woods (1999) explore the idea of cosmopolitan elites when writing on 'professional-citizens', whom they suggest have allegiances primarily to their occupation rather than to state or public; the rights and duties of national citizenship are displaced at the expense of claims for professional legitimacy and autonomy. Others working on such powerful and influential groups as architects (Kennedy 2004), journalists (Hannerz 2004), politicians and their consultants (Mayhew 1997) and academics (Bourdieu 1989) have also suggested that they are at the forefront of this struggle for a range of trans-national capitals.

Yeoh 2004). This shift in focus from elite forms of cosmopolitanism focused on a mobile trans-national class to a range of more diverse expressions of cosmopolitanism has attempted to 'open up new theoretical and empirical horizons and contemplate the existence of non-intellectual forms of inclusive thinking and acting ... essential for understanding the process of bridging boundaries and for fighting more effectively against exclusion' (Lamont and Aksartova 2002: 18). Cosmopolitanism scholarship has been reinvigorated by these attempts, which have focused on 'real world' transformations, rather than utopian projections, leading to a search for theoretical and social models that provide some analytical purchase as well as a description of a contested 'cosmopolitan identity'. As a corollary to this, much of this more critical recent work in the field of cosmopolitanism has been 'combined with a critique of the ethically deficient globalism embodied in neo-liberal modes of thought' (Falk 1996: 57).

A central argument of this emerging work has been to suggest that we must recognize that 'cosmopolitanism has been a constant feature of everyday social and political life for a very long time' (Rumford 2005: 4). In her notable contributions to this emerging field of cosmopolitan study, Michele Lamont suggests that academic agendas must be extended to assess how people engage in cosmopolitan practice in 'everyday life' across ethnic, national and structural contexts. For example, by addressing the potential of cosmopolitan forms of communication between working-class people in the US and France, Lamont suggests that cosmopolitanism is better understood as a stance, as an approach to transcending particularized difference, rather than a fixed descriptor of an elite identity (Lamont 2000). Lamont has thus called for attention to be paid to the range of cultural repertoires that people across the whole of society draw upon – 'everyday practical cosmopolitanisms' – to overcome different social and symbolic barriers, such as racism (see, for example, Lamont 2002; Lamont and Aksartova 2002). Certainly such 'everyday cosmopolitanism' is an important yet hitherto underdeveloped research area for social science. Lamont's work reminds us that multiple expressions of cosmopolitanism can be found across many sections of society; conceptualizing cosmopolitanism as a stance designed to overcome boundaries of many kinds also guards against conflating cosmopolitanism simply with the mobility experienced by an intellectual and cultural European elite.

A further tension in much of the literature on cosmopolitanism relates to the exact function of this scholarship; frequently there is ambiguity between cosmopolitanism as an analytical tool and its use as a solely descriptive category. Is cosmopolitanism 'a methodological concept which helps to overcome methodological nationalism and to build a frame of reference to analyse the new social conflicts, dynamics and structures' (Beck 2002: 18) or, rather, a way of describing societies or groups – 'Paris is cosmopolitan', 'high-profile architects are cosmopolitan'? The prevalence of descriptive versions of cosmopolitanism has led to the term being casually applied as if to denote some kind of identity, frequently delineated in opposition to 'locals' or 'nationals'. If cosmopolitanism is to provide a useful and critical framework for social scientific research, this issue must be resolved. What concrete research agendas does a cosmopolitan framework afford us, and what conceptual clarity does such theorizing provide?

Cosmopolitanism as anti-essentialism: contesting identities

As Lamont's work ably demonstrates, contestation is a centrally important aspect of the cosmopolitan project, with challenges to essentialized identity boundaries central in allowing the programme to go beyond simple description. Linking cosmopolitanism with such challenges to the boundaries of collective identities – and other associated categories that are frequently essentialized – in a critical and reflexive way is crucial, as it provides a clear conceptual focus, not to mention empirical research agenda, so often lacking in cosmopolitan theorizing. Vitally, we need to recognize that 'while important work is being done by scholars in several fields on how symbolic boundaries translate into social boundaries, it should be accompanied by parallel studies of the reverse process, where the elimination of social boundaries begins with the deconstruction of symbolic ones' (Lamont and Aksartova 2002: 12). So doing moves the discourse beyond the tendency to either utopian wishful thinking or description that is in evident in much contemporary cosmopolitanism.

Indeed, situating struggles for equality at the heart of cosmopolitan discourse signals an attempt to move beyond the simple description of an elite European reality modelled on a highly mobile class and towards a programme for social change. In order to move beyond this current impasse, cosmopolitanism must provide a framework for understanding the wide range of strategies people across societies use to challenge exclusionary discourses such as racism and ethno-nationalism. Cosmopolitanism, then, ultimately requires a rethink of political and social responsibilities, including a change in the way we perceive the boundaries – both symbolic and physical – between groups. Cosmopolitanism can thus be invoked as a way to 'avoid pitfalls of essentialism or some kind of zero-sum, all-or-nothing understanding of identity issues within a nation-state framework' (Vertovec and Cohen 2002: 3). Arguably it is also a commitment to questioning – and challenging – such boundaries that helps to prevent cosmopolitanism from descending into a type of cultural voyeurism, in which cosmopolitanism is merely a way for those with the competencies to transcend immediate constraints of time and space to appropriate many different cultures (Skeggs 2002). We should not need the example of Kant's geographical fixity to remind us that the value of cosmopolitanism is not related to the amount of travel undertaken or the degree of cultural 'difference' we consume; cosmopolitanism takes multiple and ubiquitous forms relative to the overcoming of essentializing identities. It could be suggested that cosmopolitanism must be underpinned by more radical notions of reflexivity and contestation than is currently the case, and that it is vital to situate what Beck (2002: 19) refers to as 'inclusive oppositions' – contestations of essentialized identities based in the national – at the heart of cosmopolitanism.

This version of cosmopolitanism is engaged with everyday practice and is, thus, far removed from 'wishful thinking primarily concerned with projecting the cosmopolitan intentions of the scholar' (Beck 2002: 18). Such cultural contestation is just as likely – probably more likely – to take place in the context of travelling away to support a football team or to see a gig as it is at an international academic conference on cosmopolitanism.[3] While it is primarily elites who have the capacity to frame – and crucially to codify – the values associated with a wide range of cultural and political meanings (for example, Bourdieu 1989; Skeggs 2002) cosmopolitanism is underpinned by the potential of reflexive contestations.[4] This is what Lamont and Molnár call 'boundary work', which would entail an assessment 'not only [of] the construction but also [of] the transcending of boundaries, as well as … their strength and permeability' (cited in Lamont and Aksartova 2002: 7). Crucially in this context, Lamont's perspective does facilitate analysis of the constructive processes by which boundaries are drawn, while also providing a framework for understanding their transcendence.

Such contestation could take the form of post-national 'duties', human rights, cultural exchanges or – as is the argument here – challenges to essentialized identities. Accordingly, cosmopolitanism offers us a useful way of thinking about expressions of collective identities in broadly post-national conditions. The idea of cosmopolitan citizenship is salient here, with 'new transnational political spaces not "contained" by modern nation-states as grantors of rights and imposers of obligations' (Isin and Woods 1999: 91), as it harbours some potential for identities to be formulated in opposition to, for example, nationalist discourses. Indeed, Isin

3 What Beck has referred to as 'methodological nationalism' (Beck 1998, 2000, 2002, 2003) is an academic expression of the same tendency.
4 It is an irony that in 'information rich' societies, public and political discourses are increasingly distorted and dominated by economic imperatives, and manipulated by a range of expert groups. Leon Mayhew (1997) has argued that a 'new public' has emerged, which is particularly susceptible to manipulation by professional specialists, who erode some of the fundamental bases of the ideal-type public sphere as conceptualized by Habermas (1989). According to Mayhew the potential for democratic association and authentic cultural exchange is distorted in the 'new public', as discourse is dominated and colonized by experts, especially experts in the fields of political communication/lobbying, market research and the media. Via these distorting elements 'public opinion' as such becomes led by an elite group with massive political influence – as Mayhew (1997: 5) reminds us, 'rhetoric calculated by experts [is] a type of coercion'.

and Woods view the potential of cosmopolitanism precisely as a way of contesting notions of sovereignty tied to the nation state, and of questioning the capacity of the nation state to support identities and to provide for a range of populations. Castells forwards a similar argument – albeit with different emphases – when writing of 'resistance identities', which are collective identities 'generated by those actors that are in positions/conditions devalued and/or stigmatized by the logic of domination' that are aimed at building 'trenches of resistance and survival on the basis of principles different from, or opposed to, those permeating the institutions of society' (Castells 1997: 8).

For Hannerz (1990), cosmopolitanism involves a tension between a 'mastery' of other cultures and a 'surrender' to them, within the framework of the adoption of a pluralist stance based on tolerance; the intention is not to colonize or change other cultures, but, rather, to appreciate their value. Hannerz's argument, as I understand it, still has elitist connotations, as the culturally cosmopolitan are distinct from many other groups, for example working-class migrants (see Lamont 2000), who do not necessarily possess the much-valued cultural capitals associated with distance and reflexivity (Bourdieu 1989; Bourdieu *et al.* 1999). A further flaw in Hannerz's argument lies in his juxtaposition of 'cosmopolitans and locals'; distinguishing between cosmopolitans and locals is not a useful dichotomy, as we are necessarily both, simultaneously.

Cosmopolitanism is defined by Beck as a kind of 'internal globalization' that 'transforms everyday consciousness, with issues of global concern becoming part of the everyday local experiences and the "moral life-worlds" of the people' (Beck 2002: 17). Bauman (2001) characterizes this increased interdependence and interconnectedness of morality by suggesting that 'nothing that happens anywhere on earth can be safely left out of account in calculations of causes and effects of actions: nothing is indifferent or of no consequence, to the conditions of life anywhere else'. Certainly, normative constructions of cosmopolitanism emphasize commitment to universalized values such as human rights. Cosmopolitanism in fact attempts the resolution of one of modernity's central tensions, that between the particular and the universal. The promise of cosmopolitanism lies in its capacity to engage with both the particularized understandings of culture (for example national identities) and also with universal dimensions (such as 'civilizations' and human rights). So, by viewing culture as the domain of the particular and civilization as the universal realm, cosmopolitanism reconciles the existence of particularized national cultures, on the one hand, with the cosmopolitan ideal of the universality of civilization – perhaps in the form of universalized human rights – on the other (see Delanty and Jones 2002).

This approach is typified by Martha Nussbaum's impassioned plea for a cosmopolitanism that pledges allegiance to 'the worldwide community of human beings' (Nussbaum 1996: 4). This universalized conception of cosmopolitanism demands that national boundaries are not 'morally salient'; herein lies both the strength and weakness of solely normative conceptions of cosmopolitanism. In arguing for the creation of a moral community over and above national boundaries, Nussbaum attempts to use cosmopolitanism to bridge globalization's deficit, and to introduce a universalized humanist dimension as a challenge to particularized interests, identities and affections. What supporters of this normative cosmopolitan perspective argue for is universalized political, social and cultural 'engagement' beyond the boundaries of the nation state.

However, a generalized moral argument is an insufficient basis for cosmopolitanism. As Zolo (1997) argues, such universalized human rights discourses become useful only when they operate in a substantive sense, for example when such rights can be clearly and unambiguously defined and are 'positive' rights in that they are legally enshrined (as opposed to being operable only on an abstract, moral level). Acknowledging an abstract notion of human rights as the basis of cosmopolitanism raises a number of other issues. For example, almost all contemporary nation states would probably express a commitment to the *idea* of human rights, regardless of how they actually proceed in this regard. This is brought into sharp focus by a number of recent world political events: Tony Blair's desire to remove the UK from the 1951 Geneva convention so as to avoid its responsibility to receive asylum seekers could be cited in this context, as could the US government's treatment of those people held at Guantanamo Bay and accused of terrorist acts.

In support of the work of Michele Lamont, who calls for challenges to inequalities (including – but not limited to – anti-racism) to be situated at the heart of cosmopolitanism, it is interesting to counterpoise a 'passive' cosmopolitanism against an 'active' one. A more active understanding of cosmopolitanism posits a radicalized approach to everyday life, and also to the essentialized, exclusionary discourses that maintain inequalities of many kinds. If we are to release the critical conceptual potential within cosmopolitan perspectives we must guard against solely normative projections of the cosmopolitan (see below). It is also important to make it a sufficiently critical category for it to be able, for example, to support challenges to racism as an essentializing and exclusionary discourse. There is a real danger that constructions of cosmopolitanism overlook the very real – and persistent – inequalities that exist within and between societies across the world. Without this focus, we are left with a primarily descriptive category that relates only to a narrowly defined *European* experience. In fact, Ulf Hannerz has defined the cosmopolitan in contrast to the tourist: rather than just being a travelling citizen, the cosmopolitan adopts just such a plural attitude towards other cultures or, as he puts it, an 'intellectual and aesthetic stance towards divergent cultural experiences, a search for contrasts' based around a 'willingness to engage with the other' (Hannerz 1990: 127). Here the cosmopolitan is viewed as possessing the reflexive cultural competencies that enable him or her to exist within new systems of meaning and to engage in a wide range of cultural contexts. Crucially, though, the cosmopolitan always remains slightly detached from any one fixed identity or cultural discourse, by retaining the capacity to transcend locale thanks to the aforementioned stance.

Cosmopolitanism is, then, fundamentally an anti-essentialist discourse: 'The conception of cultures as homogeneous unities of language, origin and political identity, as maintained by methodological nationalism, is the exact opposite of the cosmopolitan self-conception' (Beck 2002: 37). Clearly the nation has historically been one significant way in which borders have been constructed and maintained, with essentialized discourses – such as nationalism and xenophobia – closely linked to the development of the nation state. As is argued here, cosmopolitanism is concerned with a degree of transgression of such boundaries and of contestation of such essentialized identities, so it is useful to contrast this approach with the nationalist logic of delineating identities around more fixed characteristics, such as 'race', class, gender or national identity. Much of cosmopolitanism's appeal is in the fact that it helps us move beyond a nation-centric view of the world and accordingly to throw off the constraints of nationalism – in both its methodological (Beck 2000) and other manifestations. Indeed, a major allure of cosmopolitanism is that it allows us to think of new forms of social engagement beyond identities and roles tied to the nation state.

The cosmopolitan discourse is concerned with transcending the boundaries that have been responsible for the emergence and institutionalization of exclusionary political discourses such as racism, nationalism, xenophobia, homophobia and sexism. By citing allegiances to universalized discourses that transcend particularistic national contexts, cosmopolitans strive to challenge such ideologies and ethno/cultural-centric approaches. However, such conceptions also illustrate something of the aforementioned paradox of cosmopolitanism, inasmuch as commitments to normative universals are difficult to conceptualize without some link to a bounded political community. It is arguably this tension that has led to the (re)emergence of interest in the potential of Europe as a post-national political and cultural community to support such cosmopolitan forms of social, cultural and political organization.

European cosmopolitanism or cosmopolitan Europeans?

Linking cosmopolitanism to Europe raises many issues pertinent to the previous discussion. In addition to the useful contributions from theorists seeking to radicalize the concept (as assessed above), in recent years cosmopolitanism has been reinvigorated by a number of social and political theorists who have sought to integrate studies on Europe with cosmopolitanism (see for example Delanty and Rumford 2005; Rumford 2005). Certainly, critical approaches to the construction and maintenance of European boundaries suggest that social transformations associated with the much-contested process of Europeanization offer considerable potential for those interested in cosmopolitanism. While many have celebrated (Archibugi 1998) – or at least sought to situate (Delanty and Rumford 2005) – the European project as a post-national one capable of transcending particularized (such as nationalized) assumptions and identities while engaging fully with more universalized expressions (such as 'diversity' or human rights), it is clear that the construction of 'Europe' raises a number of other issues highly pertinent to the cosmopolitan discourse. Accordingly, then, cosmopolitanism can be a useful framework within which to assess Europeanization and the associated political developments, but crucially only if it asks the right types of question.

However, given the need for cosmopolitanism discourse to go beyond boundaries of many kinds, it seems somewhat strange that some scholars are trying to construct new ones around it. Initially it is important to attempt to square what appears to be a circle with regard to cosmopolitanism and Europe: while linking cosmopolitanism to Europe does reinvigorate the cosmopolitan project for the reasons discussed below, arguably there is an inherent danger in trying to territorialize cosmopolitanism in such a way. Why should cosmopolitans feel the need to territorialize the concept and so raise a number of the problems – such as particularization and essentialization – that it sets out to transcend? It is understandable though that, even in the face of such issues, some call for us to link cosmopolitanism to Europe.

David Harvey, who has written on the 'banality' of the apolitical and placeless versions of cosmopolitanism, suggests that true cosmopolitanism cannot be based on a passive, despatialized relationship to abstracted global struggles and politics; for Harvey a cosmopolitan vision in the absence of a recognition of geographical differences and a strong engagement with the particularities of the local context is not a feasible project (Harvey 2000: 556–58). He argues that any meaningful cosmopolitanism must go beyond simply passive contemplation of global citizenship, human rights or other universal conceptions. In emphasizing the active foundations of cosmopolitan engagement, Harvey reminds us of the central features of the discourse, inasmuch as it entails a relationship between particulars and universals, local issues informed by global concerns. Similarly, Tim Brennan has argued that 'if we wished to capture the essence of cosmopolitanism in a single formula, it would be ... a discourse of the universal that is inherently local – a locality that is always surreptitiously imperial' (Brennan, cited in Robbins 2002: 33). In short, Harvey's argument would lead us to value the importance of place to cosmopolitan visions, as it allows us to territorialize – and potentially to operationalize – this most elusive of categories.

Furthermore, the radicalized reflexivity with regard to political, cultural and social boundaries – suggested earlier in this chapter as being fundamental to cosmopolitanism – is clearly in evidence in the research literature on Europe. The highly complex and frequently ambivalent relation between national and 'European' politics (including the extent to which the two can be disentangled) is an example of this, and one which raises a number of expressions of cosmopolitan tensions. For example, the Europeanization of protest (Imig and Tarrow 2001), facilitated in part by advances in information and communication technologies (Castells 1997),[5] has given the imperatives of cosmopolitanism (as sketched earlier in this chapter as well as elsewhere in this volume) a tangible focus. A wide range of protest movements have successfully 'Europeanized' their struggles, which are frequently against national governments. The Europeanization of protest provides a useful research agenda within the cosmopolitan debate, as not only does it assess the extent to which *citizens* are concerned with contesting power in 'Brussels' as opposed to in national political spheres, but it also speaks to contestation around identity boundaries of many kinds (for numerous examples of this type of engagement see Imig and Tarrow 2001).

A fundamental condition of cosmopolitan research on Europe must be that the boundaries of Europe are not drawn too narrowly; it must also be recognized that the codifications of European identity are fraught with even more problems than are those of national culture. Of course, there is a considerable body of scholarship – broadly in the constructivist tradition – that draws attention to the politicized nature of the constructions of European boundaries. In this context Gerard Delanty's work *Inventing Europe: Idea, Image, Reality* – which charts the political and cultural construction of the European project – and Chris Shore's *Building Europe: The Cultural Politics of European Integration* – which interrogates the highly politicized images associated with the emergence and maintenance of the European Union (EU) – could both be mentioned (Delanty 1995; Shore 2000).

---

5 In a related debate it has been suggested that the information society is one such space in which a cosmopolitan engagement could take place (see for example Castells 1996, 1997). In these formulations the information society is seen as a decentred, post-national space based on the flows of electronic information and communication. In his now familiar argument Manuel Castells suggests that this space is the ultimate expression of global civil society, as it is decentred and disparate enough to operate beyond the regulatory capacity of the nation state. The important link between Castells' idea of information-rich elites and cosmopolitanism is that the type of knowledge possessed by cosmopolitan elites is not tied to place; rather, it is flexible, transferable and decontextualized.

Both books draw attention to the ultimately contested nature of the cultural construction of Europe; maintaining a critical distance from the symbols of Europe and questioning the claims of the EU to represent a truly cosmopolitan project remind us of the ultimately constructed nature of the boundaries that conscribe Europe. Similarly, Ash Amin's work on Europe could also be cited in this context, as it encourages us to guard against associating Europe too narrowly with religious or ethnic traditions (Amin 2004). Such critical reflexivity hints at a grounded basis for a more truly cosmopolitan engagement around Europe.

Certainly, while 'Europe' is perhaps a sufficiently open and contested category that can support such analysis and enquiry, we must keep in mind the dangers of simply replicating existing problems of the nation state – and the associated essentialized boundaries and identities it fostered in the modern age – on a European level. Indeed, while the EU may seem to deal effectively with universalism relative to national particularism, ethnocentric conceptions of Europe still dominate many contemporary debates, in which Europe is typically equated with a narrow heritage – often Christian – exclusive of the many ethnic and secular cultures that now exist in Europe (Delanty 1995; Holmes 2000). Such conceptions of European civilization raise major concerns. For example, European Jews and Muslims cannot too easily identify with a Europe that looks to such an ethnocentric version of European heritage to maintain pseudo-ethnicized or essentialized categories. It is crucial therefore that cosmopolitan scholarship reminds us of these dangers; this type of research on Europe furthers Lamont's argument for cosmopolitanism to place questions of 'boundary work' – in terms of construction, maintenance and transgression – at the centre of its project.

It has been suggested that it may be favourable to construct a European cultural identity in such a way that takes account of conflict, crisis and Europe's turbulent past. For example, the notion that the Holocaust should be remembered as a European, rather than distinctly German, trauma emerged in the Intergovernmental Conference on the Holocaust in Stockholm in January 2000. The commemoration of the Holocaust as a European memory necessitates the disassociation of this genocide from the symbols of any one nation.[6] Levy and Sznaider (2002) explicitly develop such arguments with reference to the arguments assessed earlier when they discuss the emergence of cosmopolitan collective memory around the Holocaust commemoration.

In a stark reminder of the dangers associated with constructing quasi-national, essentialized boundaries around Europe, a number of high-profile academic

6   Similarly, such reflexivity towards the Europeanization of the Holocaust is evident in the architect Daniel Libeskind's Jewish Museum in Berlin, in which he uses a range of symbolic narratives to situate the building – and the huge loss of life in the Second World War – as 'post-national' (see Delanty and Jones 2002).

commentators have suggested that an emergent European public sphere could crystallize around opposition to the US government's so-called 'war on terror' (see Markovits 2005 for an overview of these arguments). Those who would like to 'Europeanize' cosmopolitanism have drawn on a range of broadly anti-US – as distinct from anti-war or anti-state – feeling. The dangers of such an approach barely need to be spelled out here; suffice to say that replicating the very essentialized identity boundaries and exclusionary discourses that cosmopolitanism is supposed to transcend in this way simply amplifies the particularizing tendencies of the nation state to a bigger stage. While such 'other' discourses may well give to the idea of Europe a coherence that it hitherto lacked, the cost of such integration is high and potentially disastrous.

So, while it may be true that 'The first international model which begins to resemble the cosmopolitan model is the European Union' (Archibugi 1998: 219), we must also be very clear about the inherent dangers of associating Europe too closely with the EU (Burgess 2002). It is clear in these various studies that what is being discussed is a cosmopolitan approach or a stance, rather than a cosmopolitan identity. By embracing such a political programme, cosmopolitanism is also given a tangible analytical focus. Crucially, though, the aforementioned reflexivity and anti-essentialism, suggested here as being fundamental to any credible cosmopolitanism, should remind Europeans that Europe is not the world, and at the same time encourage them to raise pertinent questions about the construction of the boundaries that presently conscribe and define Europe. In other words, we must guard against constructing cosmopolitanism in such a way that essentializes Europe, reifying a European elite and thus repeating the worst mistakes of detached and exclusive constructions of the nation in an earlier modernity. Cosmopolitanism cannot be considered as some form of 'identity capital' that people compete for, where we decide whether or not people are or are not cosmopolitan; this is not to do with an identity, or the quest for an identity.

Conclusion

The notion of a distinctly European cosmopolitanism seems something of a contradiction in terms, given that cosmopolitanism is predicated on the transcendence of boundaries. This chapter has argued that to move beyond this impasse, the European cosmopolitan project must actively challenge exclusionary identity discourses, both within and beyond the confines of the nation state. A key challenge within this cosmopolitan paradox is to construct a model that guards against the essentialization of 'European' and other identity boundaries; situating such struggles around identity at the heart of cosmopolitanism signals an attempt to move beyond the description of an elite 'European' reality modelled on a highly mobile class and – at the same time – reinvigorates the concept with a critical dimension lacking in much contemporary discussion. Asking these sorts of crucial questions would allow us to move beyond cosmopolitanism as either simple descriptions of elite realities or utopian projections detached from the lived realities of many. It is through addressing this research agenda that cosmopolitan scholarship can both recapture something of a commitment to social justice beyond particularized constructions of collective identity and at the same time provide a theoretical framework within which to understand the social transformations of our time (within and without Europe).

We live in a Europe of extreme inequalities; some cosmopolitan theorizing is in danger of compounding these injustices by fetishizing mobility and stigmatizing fixity. Although populations are in general more mobile now, the consumption of space is still a fundamental characteristic of an elite who stand in stark contrast to an expanding population of excluded people who are very much bounded by place. Cosmopolitanism is currently an intellectual and political concept that is sufficiently fluid to be recast as a challenge to persistent forms of inequality and discriminatory ideology, and placing such struggles at the centre of the cosmopolitan agenda makes it possible to realize something of cosmopolitanism's potential. Although such calls have frequently led to solely normative constructions of cosmopolitanism, which add little to our conceptual understanding of identities in changing societies, it is by framing such arguments via anti-essentialized constructivist reflexive theorizing – broadly speaking what Beck has called a methodological cosmopolitanism – that cosmopolitanism also provides an approach of use to social science.

References

Amin, A. (2004) 'Multi-ethnicity and the idea of Europe', *Theory, Culture and Society*, 21(2), 1–24.

Archibugi, D. (1998) 'Principles of cosmopolitan democracy', in A. Archibugi, D. Held and M. Kohler (eds), *Re-imagining Political Community: Studies in Cosmopolitan Democracy*, Cambridge: Polity Press, pp. 198–228.

Bauman, Z. (2001) 'Wars of the globalization era', *European Journal of Social Theory*, 4(1), 11–28.

Beck, U. (1998) 'Cosmopolitan manifesto', *New Statesman*, 20 March.

Beck, U. (2000) 'The cosmopolitan perspective: sociology of the second age of modernity', *British Journal of Sociology*, 51(1), 79–106.

Beck, U. (2002) 'The cosmopolitan society and its enemies', *Theory, Culture and Society*, 19(1–2), 17–44.

Beck, U. (2003) 'Rooted cosmopolitanism', in U. Beck, N. Sznaider and R. Winter (eds), *Global America? The Cultural Consequences of Globalization*, Liverpool: Liverpool University Press.

Bourdieu, P. (1989) *Distinction: A Social Critique of the Judgement of Taste*, London: Routledge.

Bourdieu, P., Accardo, A. and Parkhurst Ferguson, P. (1999) *The Weight of the World: Social Suffering in Contemporary Society*, Cambridge: Polity Press.

Burgess, J. P. (2002) 'What's so European about the European Union? Legitimacy between institution and identity', *European Journal of Social Theory*, 5(4), 483–98.

Castells, M. (1996) *The Network Society*, Oxford: Blackwell.

Castells, M. (1997) *The Power of Identity*, Oxford: Blackwell.

Charlesworth, S. (2000) *The Phenomenology of Working Class Experience*, Cambridge: Cambridge University Press.

Delanty, G. (1995) *Inventing Europe: Idea, Identity, Reality*, London: Macmillan.

Delanty, G. and Jones, P. (2002) 'European identity and architecture', *European Journal of Social Theory*, 5(4), 453–66.

Delanty, G. and Rumford, C. (2005) *Rethinking Europe: Social Theory and the Implications of Europeanization*, London: Routledge.

Falk, R. (1995) 'The world order between inter-state law and the law of humanity: the role of civil society institutions', in D. Archibugi and D. Held (eds), *Cosmopolitan Democracy*, Cambridge: Polity Press, pp. 163–79.

Falk, R. (1996) 'Revisioning cosmopolitanism', in J. Cohen and M. C. Nussbaum (eds), *For Love of Country: Debating the Limits of Patriotism*, Boston, MA: Beacon Press, pp. 53–60.

Habermas, J. (1989) *The Structural Transformation of the Public Sphere*, Cambridge: Polity Press.

Hannerz, U. (1990) 'Cosmopolitans and locals in world culture', in M. Featherstone (ed.), *Global Culture: Nationalism, Globalization and Modernity*, London: Sage, pp. 237–52.

Hannerz, U. (2004) *Foreign News: Exploring the World of Foreign Correspondents*, Chicago, IL: Chicago University Press, pp. 237–51.

Harvey, D. (2000) 'Cosmopolitanism and the banality of geographic evils', *Public Culture*, 12(2), 529–64.

Holmes, D. (2000) *Integral Europe: Fast-Capitalism, Multiculturalism, Neofascism*, Princeton, MA: Princeton University Press.

Imig, D. and Tarrow, S. (eds) (2001) *Contentious Europeans: Protest and Polity in an Emerging Polity*, New York: Rowman and Littlefield.

Isin, E. and Woods, P. (1999) *Citizenship and Identity*, London: Sage.

Kennedy, P. (2004) 'Linking the local and the global: transnational architects in a globalizing world', in F. Eckhard and D. Hassenpflug (eds), *Urbanism and Globalization*, Frankfurt: Peter Lang, pp. 231–50.

Lamont, M. (2000) *The Dignity of Working Men: Morality and the Boundaries of Race, Class, and Immigration*, Cambridge, MA: Harvard University Press.

Lamont, M. and Aksartova, S. (2002) 'Ordinary cosmopolitans: strategies for bridging racial boundaries among working-class men', *Theory, Culture and Society*, 19(4), 1–25.

Levy, D. and Sznaider, N. (2002) 'Memory unbound: the Holocaust and the formation of cosmopolitan memory', *European Journal of Social Theory*, 5(1), 87–106.

Markovits, A. S. (2005) 'European anti-Americanism (and anti-Semitism): ever present though always denied', Centre for European Studies working paper no. 108, Harvard University. Available at http://www.people.fas.harvard.edu/~ces/publications/docs/pdfs/Markovits.pdf (last accessed January 2007).

Mayhew, L. (1997) *The New Public: Professional Communication and the Means of Social Influence*, Cambridge: Cambridge University Press.

Mignolo, W. (2002) 'The many faces of cosmo-polis: border thinking and critical cosmopolitanism', in C. A. Breckenridge, S. Pollock, H. K. Bhabha and D. Chakrabarty (eds), *Cosmopolitanism*, Durham, NC: Duke University Press, pp. 721–48 (special issue of *Public Culture*, 12(3)).

Nussbaum, M. (1996) 'Patriotism and cosmopolitanism', in J. Cohen (ed.), *For Love of Country: Debating the Limits of Cosmopolitanism*, Boston, MA: Beacon Press, pp. 2–17.

Robbins, B. (2002) 'What's left of cosmopolitanism?', *Radical Philosophy*, 116, 30–37.

Rumford, C. (2005) 'Cosmopolitanism and Europe: towards a new EU studies agenda?', *Innovation*, 18(1), 1–9.

Shore, C. (2000) *Building Europe: The Cultural Politics of European Integration*, London: Routledge.

Skeggs, B. (2002) 'Becoming cultural', presented to the School of Sociology and Social Policy, University of Liverpool, 1 May.

Urry, J. (2000) *Sociology Beyond Societies*, London: Routledge.

Vertovec, S. and Cohen, R. (2002) 'Introduction: conceiving cosmopolitanism', in S. Vertovec and R. Cohen (eds), *Conceiving Cosmopolitanism: Theory, Context and Practice*, Oxford: Oxford University Press.

Yeoh, B. S. A. (2004) 'Cosmopolitanism and its exclusions in Singapore', *Urban Studies*, 41(12), 2431–45.

Zolo, D. (1997) *Cosmopolis: Prospects for World Government*, Cambridge: Polity Press.

Part II
Europe and the Cosmopolitan Public Sphere

CHAPTER 6

Out of Europe: Human Rights and Prospects for Cosmopolitan Democracy

Kate Nash[1]

If, as theorists of cosmopolitanism argue, sociology must break out of 'methodological nationalism', and reject nation-based concepts of society and politics (Beck 2002, 2003), it is equally necessary to recognize the continuing importance of the organization of social, cultural and political life within and in relation to states. Here we are concerned with how such organization affects prospects for global justice. More concretely, the chapter is concerned with the contribution of the expanding international human rights regime to cosmopolitan democracy. In particular, it is concerned with the possibilities that discourses of human rights may offer for the formation of solidaristic political identities beyond the national state in Europe, where the institutions of the European Union (EU) and the human rights system of the Council of Europe offer the closest approximation to a working model – albeit regionally limited – of 'actually existing' cosmopolitan democracy. I argue that Europe does provide important resources for cosmopolitan democracy, but that building a common European identity is counterproductive if cosmopolitan democracy is the aim. At best, cosmopolitan democracy will develop out of nationalism reworked. Developed in such a way, cosmopolitan democracy is unlikely to be as unequivocally attractive as it is represented in the purely moral terms of liberal philosophy. Sociological research on the *meanings* of human rights is necessary: moral ambiguity in extending human rights cannot be avoided and must be confronted if cosmopolitan democracy is to be anything more than a dream.

1 I would like to thank *Cultural Politics* for permission to reprint some material that appeared in 'Political culture, ethical cosmopolitanism and cosmopolitan democracy' (*Cultural Politics*, 2(3), 2006), and thanks to John Armitage, Kirsten Campbell, Chris Rumford and Neil Washbourne for helpful suggestions on how to improve it.

Kate Nash

Cosmopolitan democracy and human rights

The Universal Declaration of Human Rights (UDHR), adopted at the United Nations (UN) in 1948, was novel in encoding human rights in an international rather than a national setting. For the first time, the individual is the subject of international law rather than, or more accurately as well as, states (Held 1995; Henkin 1990: 34–37). Humanity is thereby figured, in principle, as a political community in which the individual may make claims against his or her state, and is supported in doing so by other nation states, organized internationally.

As sociologically sensitive normative political theory, proposals for cosmopolitan democracy build on the principles of the UDHR, by putting human rights at the centre of projects for global social democracy; in such proposals, the state is displaced as the centre of legal and democratic legitimacy, to become just one node in a network of institutions and organizations securing human rights operating at different levels, from a reformed UN to governing bodies of local regions (Archibugi 2004; Archibugi *et al.* 1998; Beetham 2000; Held 1995, 1999, 2002, 2003; Held and McGrew 2002). As expounded by David Held and his collaborators, cosmopolitan democracy is indeed a form of global social democracy. It involves: the redistribution of wealth within and across regions, to enable basic welfare needs to be met across the world; regulation of labour, social and health standards everywhere; and the empowerment of all in regional, national and global institutions (Deacon 2003). It is *global* because, although cosmopolitan democracy involves multiscalar governance, it requires international institutions to become more integrated and to take on policy-making in such a way as to make the global demos a political community for decisions that cannot be taken at a regional, national or local level. Ultimately, cosmopolitan democracy requires the formation of a global political community, as one of a plurality situated at different geographical scales according to the issue in question (Held 2003: 195).

Human rights are a resource for cosmopolitan democracy because, although human rights are more commonly associated in the West with individual civil rights, social and economic rights are an important aspect of the UDHR. Supported by the International Covenant on Economic, Social and Cultural Rights (ICESCR) of 1966, the UDHR calls for the observance of comprehensive rights to welfare as well as civil and political rights. As article 22 of the UDHR puts it: 'Everyone ... is entitled to realisation, through national effort and international co-operation and in accordance with the organisation and resources of each State, of the economic, social and cultural rights indispensable for his dignity and the free development of his personality'. For cosmopolitan democrats, the fact that social and economic norms are to be considered as *rights* (even if there are questions over their justiciability) is important. The creation of global social solidarity and the integration of international institutions are desirable only insofar as they are compatible with the rule of law and democratic accountability, and the language of rights legitimizes reform within these limits.

Advocates of cosmopolitan democracy have given a good deal less attention to how the political will to achieve it might be formed than to analysing the shortcomings of the present international states system and to proposals for global, national and local institutional reform. One of the main problems for the 'how' of cosmopolitan democracy is that it requires a system of global governance, however loosely networked at different scales, to perform the functions of a world state in terms of regulation and redistribution, but it could function as such only by relying on the legitimate monopoly of the means of coercion that is possessed by states. In principle, cosmopolitan democracy involves the devolution of democracy to the lowest possible geographical scale, but as the rule of law depends ultimately on force, the nation state remains crucial. The realization of cosmopolitan democracy requires that nation states enforce international human rights law. As David Held puts it, in a characteristically optimistic turn of phrase: 'The principles of individual democratic states and societies could come to coincide with those of cosmopolitan democratic law … and democratic citizenship could take on, in principle, a truly universal status' (Held 1995: 232–33).

The most compelling arguments for cosmopolitan democracy are based on the way in which nation states are losing control of the processes and events that directly concern their citizens. Globalization – the time–space compression associated with economic deregulation, the spread of ideas and images through new technologies, and the increasing likelihood of cross-border environmental risks – requires states to cooperate in order to regain a degree of control over processes that affect their populations. To a greater or lesser extent in different cases, states are 'internationalizing' in processes of globalization that result in the erosion of state autonomy, of capacities to mobilize and to dispose of resources for effective domestic and international policy-making. They are also 'internationalizing' in the sharing of state sovereignty, as a result of integration in international policy networks associated with the World Trade Organization (WTO), the North Atlantic Treaty Organization (NATO), the EU and so on (Held 1995: 99–100; Jessop 1997, 1999). Theorists of cosmopolitan democracy see the tendency for states to give up their historic claims to absolute sovereignty and to share jurisdiction with other states as potentially enabling individuals to gain greater control over processes that affect them through democratic forums at different geographical scales.

On the other hand, critics of cosmopolitan democracy argue that evidence of the decline of the nation state has been exaggerated, and that because states retain unrivalled capacities for control over social and economic processes there is currently no other locus of democratic decision-making that has anything like comparable legitimacy (Axtmann 2002; Kymlicka 1999). Trans-national social movements and activist networks are growing in importance, and participation in national elections is in decline – no doubt linked, in part, to the perceived effects of globalization – but decision-making at the international level is far from democratic, whether democracy is conceived of as merely procedural or as more participatory (Dahl 1999; Habermas 2001a; Urbinati 2003). Non-governmental organizations (NGOs), including international NGOs (INGOs), have undoubtedly advanced the human rights agenda in ways that are promising for cosmopolitan democrats, but even the largest membership-based organizations like Amnesty International do not begin to overcome the 'democratic deficit' of international institutions.

Cosmopolitan democracy models a theoretically virtuous circle between democracy and human rights insofar as global regulation and redistribution are required in order to achieve democratic empowerment at different levels within what are currently the territories of nation states. According to the arguments of cosmopolitan democrats, there is a need for strong supranational institutions, precisely in order to facilitate democracy at all levels, including at the national level. This is clearer in the South than in the North, but it applies to all states insofar as they are subject to restructuring through economic globalization. Turning conventional wisdom in the North on its head, Abdullah An-Na'im (not himself an advocate of cosmopolitan democracy as such) argues that respect for human rights in the post-colonial states of Africa depends on the 'international community' to radically restructure the institutions of social and economic human rights (rather than simply to police civil and political rights). According to An-Na'im, legal enforcement of and respect for human rights in Africa are in crisis, in large part as a result of the lack of capacity of post-colonial states: because elected leaders have so little control over economic resources, democratic decision-making has no legitimacy and anarchy is the consequence (An-Na'im 2002). Global social democracy is, therefore, not *additional* to, and potentially damaging for, democracy at the national level. International regulation and redistribution are required for democracy at the national level to be in any way effective. Globalization means that democracy cannot be realized solely at the level of independent nation states, but only through the cooperation of states working together in international institutions, mandated by their citizens to achieve conditions of economic stability that make control over the conditions of social life possible.

However, there is an obvious missing link in the virtuous circle that links human rights and cosmopolitan democracy. If democracy at the level of the nation state is currently the only legitimate form, however imperfect, if democracy at all levels depends on global regulation and redistribution, and if those agreements can be made only by the leaders of nation states, then support for extensive human rights must be created within democratic nation states. In particular, it must be created within the globally powerful nation states of the North. Support for the reforms necessary for cosmopolitan democracy would take us far beyond what already exists in terms of a democratic mandate for the institutionalization of international human rights. As it is, elected politicians are mandated to represent nation states, to work with bureaucrats of the internationalizing state, diplomats and international lawyers to ratify human rights treaties, to write country reports to the UN, to take decisions over budgets for international aid, foreign policy and military commitments, and so on. Decisions made at the international level are rarely prominent in the manifestos politicians are elected to enact. Moreover, negotiations take place in relation to a very limited range of human rights. The 'Washington consensus' continues to dominate economic regulation at the international level and the commitment to human rights in the North is overwhelmingly to civil and political rights, to which we may subscribe with ethnocentric pride and without fear for our comfortable lifestyles.

Cosmopolitan democracy requires that support for human rights is generated within nation states, either as consent to global reform brought about by elected political leaders, or as active demands that push politicians into reform. Reform seems unlikely unless voters bring leaders to account if they fail to sign or ratify human rights treaties (the US, for example, has signed the ICESCR but has not ratified it) or oblige them to live up to the human rights treaties that states have signed and ratified. As Julie Mertus has argued concerning US promises for a foreign policy guided by human rights, unless citizens call governments to account for failing to live up to their own rhetoric, double standards will continue in practice (Mertus 2004).

For reasons of democratic legitimacy as well as for practical reasons, cosmopolitan democracy requires more than institutional reform from above. It also requires the formation of a political culture within which world citizens situated in local and national political practices are oriented towards global social justice. As Held (2003: 167) notes, states must stop treating international governmental organizations as outposts of national politics, and to begin to see them as making public policy for the world. Leaders with a democratic mandate from their citizens must cease acting in 'the national interest' and citizens must encourage them to do so. Effectively, cosmopolitan democracy requires that the citizens of a nation state dissolve the national political community to which they belong, at least where policies concern issues which do not neatly fit inside state borders. Only then will nation states 'wither away' as the sole centres of legitimate power over their territories (Held 2002: 33).

The promise of Europe

Although Europe currently falls far short of the demanding criteria for a fully functioning cosmopolitan democracy, the political and legal integration of European institutions nevertheless appears to many theorists to offer the best hope of incubating and growing global social democracy. It is important to distinguish analytically here between institutions and political culture, between actually existing political and legal integration in Europe and the symbolic resources of the legacy of European history and thought. It is also useful to distinguish between relations within Europe as a single, if complex, 'domestic' political space, and relations extending beyond it, in terms of an integrated European 'foreign' policy – even if globalization and global politics, including human rights norms, make such a distinction a good deal less clear cut in practice.

Within Europe, in terms of institutions, Europe resembles cosmopolitan democracy to a greater degree than any previously or currently existing political arrangements in the world. European political and legal institutions have achieved a level of integration beyond the nation state that most closely resembles what would be required by cosmopolitan democracy at the regional, national and local levels, including mechanisms for enforcing human rights within nation states (Held 2003: 101). In the case of human rights, institutional integration guarantees both positive and negative rights for citizens and non-citizens to an unprecedented and unparalleled degree, through the European Court of Human Rights, the European Court of Justice, the European Parliament and above all through governments, which are legally bound to adhere to the European Convention on Human Rights (ECHR).

The relationship between Europe and the rest of the world is much less established: there is no EU foreign policy, no unified European military force and no obvious agreement of interests between member states on these topics. Foreign policy beyond Europe remains largely the remit of individual states, networked into distinctive military alliances and socio-economic institutions that grew up during the Second World War and the Cold War. Similarly, in terms of human rights, beyond the considerable integration that we have noted, individual states have their own relationships to the UN system of monitoring and ensuring human rights, and are bound by the treaties and conventions into which they have entered.

Arguments for an integrated European 'foreign policy' rely, therefore, on more 'ideal' characteristics of Europe, rooted in history and culture rather than found in existing European institutions. The most interesting intervention arguing along these lines is undoubtedly the letter written by Jürgen Habermas, signed by himself and Jacques Derrida and published in both the *Frankfurter Allgemeine Zeitung* and *Liberation* in 2003 in response to the Iraq war (discussed also in Chapter 1). Its purpose was twofold: it was an attempt to bring about a relationship of Europe to the rest of the world by rational means, by listing the reasons that give Europe – or, rather, 'core' Europe – common cause and a common identity as an independent and countervailing force with regard to US foreign policy; and at the same time it sought performatively to bring about a European public sphere, to begin a debate and realize a common European identity, by publishing the letter on the same day as others written on the same theme and for the same purposes in leading newspapers in Italy, France, Spain and Switzerland (see also Habermas and Derrida 2005).

Habermas's and Derrida's letter represents a kind of 'European Declaration of Independence' (Levy *et al.* 2005: xvi), seeking to free Europe from US influence. In contrast with the US, according to Habermas and Derrida, 'core Europe' (which does not include the UK, nor the new Eastern European member states of the EU) shares a number of common characteristics that distinguish it from the US: the secularization of public affairs; a reflexive appreciation of difference, including, as a result of decolonization, that of non-Europeans; sensitivity to the paradoxes of progress; trust in the state over the market; lack of tolerance for the use of force against persons; and the desire for a non-Eurocentric foreign policy organized by a reformed UN. From Habermas's writings elsewhere on global governance (Habermas 1998, 2001b), we can take it that his aim for a united European foreign policy is the realization of what we are here describing as cosmopolitan democracy, or global social democracy, a potentially important contribution to which, Habermas suggests, would be the development of a distinctively European identity and orientation towards the non-European world.

The aim of Habermas's and Derrida's letter is, then, to prompt Europe to realize its 'ideal' self, to become unified around what is or should be its common destiny as a political community and a project for the global common good as cosmopolitan democracy. In order to do so, however, there is one major obstacle to overcome: 'Europeans' do not conceive of themselves as such in terms of their political identifications. While there is a rather minimal, and highly contested, commitment to European institutions on the part of European citizens, there is no common European political identity among the general population of member states. Nation states retain an appeal for the 'peoples' in whose name they exercise their considerable economic, political, military and environmental power.

Given Europe's leading role in institutionalizing human rights, it is surprising that the 'European Declaration of Independence' did not mention them, except implicitly in terms of the 'UN system'. It is true that a commitment to human rights does not neatly distinguish Europe and the US. The US has at least an equal claim to world leadership in human rights, both as a matter of recent historical fact – in setting up the UN and in establishing the conditions for the recovery of Europe itself after the Second World War – and in terms of its Enlightenment antecedents as a nation (while the American Declaration of Independence was somewhat more limited than the French Declaration of Human Rights, it was similar in form). However, it is also widely agreed that US policy with regard to human rights is so contradictory as to deserve the label 'American exceptionalism': although the US has historically taken the lead in extending human rights to other countries – very successfully in many cases – and, with a couple of notable exceptions, including the use of capital punishment for juveniles, generally complies in most of its domestic laws with international norms, the US systematically refuses itself to ratify core treaties, tolerates double standards on the part of its allies and generally blocks any human rights initiatives that might affect its own sovereign domestic and foreign policy decisions (Ignatieff 2005). Indeed, 'American exceptionalism' is so well established as to be *justified* as such by Robert Kagan in an almost precisely parallel argument to that of the European philosophers, in which he posits the differences between the US and Europe as positive and necessary, even for Europe's own peace and prosperity (Kagan 2004).

Nevertheless, although it is possible to argue for a distinctive European history of human rights, it is not clear that even a genuine and unwavering commitment to human rights is compatible with the European *identity* that Habermas and Derrida are proposing. Certainly, in terms of European 'domestic' policy, human rights institutionalized in law and public policy unify Europe from within to a very high degree. Crucially, however, such uses of human rights do not rely on a 'thick' common identity. Indeed, if human rights are to succeed, as they do to a certain extent, in protecting unpopular minorities, including racialized ethnic minorities, from the democratic majority, a quasi-ethnic and already racialized European identity may well be as problematic as ethnic nationalism. A genuine commitment to universal human rights would mean an end to 'fortress Europe', not necessarily in terms of uncontrolled immigration, but certainly in terms of guaranteed possibilities for asylum seekers, building more positive images of immigration and treating all individuals, citizens or not, as full legal persons (Balibar 2004; Benhabib 2004). A Europe of human rights cannot mean replacing a loosely federated collection of parochial nation states with a bigger, more closely integrated and positively asserted but equally parochial European identity.

In terms of European foreign policy, it is also unclear what contribution a commitment to human rights might make if its main purpose is to support a reformed UN system as a counterbalance to US power. European states can reasonably claim to have adopted, at least in theory though always failing in practice, a principled orientation towards the rest of the world in legally binding themselves into the UN and European human rights systems. In other respects, however, there is no reason to see European states as less partial and realist than others – although without the US's military, economic and political power. If Europe had such power, founded on the strategic aims of bringing the US into line, how likely is it that it would act in any more principled way on the world stage than any other state oriented towards ensuring its own position? Again, there would seem to be no particular advantage to the world outside Europe in European states exchanging national parochialism for European parochialism.

If cosmopolitan democracy is the aim, it is far from evident that uniting Europe around a common identity is valuable as a means. A European identity existing as one of a plurality, alongside and intertwined with other political identities within the EU system – local, national, trans-national – would no doubt be of benefit to European citizens in facilitating a range of policies more appropriately decided at the European level, especially concerning welfare measures requiring 'thick' solidarity, but it is unclear how it would contribute substantively to cosmopolitan democracy, which requires an ethical orientation towards human beings as such. On the contrary, what is required is that, alongside and intertwined with these particular identities, there should *also* be a cosmopolitan dis-identification from the particular, and an orientation towards the horizon of the universal, an identification with humanity (see Appiah 1998). If the conditions for such a cosmopolitan orientation already exist within Europe, it is in the nation state – where thick nationalist identities continue to exercise an attraction that makes European identity itself unthinkable for some time, except among that small minority of 'frequent travellers' (Calhoun 2002) – that they must be fostered.

Ethical cosmopolitanism within the nation state

As a matter of empirical fact, human rights require states. Insofar as international human rights are more than moral principles or political ideals, they are guaranteed and administered by states, established in international law as binding and detailed agreements between states and incorporated into domestic law. Human rights are made and enforced by states, which are represented as sovereign and as representing peoples or nations, which vary a great deal in their capacities, which are located in hierarchies of economic, military and political power, and which continue to serve as the locus of elite decision-making, even where the state no longer resembles anything like the ideal typical nation state and where human rights are those of the individual, rather than of the people. It is within societies organized around nation states that cosmopolitan (dis)identification must be fostered if cosmopolitan democracy is to become a real possibility.

Seyla Benhabib (2004) makes of this empirical fact a normative problem, and argues that in the tension, and sometimes outright conflict, of principle between membership of democratic communities – organized as they currently are around nation states – and human rights, there is a real dilemma for political theorists. If sovereign self-determination is itself a human right and membership of bounded political community is a prerequisite for democracy, what is the legitimate scope of supposedly universal human rights, which – morally – should recognize no boundaries? What political institutions enable legitimate limits on human rights to be established within bounded, democratic communities?

Benhabib's answer to this question is of interest here because, while recognizing the importance of *subjectivity* to the formation of political will as a necessary condition for the development of a cosmopolitan schedule of human rights, her analysis avoids the impasses of *identity* as a limitation on the principles of human rights. Benhabib argues that, in Europe especially and in relation to the question of migration with which she is concerned, we may be seeing the emergence of 'ethical cosmopolitanism', that is, an open-ended orientation towards possible membership of democratic communities that is not based on cultural identity and that is being fostered by European integration of human rights norms into national societies. She suggests that the institutionalization of human rights in Europe is providing propitious conditions for 'jurisgenerative politics': through the 'democratic iteration' of international human rights norms by democratic legislatures, 'Cosmopolitan norms are becoming embedded in the political and legal culture of individual polities' (Benhabib 2004: 177).

I am less concerned in this chapter with Benhabib's normative question of legitimacy than with using her theoretical framework to address a sociological question: how likely is it that a cosmopolitan orientation will develop within national public spheres alongside the institutionalization of human rights? Benhabib herself, despite opening up the question of subjectivity, does not develop this aspect of her theory in the case studies she discusses, as she focuses more on developing the normative principles of democratic iteration through which human rights norms should be made law as a result of media debate and the mobilization of migrant organizations. However, her idea of 'jurisgenerative politics' – as practices that engage embodied, feeling, active human beings in reflexively using human rights norms for various ends, constructing 'ethical cosmopolitanism' along the way as an orientation to human rights, and assuming, imposing or questioning limits to their application according to the membership of a political community conceived at different scales – is potentially very useful for sociological analysis of incipient cosmopolitan sensibilities that may be developing within the boundaries of nation states and that are, as I have argued, a necessary condition for the growth and development of cosmopolitan democracy.

By way of a preliminary exploration of the fruitfulness of Benhabib's theoretical framework for sociological research on the possibilities of popular cosmopolitan (dis)identification within the nation state, we will consider two examples from the UK, one of 'domestic' human rights and one of 'foreign policy' guided by principles of human rights. Although the close alliance with the US puts the UK out of the European 'core' as characterized by Habermas and Derrida, in all other respects it is in an ambiguous rather than an antithetical position with regard to 'European values'. With regard to human rights, the same Blair government that supported the Bush administration's determination to go to war in Iraq was also the government that incorporated the ECHR into UK national law in the 1998 Human Rights Act (HRA), to create a written quasi-constitution. The UK may, therefore, provide a critical example for the research I am proposing, in that, insofar as the parameters of human rights law are currently being worked out in the UK, it should offer a propitious environment for the development of ethical cosmopolitanism.

A dramatic case in which the HRA effectively bound the UK parliament is in relation to the government's derogation from the ECHR in order to detain, for an indefinite period and without charge, terrorist suspects who could not be deported as their status as political asylum seekers had been accepted, in accordance with international human rights. In December 2004, when sixteen suspects had been detained without charge for three years, the Law Lords ruled that the government's derogation from human rights was illegal: the anti-terrorist measures were disproportionate because there was no public emergency that would warrant a suspension of such fundamental rights; and they were discriminatory because only non-citizens were detained, while citizens who were suspects were subject to surveillance but did not lose their liberties (*A and Others v. Secretary of State for the Home Department*, 3 All ER 169). As a result (at the time of writing), the Home Secretary has created a range of 'control orders' up to and including house arrest for both British and non-British detainees – enabling him to get round the charge of discrimination (though not that of disproportionality, which will surely be challenged in the European Court of Human Rights, as domestic remedies are now exhausted).

The anti-terrorist legislation in the UK and the legal battles that have been fought over it are undoubtedly examples of jurisgenerative politics. At each step of the way, the UK government has been constrained by and has had to find ways to work within international human rights norms in Europe and domestic law. Moreover, it could be argued that in ending discrimination between citizens and non-citizens, the Lords made a cosmopolitan interpretation of human rights: they upheld the spirit of human rights after the UDHR in supporting the rights of individual persons as such against the privileging of national citizens' rights over those of non-nationals. In this respect the Lords' re-iteration of the HRA represents an instance of 'cosmopolitan law' (Held 2002; Hirsh 2003).

On the other hand, although the institutionalization of human rights was significant in confirming cosmopolitan norms within the state, it is unclear how that might have contributed to 'ethical cosmopolitanism' as an inter-subjectively supported orientation among the general population. It is notable that there was very little public protest against the detention of the suspects *before* the Lords' ruling; and coverage in the news media of the law and its enforcement did not make much of an issue of discrimination against non-citizens. A great deal more media attention was given to the difficulty of the government in responding to the Law Lords' decision and to the issue of control orders and house arrest, which apply to UK citizens as well as to non-citizens, than to the detentions of non-national terrorist suspects. Media concern over powers claimed by the Home Secretary to prevent terrorism following the Lords' ruling was with perceived threats to what the shadow Home Secretary referred to in parliamentary debate in February 2005 as 'long-standing principles of British liberty' at least as much as with international human rights. On the face of it, the democratic iteration of the legitimacy of nation states for national citizens appears to have been at least as impressive in this jurisgenerative politics as ethical cosmopolitanism.

The second example of jurisgenerative politics concerns 'foreign policy'. It also concerns a type of jurisgenerative politics that does not go through lawyers and courts, but addresses governments directly – necessary where human rights treaties are more clearly aspirational than justiciable, as in the case of social and economic rights.

A prominent attempt to realize global social democracy that has drawn explicitly on social and economic human rights is the 'Drop the Debt' campaign, which mobilized a great deal of support from below to put pressure on politicians in the North. Jubilee 2000, the main campaigning network in the North, collected 24 million signatures across the world and presented them to G8 leaders in Cologne in 1999 to support cancelling the debt of all developing countries by the millennium. Although Jubilee 2000 is a trans-national social movement, working across Europe and North America and affiliated with Jubilee South in the developing world, its aims are to target national governments, to put pressure on them from below rather than through international institutions (Buxton 2004). The campaign directly concerns human rights because one of the main arguments for debt cancellation is that illegitimate debt directly contravenes basic social and economic rights where repayment is made possible only by reducing state provision of essentials like water, food, health care and education (Millet and Toussaint 2004: 124–25). Jubilee 2000 made human rights a focus of its campaign – the debt should be dropped for reasons of justice, not charity.

The 'Drop the Debt' campaign grew into the more ambitious 'Make Poverty History' campaign in the UK, which culminated in a huge upsurge of public support for the Live 8 concert in Hyde Park in July 2005, protests in Scotland around the G8 meeting itself, which took place a few days later, and practically an overnight consensus in the British media that all the demands of the campaign for full debt cancellation and long-term aid should be met (see also Chapter 4). In terms of the rhetoric of the UK government, European leaders, and even US President George Bush, moreover, the campaign was pushing at an open door as promises were made all around to cancel debt, increase aid and introduce a range of measures to boost African economies. Surely here there is evidence of ethical cosmopolitanism?

In fact, any conclusion to this effect is not so straightforward. For one thing, nationalist imagery was prominent throughout media coverage of the campaign. For example, the emergence of 'Make Poverty History' into the mainstream news began during the reporting of Chancellor Gordon Brown's tour of Africa in January 2005. In various speeches Brown linked responses to suffering in Africa to the generosity shown by the British people to those affected by the tsunami disaster and made reference to 'Britain leading the world' in cancelling debt (Brown 2005). Despite the fact that the UK, in a dominant position within the structures of global economic governance, with special voting rights in the International Monetary Fund and the World Bank, membership of the G8 and so on, might well be thought to be part of the problem as well as part of the solution, the 'Make Poverty History' campaign was constructed as a matter of national pride from the very beginning. British patriotism was enhanced by the country's generosity rather than troubled by its implication in maintaining the conditions of global poverty.

Moreover, the construction of what we might call 'cosmopolitan nationalism' must be understood in a context in which, in mainstream political rhetoric and media coverage, the human rights dimension of the 'Drop the Debt' campaign practically disappeared in 'Make Poverty History' (see Nash 2006 for a fuller discussion). Given that there is no legal basis for linking poverty with human rights, it may be that it is not especially productive to link them politically. It is certainly *possible* to link human rights and poverty to mobilize certain constituencies, as the Jubilee 2000 campaign showed. However, the fact that experienced politicians felt that such a link was not worth making for the general public, despite this limited but striking success, nor for other national leaders, is in itself noteworthy. It suggests that the extension of human rights norms may offer little promise of building the trans-national solidarity on economic issues required for global social democracy. On the contrary, the construction of 'cosmopolitan nationalism' suggests that it is less human rights and justice that were at stake than a media-hyped, event-led, image-driven feeling that 'we' (great British) must do something for 'them' (poor Africans).

Conclusion

Cosmopolitanism has a very clear appeal for moral philosophers and liberal political theorists (e.g. Nussbaum 1996). This chapter has discussed the appeal of cosmopolitanism to more sociologically sensitive political theorists, who understand it as one, highly desirable, possible development of the existing political institutions of global governance and especially, given their universalist impetus, of human rights encoded in international law and public policy. However, I have been concerned to argue that even theorists of cosmopolitan democracy and ethical cosmopolitanism, while providing theoretical frameworks that are indispensable to thinking through and investigating the best possible outcomes of global governance today, have given insufficient attention to *how* global social democracy might be realized. Though the point of this chapter has really been to plea for more research in this area, certain conclusions have been reached along the way.

Above all, it seems likely that, insofar as it must develop within national public spheres – not only for reasons of democratic legitimacy, as Benhabib has argued, but also, simply, because no public sphere beyond the national actually exists – cosmopolitanism will be bound up with nationalism, in ways that are neither clearly progressive nor morally attractive, and that may be highly problematic. Nationalism has historic links with racism and imperialism that are difficult to disentangle in practice, and that always threaten to become dominant. Human rights do offer tools to combat racism and imperialism, as they do to counteract domination and inequalities of all kinds. But in practice human rights are not static, decided once and for all, administered neutrally. They are never, in practical terms, universal. If, as I think the examples I have discussed indicate, any extension of human rights into cosmopolitan democracy can work only off and through existing commitments to national interests and national identities on the part of privileged populations in the North, there will be ever-present dangers in the extension of human rights as cosmopolitan democracy. My point here is not that we should give up on human rights, nor on hopes for cosmopolitan democracy. It is only that we should be aware of the dangers that the extension of human rights into cosmopolitan democracy inevitably presents, given that it necessitates the formation of popular will for its realization.

References

An-Na'im, A. A. (2002) 'The legal protection of human rights in Africa: how to do more with less', in T. R. Kearns (ed.), *Human Rights: Concepts, Contests, Contingencies*, Ann Arbor, MI: University of Michigan Press, pp. 89–116.

Appiah, K. (1998) 'Cosmopolitan patriots', in P. Cheah and B. Robbins (eds), *Cosmopolitics:*

Thinking and Feeling Beyond the Nation, Minneapolis, MN: University of Minnesota Press, pp. 91–114.

Archibugi, D. (2004) 'Cosmopolitan democracy and its critics: a review', *European Journal of International Relations*, 10(3), 437–73.

Archibugi, D., Held, D. and Kohler, M. (eds) (1998) *Re-imagining Political Community: Studies in Cosmopolitan Democracy*, Stanford, CA: Stanford University Press.

Axtmann, R. (2002) 'What's wrong with cosmopolitan democracy?', in J. Williams (ed.), *Global Citizenship: A Reader*, Edinburgh: Edinburgh University Press, pp. 101–13.

Balibar, E. (2004) *We, the People of Europe: Reflections on Transnational Citizenship*, Princeton, MA: Princeton University Press.

Beck, U. (2002) 'The cosmopolitan perspective: sociology in the second age of modernity', in S. Vertovec and R. Cohen (eds), *Conceiving Cosmopolitanism: Theory, Context, and Practice*, Oxford: Oxford University Press, pp. 61–85.

Beck, U. (2003) 'Toward a new critical theory with a cosmopolitan intent', *Constellations*, 10(4).

Beetham, D. (2000) *Democracy and Human Rights*, Cambridge: Polity Press.

Benhabib, S. (2004) *The Rights of Others: Aliens, Residents and Citizens*, Cambridge: Cambridge University Press.

Brown, G. (2005) 'Remarks by the Right Honourable Gordon Brown MP, Chancellor of the Exchequer, on debt relief', 14 January. Available at http://www.hm-treasury.gov.uk/newsroom_and_speeches/speeches/chancellorexchequer/speech_chx_140105.cfm (last accessed January 2007)

Buxton, N. (2004) 'Debt cancellation and civil society: a case study of Jubilee 2000', in P. Gready (ed.), *Fighting for Human Rights*, London: Routledge, pp. 54–77.

Calhoun, C. (2002) 'The class consciousness of frequent travellers: towards a critique of actually existing cosmopolitanism', in S. Vertovec and R. Cohen (eds), *Conceiving Cosmopolitanism: Theory, Context, and Practice*, Oxford: Oxford University Press, pp. 86–109.

Dahl, R. (1999) 'Can international organizations be democratic? A skeptic's view', in C. Hacker-Cordon (ed.), *Democracy's Edges*, Cambridge: Cambridge University Press.

Deacon, B. (2003) *Global Social Governance Reform*, Globalisation and Social Policy Programme, Sheffield University.

Habermas, J. (1998) *The Inclusion of the Other*, Cambridge, MA: MIT Press.

Habermas, J. (2001a) 'The postnational constellation and the future of democracy', in M. Pensky (ed.), *The Postnational Constellation*, Cambridge: Polity Press, pp. 58–112.

Habermas, J. (2001b) *The Postnational Constellation: Political Essays*, Cambridge: Polity Press.

Habermas, J. and Derrida, J. (2003) 'February 15, or, what binds European together', *Frankfurter Allgemeine Zeitung/Liberation*, 31 May.

Habermas, J. and Derrida, J. (2005) 'February 15, or, what binds Europeans together: plea for a common foreign policy, beginning in core Europe', in D. Levy, M. Pensky and J. Torpey (eds), *Old Europe, New Europe, Core Europe: Transatlantic Relations After the Iraq War*, London: Verso, pp. 3–13.

Held, D. (1995) *Democracy and the Global Order: From the Modern State to Cosmopolitan Governance*, Cambridge: Polity Press.

Held, D. (1999) 'The transformation of political community: rethinking cosmopolitanism in the context of globalization', in C. Hacker-Cordon (ed.), *Democracy's Edges*, Cambridge: Cambridge University Press, pp. 84–111.

Held, D. (2002) 'Law of states, law of peoples: three models of sovereignty', *Legal Theory*, 8(1), 1–44.

Held, D. (2003) 'Global social democracy', in A. Giddens (ed.), *The Progressive Manifesto*, Cambridge: Polity Press.

Held, D. and McGrew, A. (2002) *Globalization/Anti-globalization*, Cambridge: Polity Press.

Henkin, L. (1990) *The Age of Rights*, New York: Columbia University Press.

Hirsh, D. (2003) *Law Against Genocide: Cosmopolitan Trials*, London: Glasshouse.

Ignatieff, M. (2005) *American Exceptionalism and Human Rights*, Princeton, MA: Princeton University Press.

Jessop, B. (1997) 'Capitalism and its future: remarks on regulation, government and governance', *Review of International Political Economy*, 4(3), 561–81.

Jessop, B. (1999) 'Narrating the future of the national economy and the national state: remarks on remapping regulation and reinventing governance', in G. Steinmetz (ed.), *State/Culture*, Ithaca, NY: Cornell University Press, pp. 378–405.

Kagan, R. (2004) *Of Paradise and Power: America and Europe in the New World Order*, New York: Vintage.

Kymlicka, W. (1999) 'Citizenship in an era of globalization: commentary on Held', in I. Shapiro and C. Hacker-Cordon (eds), *Democracy's Edges*, Cambridge: Cambridge University Press, pp. 112–29.

Levy, D., Pensky, M. and Torpey, J. (2005) 'Editors' Introduction', in D. Levy, M. Pensky and J. Torpey (eds), *Old Europe, New Europe, Core Europe*, London: Verso, pp. xi–xxix.

Mertus, J. A. (2004) *Bait and Switch: Human Rights and U.S. Foreign Policy*, New York: Routledge.

Millet, D. and Toussaint, E. (2004) *Who Owes Who? 50 Questions About World Debt*, London: Zed.

Nash, K. (2006) 'Mediating human rights in the national public sphere: the Pinochet case', paper presented at the 'Crossing the Boundaries' conference, Centre for the Study of Human Rights, London School of Economics, 24 March 2006.

Nussbaum, M. (1996) 'Patriotism and cosmopolitanism', in J. Cohen (ed.), *For Love of Country: Debating the Limits of Cosmopolitanism*, Boston, MA: Beacon Press, pp. 2–17.

Urbinati, M. (2003) 'Can cosmopolitical democracy be democratic?', in D. Archibugi (ed.), *Debating Cosmopolitics*, London: Verso, pp. 67–85.

CHAPTER 7

The European Information Society: A New Public Sphere?

Barrie Axford and Richard Huggins

Prescriptions for trans-national, even cosmopolitan, democracy in Europe conjure two well worn but still robust counterarguments. Curiously, they are voiced both by realist critics of the European project and by those who are sympathetic to the goal of a united Europe but dismayed by the difficulties in surmounting usual politics. Both arguments subsume the litany of the 'democratic deficit' which is held to vitiate the legitimacy of European institutions. The first argument opines that because the European Union (EU) is not a state in the sense of a territorially defined political community, it can never support a true demos. The second, a corollary of the first, is that in the absence of a demos there are no real opportunities for 'substantive public engagement', the hallmark of competent citizenship and republican democracy (Chryssochoou 2002).

The nub of such complaints is that the EU – whether as a form of advanced multilateralism, a system of multiscalar governance or a network polity – does not, perhaps cannot, fulfil the 'imaginary suppositions of democracy' (McLennan 1995: 37), whereby 'a' people have a shared commitment to core definitions of value and play a part in how such value is allocated. Of course, the force of these arguments turns in some measure, possibly altogether, on what we understand by the concepts of 'citizenship' and 'demos', especially when applied to a transnational polity. In the EU context, it is common to identify the trappings of formal citizenship and treaty-based rights and perhaps a dash of something thicker, whereby 'Union citizenship carries an undisputed political weight, a kind of "deep symbolism", with crucial implications for the embodiment of a stronger *Gemeinschaft* element at the grassroots' (Chryssochoou 2002: 6). Available data on public attitudes (Eurostat 2004) may qualify such a bold claim and, given the paucity of richer, qualitative studies of citizenship practice in the EU, it is still wise to be cautious.

Evidence for a unified, self-conscious European demos is indeed scarce, and some would say non-existent. Given the barriers to a sense of common political community and a 'community of culture' (Bauer 1907: 34) in the EU, this is hardly surprising. At the same time it is clear that diverse and attentive publics formed around issues and mobilized as interests are a highly visible feature of European policy discourses. These constituencies can be seen at different scales (local, regional, national, European) or are multiscalar (trans-national). Indeed, some have been constructed without regard for borders and scales at all and are not predicated on the existence of EU institutions. Such relatively open networks sometimes instantiate European-wide communities of interest and affect, but how far constituent actors are 'Europeanized' through such encounters is open to question, even if there were an agreed sense of what that term implies (Pollack 2005).

But what is really lacking, according to many observers, is firm and growing evidence of practical citizenship, that is, of participatory opportunities that instantiate and express the democratic potential of the demos in the exercise of political authority, and which promote both expressive and purposive rationality. Of particular concern is the alleged dearth of civic spaces (including communication spaces) and that 'vast middle ground of communal activity and communication between private life and large-scale institutions' (Evans and Boyte 1986: 89), as only in such spaces can the ideal of common good and common identity be promoted and sustained. This is another way of saying that the EU lacks public spaces to deliver 'civil society's capacity for self-organisation', communication and self-reflection (Calhoun 2004; see also Calhoun 1993). Within these spaces citizens can achieve civic and communicative competence, or 'the institutional capacity of citizens *as* social equals to enter the realm of political influence with a view to sustaining a vital public sphere' (Chryssochoou 2002: 8). Individual actors not only become more reflexive agents, but social analysts and critics, thus enacting a sort of institutional reflexivity.

To reiterate: conventional wisdom has it that the EU has not met the conditions necessary for the institutionalization of a public sphere based on the discursive qualities of free public deliberation. This is bad news, runs the argument, because a vital public sphere is needed to sustain civic governance and to turn diffuse issues into topics of genuine public concern and debate (Chryssochoou 2002). But if we are trying to grasp the vagaries of trans-national polity construction, why not be more relaxed about the imagined qualities of a European demos and of a/the European public sphere? Even to entertain this question we have to step outside the liberal territorialist model of democracy.

Why? Because an examination of the 'imaginary suppositions' of democracy usually reveals the continuing salience of the liberal territorialist model of the organization of political space and of methodological nationalism as the toolbox with which the world is still analysed (Axford 2006; Beck 2003; Shaw 2003). Indeed, much discussion of the construction of a European polity still takes place within at least implicit Cartesian models of political space, liberal discourses about the boundaries of political community, and what Shapiro (1997) calls 'neo-Tocquevillian' assumptions about the natural spaces of civic association and communication (Axford 2006; Brenner 1999).

Even if we can dispense with the epistemological blinkers around 'imagining democracy' – territorial space, 'bounded solidaries' and 'thick' identities – and recognize that there can be no easy and obvious transference of the liberal territorial paradigm for democracy to the EU, we are still left with a problem, and it is this: if democracy within the state requires a healthy public sphere, to what extent must governance across the EU be underpinned by a European-wide public sphere in order to meet the legitimation requirements of a truly democratic system? The ideal public sphere demands 'free and unconstrained public deliberation of all matters of common concern' (Benhabib 1996: 68) and, in principle, deliberative practices given expression through the public sphere do hold out the promise of greater reflexivity and communicative rationality. But can such a strong prescription be realized in *any* pluralistic system of rule where deliberative processes are likely to be just one of many – mostly non-deliberative – means of collective decision-making? Applied beyond the national framework and the liberal territorialist paradigm, the question carries an even greater poignancy. To undo the reliance on liberal territorialist assumptions about the natural spaces of democracy, we have to relax the concept of a unified demos and a unified public sphere, and talk instead about more or less 'attentive publics' at different or multiple scales, about different ways of structuring public talk and about multiple communication spaces in which Europe may be discursively constructed.

In what follows an emphasis on public talk as a key feature of trans-national civil society enables us to focus on institutions of culture and communication as key to the theoretical analysis of polity construction and democracy promotion in Europe. We begin by looking directly at the concept of the public sphere.

The public sphere

For all its iconic status in accounts of liberal territorial democracy, the concept of the public sphere is ambiguous. Seen as the communicative expression of civil society (Sassi 2001), the public sphere is also the 'space' where shared meanings are supposed to emerge from an interactive and deliberative demos. As well as being a part of theories of how the world became modern, communicative practices and institutions carry a powerful normative charge because they 'strengthen the collective identity of a national group by creating boundaries' around it (Schlesinger 2004: 9). In like vein, advocacy of a unified European public sphere is a powerful normative project, albeit one in which there is confusion about whether it should be seen as a cause or a consequence of other democracy-making practices, and because of doubt over what it is, where it is located, how it has emerged, who participates in it and what form (or forms) it takes (Splichal 2004).

Thus, Koopmans *et al.* (2000) argue that a real European public sphere requires the trans-nationalization of collective actors such as political parties, interest groups and media. Yet Thomas Risse (2003) is convinced that public spheres emerge through routine social practice (including deliberation) and should not be seen as either a direct cause or an effect of European integration. In his role as champion of 'post-national' democracy in Europe, Jürgen Habermas advocates the establishment of a European public sphere as a necessary solution to the problems of democratic deficit and social integration (Habermas 2001; see also Calhoun 2004), and sometime Portuguese Prime Minister António Guterres observes that 'Europe's greatest democratic deficit does not lie in its institutions, but in the lack of a "European public sphere"' (*Süddeutsche Zeitung*, 24 February 2000). By contrast, Jürgen Gerhards (2000) opines that the democratic deficit in the EU contributes greatly to a lack of *publicness* because the institutional cast and elitist dynamic of the integrationist project have left little room for either discursive or practical citizenship beyond the agency of collective, organized and usually corporate interests.

This is powerful stuff, but conceptual vagueness sullies the idea of the public sphere, rendering it little more than a hortatory device or a *gestalt* in which robust dialogical and deliberative practices are presumed to elevate usual politics or, through expressions of public opinion, at least hold its practitioners to account (Axford 2001; Emirbayer and Sheller 1999). Doubts about the competence of even 'appropriately educated' citizens to deliver this vision of liberal virtue have been legion (*pace* Bentham, Hegel, Kant and Lippmann) but the appeal of an idea in which liberal and republican forms of government are secured and held accountable to public opinion has always been strong (*pace*, for example, MacKinnon and Rousseau). In Habermas's seminal account of the public sphere as a product of the Enlightenment, it functions as 'a realm of social life in which something approaching public opinion can be formed' (Habermas 1974: 51; see also Habermas 1989). Unfettered access, open communication and rational debate are key features of this public sphere and the unified public so constituted confers and adjudicates on matters of common concern.

Revisionist treatments of the pristine concept, including those from Habermas himself, stress, variously: that in polyarchies there are likely to be multiple publics and thus multiple public spheres (Habermas 2001; Meyer 2005); that the universality prescribed is, or may be, confounded by the lack of 'linguistic capital' available to certain excluded or marginal groups, as well as by other conditions which exclude whole categories of people (Emirbayer and Sheller 1999: 155; Fraser 1992); and that, depending on context and motivation, deliberation may well promote communicative rationality but not purposive rationality. Finally, publics are not just 'spaces' where politics is discussed, let alone bounded spaces, but 'networks of individuals and groups acting as citizens'. These actors perform democracy in many routine ways, in and across different spaces of association (Emirbayer and Sheller 1999: 156; Wellman 2002). In other words, publics can emerge anywhere because, by definition, they are multiple, relational (networked) and interstitial (Cohen and Arato 1992; Emirbayer and Sheller 1999; White 1995). Finally, the very idea of 'a' European public sphere as a 'cohesive and unitary space' is still an analogy of the 'national' model, with bounded terri-toriality simply reimposed at the EU 'level' (Splichal 2004: 8).

Much of the confusion apparent in discussions of the public sphere arises not only from attempts to transpose national definitions of publicness – problematic as these are – to the EU but also from the operationalization of the concept itself. Slavko Splichal (1999, 2004: 9) usefully identifies five perspectives on *publicness* which open out the concept and specify key components that are often overlooked or conflated. First, a/the *public* must be seen as a social category and a material form, as well as an abstract principle or normative symbol. Publics are material agents that coalesce around key social issues. Second, *publicness* refers to the public nature of an activity, institution or space, as in 'public service broadcasting' or 'public health'. Third, the principle of *publicity* (Kant 1795) underpins the practice of democratic citizenship since it instantiates the right to exercise the public use of reason through deliberation. Fourth, a/the *public sphere* is the domain or 'imagined space' in which public discourse takes place and public opinion is articulated (Splichal 2004: 9). Located primarily in civil society, public spaces can also be inserted into the institutions of state and economy (Cohen and Arato 1992) and this point has relevance for what we will say later about the European Information Society Project. Finally, *public opinion* is the direct or mediated expression of public discourses, or public talk.

As we have noted elsewhere (Axford and Huggins 2002), direct expressions of public opinion tend to be treated with some suspicion, not least by those with an interest in maintaining authoritative sources. When sponsored by governments, even deliberative versions of public talk tend to be structured in particular ways to promote citizen input through managed consultation (Axford and Huggins 2002). Modern governments rely more and more on public relations and the strategic monitoring of public opinion to manage their own visibility (Axford and Huggins 2002). But any institutionalized and mediated form of public talk and public opinion formation is a dilution of the principle of publicity or, as Splichal (2002: 23) puts it, 'a gradual disintegration of the liberal public'. Of course, in most large-scale democracies public opinion has long been institutionalized through legislatures, different forms of mass media and opinion polling. Of late, attempts to structure public talk have taken a more populist turn and include the use of focus groups, citizens' juries, people's panels, referendums and deliberative polling techniques (Axford and Huggins 1997). Arguably, this proliferation of opportunities for public talk enhances the prospects for both reflection (even as they fragment the ideal of a unified demos) and a consensual public sphere. The ever-growing popularity of the Internet and other forms of digital communication offers even more scope for dialogue and contestation when set against the monological communication formats, or more obviously mediated publicness, of older media genres. These new technologies also appear to facilitate more spatially extensive 'networks of publicity' (White 1995: 77).

Obvious issues arise. The first rehearses the familiar caveat that even where deliberation is involved, the public/publics are only 'judicious spectators', rather than real players (Key 1964: 557). Even worse, public opinion becomes just an 'echo chamber' of official discourse. Thus the second issue bears on the possible gap between deliberative forums, which may be either only therapeutic for actors or expressions of public opinion that actually translate into policy. Of course, there may be no gap between communicative rationality and purposive rationality, but attempts to structure public talk through the strategic monitoring of public opinion, through devices for more 'open government' and through new (digital) channels and spaces for debate and deliberation should always be assessed in terms of the ends and interests they serve. So the third issue is whether a politics (and public sphere) constructed in the 'frame' of the media, as Castells (1996) has it, and in thoroughly 'mediatized' political cultures can supply sufficient outlets and resources for discursiveness and reflexivity, or anything resembling what Arendt (1998) calls 'public spaces of appearance', in which speech and action are instantiated and narrative enacts a world that is made and remade reflexively. Clearly, these are attributes of a strong form of publicness (Jonsson *et al.* 2000). The final issue concerns the need to identify publics in terms of their 'reach' across time and space (space and time 'distanciation') and thus to guard against an implicit – and sometimes explicit – territorial nationalism. As Schlesinger (2004: 10) notes, theories of social communication have tended to emphasize the boundaries around national communicative space within a wider framework of competing national cultures. He adds that 'Such a neatly demarcationist theory of social communication and public space is not tenable' (Schlesinger 2004: 10). When examining publicness in the EU, these caveats are a useful starting point.

Publicness in Europe

Discussions about Europe (the EU) as an imagined communicative space often start from the same assumptions about the need for a European public sphere to match the growing institutional competence of the EU and to address the democratic deficit (Kunelius and Sparks 2001). There is also debate about the need to 'Europeanize' discourses and how this bears on the prospects for a European public sphere. Nancy Fraser (2003: 2) argues that there is an intuitive plausibility about 'the idea of a transnational public sphere' and in Europe this conceit might be based, among other things, on the convergence of lifestyles across the continent and the 'supracentrality' of English as a language of communication (de Swaan 2001).

Habermas suggests that constitutional innovation in the EU would be a powerful fillip to the creation of a European communicative space, because a European constitution would offer the chance to define and foster a distinctive pattern of political culture, 'a common value orientation' (Habermas 2001: 64). Communicative processes (public talk) developed within this space would add to social cohesion and thus contribute to Europeanization. The assumed functionality in this relationship often depicts EU polity-building as analogous to modern nation- and state-building processes. But whatever else it is, the EU is neither of these constructs. The character of a 'Europe-wide public sphere of political communication' is also a source of contention (Habermas 2001: 64).

Debate turns on the prospects for 'a' European public sphere built through trans-national mass media versus a more pluralistic, or a less demanding, interpretation of European publicness reliant upon the growth of trans-national communication networks in particular policy or issue areas (Gerhards 2000; Van der Steeg 2002). A further nuance concerns the prior necessity or mere contingency of the 'Europeanization' of national media discourses. Of course, genuinely trans-national mass media are largely absent in Europe, or confined to elite and specialist print media such as *The Economist* and the *Financial Times*, which publish in English, or broadcast media such as *Euronews*, *Eurosport* and *Arte*. *Le Monde diplomatique* still offers parallel translation and publication in many languages, but this is not a commercial option for mass-circulation newspapers.[1] Avowedly pan-European media such as the now defunct *European* newspaper have also failed to capture even a niche market. So one might argue that the assumed centrality of media of mass communication to the creation and sustenance of a 'supra-national communicative space' (Schlesinger 2004: 17) in

---

1 In 2006 the French won approval from the EU for a 24-hour, international, Francophone television news service on the CNN model, called France 24.

fact diminishes the prospects for such a space, because they remain vehicles for national concerns, prejudices and styles.

Language barriers, cultural pluralism and (the Sky Sports and MTV television channels apart) the enduring status of the 'national' in media constructions of the audience and in journalistic values militate against the formation of a unified European public sphere (Koopmans *et al.* 2000). All such qualifications are potent because, as Schlesinger (2004: 18) notes, 'the mediated public sphere in the EU remains first, overwhelmingly national; second, where it is not national, it is trans-national and Anglophone … and third, where it is ostensibly transnational, but not Anglophone, it still decants principally into national modes of address'. We should, however, guard against any simplistic analytical dualism in which actors and discourses are either patently European or national. In a world where local and global are imbricated in so many ways, 'communicative complementarities' (Deutsch 1963) are seen in all sorts of networks (Axford 2006; Pries 2004) and in what Eriksen and Fossum (2002) call 'strong' publics (see also Eriksen 2004). In the EU these might include the European Parliament, the communication spaces opened up by cross-border regions (CBRs) and transitory forums such as the Convention on the European Constitution (Schlesinger 2004: 15).

Perhaps all strong publics look more like knowledge communities or insiders' clubs than opportunities for unfettered participation and debate, but claims that there are 'European' publics also rest on evidence that is at once intuitively appealing yet much more diffuse. Maurice Roche (2001) identifies weak forms of Europeanization in the creation of the 'meta-cultural' spaces seen in shopping practices, Europe-wide sport and in travel, to effect a rough and ready 'European-oriented cosmopolitanism' (Schlesinger 2004: 14; see also Calhoun 2002). Leaving aside some of the obvious difficulties with these examples, such claims look a mite frivolous because the very idea of being 'Europeanized' remains elusive. Evidence of cultural hybridization or believing that 'European football teams have turned into a living, breathing embodiment of European integration' (Charlemagne 2003: 42) may not provide support for the existence of communication spaces in which there is 'free and unconstrained public deliberation of all matters of common concern' (Benhabib 1996: 37) and in which the institutions of EU governance are subjected to scrutiny. Yet we have noted that the attributed centrality of the mass media to the creation and sustenance of a 'supranational communicative space' may actually diminish the prospects for such spaces, and so the need to be sensitive to other possibilities for public talk is pressing. Concentrating upon 'old' print and broadcast media serves to underwrite the liberal territorialist paradigm and methodological nationalism. In addition, the systemic features of 'old' media are less obviously suited to the demands of trans-national polity-building. National in orientation, they foster a style of communication that John Thompson (1995) calls 'quasi-mediated interaction'. This mode of communication is (or perhaps was) monological and not, for the most part, directed at clearly identified audiences. Where dialogical in style and content, it was often, and to some extent remains, the domain of the politically literate and various shades of cognoscenti.

By contrast, 'new' or digital media and forms of communication are dialogical and appear to erase signs of mediation by supplying immediacy and interactivity, by disguising the user interface in a 'fusion of art and technology' (Johnson 1997: 43; see also Axford 2001). The aesthetic and technical qualities of 'new' media also enhance the possibility for greater reflexivity between those governed and the institutions of governance. By cutting out the middleman or mediator in the shape of newspapers, programme editors, marketers and the practitioners of spin, the interactive and deliberative qualities of public talk – of participatory communication – seem to be enhanced in ways not possible in strongly mediated forms of publicness. In reality, of course, it is all rather more complex, not least because the glib distinction between 'old' and 'new' media is hard to sustain in practice (Axford 2001) and because, for all the 'borderless' logic seemingly immanent in digital technologies, the Web itself remains a text-based medium and thus subject to the trammels of linguistic nationalism in the same ways as older media.

Online public spheres

The prospects for unmediated publicness and borderless communication may be enhanced through the spread and routine uses of digital technologies, by growing numbers of people in Europe who own personal computers and have access to the Internet (Eurostat 2004) and by the exponential growth in governance online. Students of the relationships between media and politics are likely to be more cautious about the transformative impact of new communication technologies on politics than either the techno-progressives of the early 1990s or those out-and-out sceptics who treated the digitization of political communication as an instrumentality tacked on to usual politics (Axford and Huggins 2001; Norris 2001; Street 2005). Yet, among those who discern a transformation in style and content, normative judgements about the democratic propriety of the changes differ markedly. Some forms of 'retro-nostalgic' thinking (Axford 2001: 5) claim that, unlike older media, digital media actually disadvantage thicker and more deliberative forms of discourse and civic association, because their 'segmented' character provides no holistic public spaces in which we can all 'commune, grieve and celebrate' (Barber 1998: 579). By contrast, Shapiro (1997) suggests that the liberal territorial model of political space and identity is being altered by the respatializing of interest and affect consequent upon the emergence of networked spaces. Such changes are deemed by him to be both transformative and emancipatory.[2] And as Saskia Sassen (2004: 651) points out, 'computer-centred interactive technologies facilitate multiscalar transactions and simultaneous interconnectivity among those largely confined to a locality'. In so doing 'they bypass older hierarchies of scale'. Individual and collective actors connected across conventional scales of political allegiance and activism are no longer confined to domestic roles, but become actors in Europe-wide communication networks, all 'without having to leave their work and roles in their communities'. They may not have become cosmopolitan as a result, and yet they are participating in emergent European politics (Sassen 2004).

There are, of course, significant caveats to the transformative argument, and it is worth summarizing them as they bear on the qualities of publicness attributed to and sometimes actually inscribed in the European Information Society Project. First, it could be argued that the opportunities for mediation, and thus for manipulation and surveillance, are no less telling in the world of digital communication than under any other media regime. Even fast communications are seldom unmediated, and online deliberative forums or consultative devices, especially where instigated 'from above', run the risk of subsisting in a twilight world, with a status somewhere between a policy resource for governments and an exercise in group therapy. Second, even if such communication is relatively unmediated, critics remain anxious about the 'reductive simplicity' of media whose primary attribute is speed (Axford 2001; Barber 1998: 579). Third, even though information and communication technology (ICT) may permit greater visibility for a wider range of political actors and views, and facilitate what Sassen (2004) calls 'transboundary political practice', inequalities of power and limited inclusiveness (in relation to digital technologies and other strategic political resources) remain crucial biases, and the political landscape is consequently made up of insiders and outsiders. Fourth is the claim that the Internet is a medium through which people construct and reconstruct their individuality, rather than a vehicle to promote civic association and communities of affect, let alone a demos. In this light, Barry Wellman's thesis that we live in an age of 'networked individualism' is not received as the expression of approbation intended in the original account (Wellman 2002). At best, networked individualism is seen as 'demos lite', and virtual networks are only 'thin' contexts for identity formation and for deliberative public talk. Finally, technologies which carry a borderless

---

2 As well as the ubiquitous mobile phone and text messaging, political web-logs, such as European Tribune, Café Babel, Publius l'Union Européenne and Europhobia, are achieving a kind of designer chic as bespoke instruments of one-to-many communication. Most governments in the developed world are using information and communication technologies to deliver services to the public and to improve their internal organization.

'logic' remain powerful instruments in the service of the territorial state. Across Europe, national plans for an information society are aimed at promoting the competence of national citizens as actors in the competitive knowledge economy. In so doing, the technical infrastructures of the information revolution inscribe territoriality at the heart of what is also bruited as trans-national polity.

The European information society and European publicness

So it is with the grand scheme known as the European Information Society Project (EISP) and its various progeny, notably the '*e*Europe' initiative (European Commission 2001a, 2003). In its paper *The Role of eGovernment for Europe's Future*, the Commission (2003: 7) views ICT as an enabling condition for improving 'public services and democratic processes and [to] strengthen and support public policies'. Such sentiments are at a fairly high level of generality, and it is important to note that such enabling conditions are being left, in the main, to national governments to implement and sometimes to define. Indeed, the whole EISP is in some measure a mirror of, even a paradigm for, the inchoate character of the integrative project in the EU. At one and the same time it is resolutely statist and intergovernmental, as well as being a harbinger for a post-national networked polity in Europe.

From its inception in the early 1990s (European Commission 1993, 1994) the EISP was the child of two powerful and apparently contradictory logics (for an extended discussion of these see Axford and Huggins 1996, 1999). The first is the liberalizing credo of the market, embodied in the 1992 internal market process and designed to foster an open, competitive trans-national economic space. Alongside this primary goal sits the related aim of promoting a 're-imagination of community and identity in Europe' (Robins 1994: 102), through the creation of a Europe-wide communications space. These aims prescribe the Europeanization of economic and communicative behaviour and affect, or at least their profound denationalization. As Schmitter and Streeck (1991: 142) remark, this augurs a 'formal devaluation of the vast political resources which have come to be organised in and around the state'.

But the second logic challenges the first and envisages European unity as a process akin to nation state modernization, resulting in the 'isomorphism of people, territory and culture' (Collins 1990: 126). As we have noted elsewhere (Axford and Huggins 1999), some accommodation between the two logics has been achieved by promoting the EISP as a major factor in creating truly Europeanized publics, who in time will 'imagine the new community of Europe' (Robins 1994). The implied accommodation is problematic for two reasons. The first is the familiar complaint that it is much too reliant on a neo-functionalist spill-over between zones of experience to trigger radical social change. The second reason, more telling for an analysis of publicness in Europe, is that it still underwrites a holistic or 'thick' model of the public sphere. As we shall see, the kinds of publicness being facilitated under the EISP rubric are at once more routine, more hybrid and more diffuse than the 'thick' model prescribes.

The ways in which the EISP has developed continue to subvent the original principles of accelerated economic integration through interconnectivity, greater social cohesion and a sense of European identity (Bangemann 1994, 1997). However, since the mid-1990s more attention has been paid to the place of the citizen in the information society. This shift reflects a growing concern with the lack of a popular or 'people-oriented' dimension to EU policy-making and outputs. Information society policy between 1997 and 1999 incorporated a 'people dimension' which privileged two main concerns: employment strategies in an information age; and the dangers to democracy and equality of creating a 'two-tier' information society, where some individuals, groups and regions are denied the 'power of information' (European Commission 1996). At the same time, the green paper *Living and Working in the Information Society: People First* (European Commission 1996) was not much exercised by matters of e-governance and e-democracy. In a rather throw-away fashion it noted that 'democracy is not just about voting in elections' (European Commission 1996: 25) and that online provision of government information could help to enfranchise citizens.

The 1998 green paper *Public Sector Information* actually did address issues of e-governance, mainly in relation to the narrower realm of e-government, or the use of digital tools to improve the supply of information and the delivery of services to make public administration more efficient (European Commission 1998). The paper stressed the democratic virtues of what it called 'transaction services', which referred to the electronic submission of forms, such as tax returns or claims for benefits, and electronic political participation, such as referendums. In principle there is little doubt that such developments can contribute to practical citizenship and to a nascent European civic culture. But while they may raise awareness and consciousness about governance issues and processes, with the possible exception of online referendums they are not likely to promote a deliberative demos.

The next key phase of information society policy began in the run-up to the European Council meeting in Lisbon in March 2000, when plans to make Europe the 'most advanced competitive knowledge economy in the world' were set out. This 'Lisbon strategy' incorporated an 'eEurope' initiative, launched in 1999, and developed it through a series of action plans and mid-term reviews up to 2005 (European Commission 2000a, 2000b, 2002a, 2002b, 2004a, 2004b).

The key objectives of the eEurope programmes are to create a digitally literate Europe to buttress an entrepreneurial culture, to bring every citizen, home, school and business online and to ensure that the whole process is socially inclusive and builds trust and social cohesion (European Commission 2002b). A desire to avoid or alleviate 'digital divides' and to promote social cohesion is a constant theme of the *e*Europe initiative. Attempts to realize these aims appear in programmes to extend broadband access to remote regions, special measures to ensure access for the disabled and tele-working projects aimed primarily at women. One recommended way of ensuring access to the relevant technology for all is the provision of public access Internet points in such locations as public libraries. There are also measures to integrate ICT with television and mobile phones for those who do not possess computer hardware. In order to develop a pan-European information space which is fully integrated technically, the aim of system interoperability is paramount. And if all this has a pronounced 'Europeanizing' feel to it, there are occasional references in *e*Europe action plans to the potential in the information society to protect Europe's linguistic diversity.

Questions of public transparency and accountability were addressed in the white paper *European Governance* (European Commission 2001b). Although the document does not discuss the information society as such, the use of ICT is implicit in the strategies proposed to form stronger links between the Commission, EU citizens and civil society. Yet in *Towards the e-Commission* (European Commission 2001a) and *The Role of eGovernment for Europe's Future* (European Commission 2003) the emphasis is still upon instruments such as multilingual information services, interactive communication with service delivery sites and basic transaction services in the areas of public procurement and public sector recruitment. These are hardly measures calculated to foster strong, deliberative publics and to instantiate a robust form of publicity, or what Kees Brant (2002) calls '*e*Publicanism', even if they do cater for a limited form of publicity. In the Commission white paper *The Role of eGovernment*, the creation of a more visible and integrated 'European public space for EU citizens and businesses' is seen as gradually emerging from the increased networking of local, regional and national administrations across the EU, enabled by ICT (European Commission 2003: 6).

Overall, fostering a European public sphere through the EISP is not a major goal of EU policy-makers.[3] At most this project has been concerned to create

---

3 The statement is rather sweeping, although, in the context of the EISP, accurate. On the broader front of the possibilities for public sphere development through a more 'public-centred' EU communications policy, adverse comment might well be more cautious, in the light of the agenda outlined in the Commission white paper of February 2006 (European Commission 2006). In that document the Commission proposes more transparent communication between EU institutions and the publics of member states. Much is made of a 'partnership approach' to communication, one which embraces 'all the key players'. A closer look at this formulation reveals the usual suspects, in the shape of local governments, political parties and the organized voluntary sector (civil society), but very little about the much more informal networks of association and communication that nowadays exhibit all manner of public and private talk online.

enabling conditions within which public talk can take place. In fact it could be argued that its most significant contribution to the realization of a pan-European communications space to date is the Europa website (http://europa.eu/), which goes some way to provide a portal through which EU citizens can interact with the institutions of the Union and access information they require in their own language. Information society policies have been concerned, largely, with creating and maintaining information spaces and transaction services within a limited range of policy areas, encompassing education, health care and social exclusion, because public sector service provision is seen as fertile ground for technical innovation and new forms of governance.

By and large, the *raison d'être* of the EISP is to create an entrepreneurial business environment, to support this through attention to e-learning and e-literacy, and to contribute to the building of a modern public administration, one that is, to borrow a phrase from Tony Blair, 'citizen-facing'. Some of what is in train under this remit does, or will serve to, empower citizens, in the cant expression, albeit as consumers of services. However, it is some way short – indeed, hardly tries to accommodate – a fully fledged agenda for e-democracy and e-publicanism, where those concepts refer to initiatives originating in the public sphere to involve citizens in the political process and to create conditions for dialogue between citizens and governments (Brant 2002). In a speech, Paul Timmers, head of the Commission's eGovernment Unit, emphasized that while the Commission has taken up e-democracy as part of its '*e*Commission' programme for more transparent, personalized and effective services, in key aspects of the programme there is no explicit e-democracy policy at EU level (Timmers 2004).

There are, though, consultative mechanisms with resonant titles such as Your Voice in Europe (YVIE), which was set up under the Interactive Policy-Making Initiative. Designated as the Commission's single access point to a wide variety of consultations, discussions and other tools, YVIE makes use of two online instruments, available through its web portal. These consist of a 'feedback mechanism' designed to collect 'spontaneous information' from citizens and businesses about their daily problems relating to different EU policies. About 300 intermediaries (such as Euro Info Centres, European Consumer Centres and the Citizens Signpost Service) throughout the member states of both the EU and the European Free Trade Association collect difficult cases occurring every day and record them in the Commission's feedback database. Described as a 'listening device', it allows for monitoring of the implementation of existing legislation and provides input for new policy initiatives. Thousands of cases are collected annually In addition there is an 'online consultation mechanism'. This device allows the creation of online, structured questionnaires, which are answered by citizens on the Internet and from which the Commission can obtain feedback on a particular policy-related issue. The instrument can handle structured questions in an unlimited number of languages and deliver output in the required language. Several online consultations have already been carried out including the 'European Business Test Panel', a representative panel of businesses throughout Europe which is evaluating the impact of new legislative proposals.

In many ways these initiatives do underline the Commission's commitment to new forms of governance and innovative ways of encouraging real, if highly structured, devices for public talk.

Other programmes, such as Eris@, Telecities and Dialogue, intimate the ways in which electronic networks can configure a fluid pattern of European integration. In this fluid Europe there is a complex imbrication of local and European, of communication spaces populated by civic networks, provincial, national and regional networks, as well as functional networks organized around service provision, and which constitute 'circulating entities' of information exchange and public knowledge (Urry 2003: 122). None of the programmes listed above look(ed) to enhance the European public sphere *per se*, but many have contributed to the growth of multiscalar communities of communication. The same is true of the plethora of online and otherwise mediated communications that take place between non-governmental organizations (NGOs), social movements and other individuals and collectives, often across borders, to instantiate forms of trans-national practice. Very little of this practice conforms to a 'thick' or holistic model of public sphere interaction, or even to a conscious Europeanization of interest and affect. Common European themes are communicated and debated (such as the EU and the war in Iraq, the constitutional treaty) but not always with the same intensity, using the same frame of reference or out of similar meaning structures. The lack of common frameworks and understandings, as well as diversity in outcomes, such as occurred during the debates over the Iraq war, must vitiate expressions of strong 'pan-European' public opinion (Schlesinger 2004). But what is, or may be, on offer are patterns of communication and forms of publicity in which 'speakers and listeners treat each other as legitimate actors in common discourse' (Risse and Van de Steeg 2003: 2). This discourse may only just frame specific issues as being 'European', but in doing so contributes to public talk and thus to the discursive practice of making Europe.

Conclusion: a new European public sphere?

On the evidence we have presented, it would be hard to say that anything like a unified European public sphere exists. This much is common ground for most commentators on the prospects for EU democracy. Nevertheless, our argument has been that by relaxing demanding conditions for the existence of a European demos and by abjuring liberal territorialist assumptions about the 'imaginary suppositions of democracy', we can learn more about the ways in which and the sites at which a trans-national polity is being constructed. In particular, we can gain insights into the ways in which public talk of various kinds is being conducted within and across Europe. Such insights reveal the contours of practical citizenship as it is emerging in a networked polity. Of course, the concept of public talk is a much more anodyne notion than the charged idea of a 'public sphere', but it does serve to draw attention to a range of possibilities for routine as well as exotic communication and the 'spaces' in which it takes place. On the other hand, attention to the 'banal nationalism' of older, mass media (Billig 2000) reinforces the methodological nationalism of much research on European democracy. The search for measurable indicators of Europeanization in media discourses is at once understandable and frequently unhelpful.

Yet we see no bright, ready-made world of 'virtual Europeanization' in the communication possibilities opened up by digital and online technologies. How could it be otherwise, when it is impossible to separate the technical potential in new technologies from their social use by agents? Thus, the grand narrative of the EISP in some measure underwrites older paradigms of national difference and competence at the same time as it preaches convergence and the transcending of boundaries. Its various programmes promote different types of public talk and thus subvent a kind of practical citizenship, both at the EU and at the national 'levels', although this is rarely aimed at fostering deliberation. Because of this, it cannot be seen as the space of a new European public sphere. But online Europe offers many more opportunities for public talk than are entertained in the EISP, many of them unstructured and unmediated. Virtual connections 'from below' may not produce the unfettered world of communication and deliberation prescribed by public sphere theorists but, as we have noted, they offer a glimpse of a networked European polity and of communication spaces that can be untrammelled by culture and jurisdiction. To that extent, their ontologies may well have been Europeanized. More research is needed on this point.

So, when analysing forms of trans-national sociality and communication we must guard against conventional wisdom about what constitutes 'thick' and 'thin' affinities and imaginaries, since these notions are problematized by the processes of regionalization and globalization. For example, Alex Warleigh (2000) writes about the 'functional–ideational gap' which has mired the debate over EU democracy. He notes the extent to which the democracy debate has been snared by trying to prescribe an EU polity built from a liberal democratic and territorialist blueprint. Warleigh argues that the EU is already a working system of trans-national network governance, which can become a network democracy (see also Axford and Huggins 1999; Jachtenfuchs 2001). This feat may be achieved through a system of more intensive networks and communities, through more inclusive and deliberative mechanisms involving stakeholders in the policy processes, and through the activities of an increasingly vibrant constituency of NGOs and international NGOs. While the model may rely too much on the implied inclusive and consensual nature of politics and policy processes at different 'levels' in the EU, it also provides a useful insight into the potential for a 'post-national democracy' in Europe.

This is hardly the pure milk of trans-nationalism or of cosmopolitanism. It might, however, constitute a form of 'post-Enlightenment' cosmopolitanism (Venn 2002) – an amalgam of liberal and assimilationist positions, with a dash of the postmodern just visible in its flirtation with a world of heterogeneous and complex communication networks (Habermas 2003; Venn 2002). David Held recognizes that any attempt to bridge the gap between statism and what he terms 'globalism' must rework cosmopolitanism 'for another age' (Held 2002: 12) and this seems to offer a more informal 'cultural' version that rounds out the parsimony and strict universality of liberal internationalism. To the lexicon of good governance and the rule of law extended across territories, informal cosmopolitanism adds contingent identities communicated across (cyber)space. In particular, Held (2002: 12) calls for 'recognition ... of the increasing interconnectedness of political communities in diverse domains, and the development of an understanding of overlapping "collective fortunes" which require collective solutions – locally, nationally, regionally and globally'. Perhaps the creation of European communication spaces can or should aspire to no more than this because, at the very least, it shows Europe as an 'intersubjective web of reciprocities' (de Sousa Santos 1995: 14).

References

Arendt, H. (1998) *The Human Condition*, Chicago, IL: Chicago University Press.

Axford, B. (2001) 'The transformation of politics or anti-politics?', in B. Axford and R. Huggins (eds), *New Media and Politics*, London: Sage, pp. 1–30.

Axford, B. (2006) 'The dialectic of borders and networks in Europe: reviewing "topological presuppositions"', *Comparative European Politics*, 4(2), 160–83.

Axford, B. and Huggins, R. (1996) 'Media without boundaries: fear and loathing on the road to Eurotrash or transformation in the European cultural economy?', *Innovation: The European Journal of Social Science*, 9(2), 175–84.

Axford, B and Huggins, R. (1997) 'Anti-politics or the triumph of postmodern populism in promotional cultures?', *Javnost: The Public*, 4(3), 5–27.

Axford, B. and Huggins, R. (1999) 'Towards a post-national polity: the emergence of the network society in Europe', in D. Smith and S. Wright (eds), *Whose Europe? The Turn Towards Democracy*, Oxford: Blackwell, pp. 173–207.

Axford, B. and Huggins, R. (2001) *New Media and Politics*, London: Sage.

Axford, B. and Huggins, R. (2002) 'Public opinion and postmodern populism: a crisis of democracy or the transformation of democratic governance?', in S. Splichal (ed.), *Public Opinion and Democracy: Vox Populi – Vox Dei?*, Creskill, NJ: Hampton Press, pp. 166–93.

Bangemann, M. (1994) *Europe and the Global Information Society: Recommendations to the European Council*, Brussels, 26 May. Available at http://europa.eu.int/ISPO/infosoc/backg/bangeman.html (last accessed January 2007).

Bangemann, M. (1997) 'A new world order for global communication', presented to Telecom Inter@ctive '97, International Telecommunications Union, Geneva, 8 August.

Barber, B. (1998) 'Three scenarios for the future of technology and strong democracy', *Political Science Quarterly*, 113(4), 573–89.

Bauer, O. (1907) *The Question of Nationalities and Social Democracy*, translated by J. O'Donnell (2000), Minneapolis, MN: University of Minnesota Press.

Beck, U. (2003) 'Understanding the real Europe', *Dissent*, 50(3), 32–38.

Benhabib, S. (1996) *Democracy and Difference*, Princeton, NJ: Princeton University Press.

Billig, M. (2000) *Banal Nationalism*, Cambridge: Polity Press.

Brant, K. (2002) 'Politics is everywhere'. Available at http://www.degruyter.de/journals/communic/2002/pdf/27_171.pdf (last accessed January 2007).

Brenner, N. (1999) 'Beyond state-centrism? Space, territoriality, and geographical scale in globalization studies', *Theory and Society*, 28(2), 39–78.

Calhoun, C. (1993) 'Civil society and the public sphere', *Public Culture*, 5(2), 267–80.

Calhoun, C. (2002) 'Information technology and the international public sphere', presented at the ISA Conference, Brisbane, Australia, 11 July.

Calhoun, C. (2004) 'The democratic integration of Europe: interests, identity, and the public sphere', *Eurozine*. Available at http://www.eurozine.com/articles/2004-06-21-calhoun-en.html (last accessed January 2007).

Castells, M. (1996) *The Rise of the Network Society*, Malden, MA: Blackwell.

Charlemagne, D. (2003) 'How football unites Europe', *The Economist*, 31 May, p. 42.

Chryssochoou, D. N. (2002) 'Towards a civic conception of the European polity', working paper no. 33/01 of the ESRC 'One Europe or Several?' programme, Swindon: Economic and Social Research Council (ESRC). Available at http://www.one-europe.ac.uk/pdf/w33chryssochoou.pdf (last accessed January 2007).

Cohen, J. L. and Arato, A. (1992) *Civil Society and Political Theory*, Cambridge, MA: MIT Press.

Collins, R. (1990) 'National culture: a contradiction in terms?', in R. Collins (ed.), *Television, Policy and Culture*, London: Unwin Hyman, pp. 117–38.

de Sousa Santos, B. (1995) *Towards a New Common Sense: Law, Science and Politics in the Paradigmatic Transition*, London: Routledge.

de Swaan, A. (2001) *Words of the World: The Global Language System*, Cambridge: Polity Press.

Deutsch, K. W. (1963) *Nationalism and Social Communication: An Inquiry into the Foundations of Nationality*, Cambridge, MA: MIT Press.

Emirbayer, M. and Sheller, M. (1999) 'Publics in history', *Theory and Society*, 28(1), 145–97.

Eriksen, E. O. (2004) 'Conceptualising European public spheres: general, segmented and strong publics', ARENA working paper no. 3/04, Oslo: Centre for European Studies,

University of Oslo. Available at http://www.arena.uio.no/publications/wp_04_03.pdf (last accessed January 2007).

Eriksen, E. O. and Fossum, J. E. (2002) 'Democracy through strong publics in the European Union?', *Journal of Common Market Studies*, 40(3), 401–24.

European Commission (1993) *Growth, Competitiveness, Employment: The Challenge and the Way Forward into the 21st Century*, COM(93) 700 final, Luxembourg: Office for Official Publications of the European Communities.

European Commission (1994) *Europe's Way to the Information Society: An Action Plan*, COM(94), Luxembourg: Office for Official Publications of the European Communities.

European Commission (1996) *Living and Working in the Information Society: People First*, COM(96) final, Luxembourg: Office for Official Publications of the European Communities.

European Commission (1998) *Public Sector Information: A Key Resource for Europe*, green paper on public sector information in the information society, COM(1998) 585, Luxembourg: Office for Official Publications of the European Communities.

European Commission (2000a) *eEurope: An Information Society for All*, communication on a Commission initiative for the Special European Council of Lisbon, 23–24 March, Luxembourg: Office for Official Publications of the European Communities.

European Commission (2000b) *eEurope 2002 Action Plan*, prepared by the Council and the European Commission for the Feira European Council, 19–20 June, Luxembourg: Office for Official Publications of the European Communities.

European Commission (2001a) *Towards the e-Commission: Implementation Strategy 2001–2005*, Luxembourg: Office for Official Publications of the European Communities.

European Commission (2001b) *European Governance: A White Paper*, COM(2001) 428 final, Luxembourg: Office for Official Publications of the European Communities.

European Commission (2002a) *eEurope 2002: Final Report*, Luxembourg: Office for Official Publications of the European Communities.

European Commission (2002b) *eEurope 2005: An Information Society for All*, for the Seville Council Meeting, 21–22 June, Luxembourg: Office for Official Publications of the European Communities.

European Commission (2003) *The Role of eGovernment for Europe's Future*, COM(2003) 567 final, Luxembourg: Office for Official Publications of the European Communities.

European Commission (2004a) *eEurope 2005: Mid-Term Review*, Luxembourg: Office for Official Publications of the European Communities.

European Commission (2004b) *Challenges for the European Information Society Beyond 2005*, Luxembourg: Office for Official Publications of the European Communities.

European Commission (2006) *White Paper on a European Communication Policy*, COM(2006) 35 final, Luxembourg: Office for Official Publications of the European Communities.

Eurostat (2004) 'Internet usage by individuals and enterprises 2004'. Available at http://epp.eurostat.cec.eu.int/cache/ITY_OFFPUB/KS-NP-05-018/EN/KS-NP-05-018-EN.PDF (last accessed January 2007).

Evans, S. and Boyte, H. C. (1986) *Free Spaces: The Sources of Democratic Change in America*, New York: Harper and Row.

Fraser, N. (1992) 'Rethinking the public sphere: a contribution to the critique of actually existing democracy', in C. Calhoun (ed.), *Habermas and the Public Sphere*, Cambridge, MA: MIT Press, pp. 47–62.

Fraser, N. (2003) 'Transnationalizing the public sphere'. Available at http://www.republicart. net/disc/publicum/fraser01_en.htm (last accessed January 2007).

Gerhards, J. (2000) 'Europaisierung von Okonomie und Politik und die Tragheit der Entstehung einer europaischen Offentlichkeit', *Kolner Zeitschrift für Soziologie und Sozial Psychologie*, 52(40), 277–305.

Habermas, J. (1974) 'The public sphere', *New German Critique*, 1(3), 49–55.

Habermas, J. (1989) *The Structural Transformation of the Public Sphere*, Cambridge: Polity Press.

Habermas, J. (2001) 'Warum Bracht Europa eine Verfassung', *Deutschland*, 6, 62–65.

Habermas, J. (2003) 'Making sense of the EU: towards a cosmopolitan Europe', *Journal of Democracy*, 14(4), 86–100.

Held, D. (2002) 'National culture, the globalization of communications and the bounded political community', *Logos*, 1(3), 1–18.

Jachtenfuchs, M. (2001) 'The governance approach to European integration', *Journal of Common Market Studies*, 39(2), 245–64.

Johnson, S. (1997) *Interface Culture: How Technology Transforms How We Create and Communicate*, New York: Harper Collins.

Jonsson, C., Tagil, S. and Tornquist, G. (2000) *Organising European Space*, London: Sage.

Kant, I. (1795) 'An answer to the question: "what is enlightenment?"', in *Perpetual Peace and Other Essays*, trans. T. Humphrey (1983), Indianapolis, IN: Hackett.

Key, V. O. (1964) *Public Opinion and American Democracy*, New York: Knopf.

Koopmans, R., Neidhardt, B. and Pfetsch, B. (2000) 'Conditions for the constitution of a European public sphere', presented at the Euroconference 'Democracy Beyond the Nation-State', Athens, 5–7 October.

Kunelius, R. and Sparks, C. (2001) 'Problems with a European public sphere', *Javnost: The Public*, 8(1), 5–20.

McLennan, G. (1995) *Pluralism*, Buckingham: Open University Press.

Meyer, C. O. (2005) 'The Europeanization of media discourse: a study of quality press coverage of economic policy co-ordination since Amsterdam', *Journal of Common Market Studies*, 43(1), 121–48.

Norris, P. (2001) *Digital Divide: Civic Engagement, Information Poverty and the Internet Worldwide*, Cambridge: Cambridge University Press.

Pollack, M. A. (2005) 'Theorizing the European Union: international organization, domestic polity or experiment in new governance?', *Annual Review of Political Science*, 8, 357–98.

Pries, L. (2004) 'Transnationalism and migration: new challenges for the social sciences and education', in S. Luchtenberg (ed.), *Migration, Education and Change*, New York: Routledge, pp. 1–24.

Risse, T. (2003) 'An emerging European public sphere? Theoretical clarifications and empirical indicators', presented to the annual meeting of the European Union Studies Association (EUSA), Nashville, TN, 27–30 March.

Risse, T. and Van de Steeg, M. (2003) 'An emerging European public sphere? Empirical evidence and theoretical clarifications', presented to the conference 'Europeanisation of Public Spheres, Political Mobilisation, Public Communication and the European Union', Berlin, 20–22 June.

Robins, K. (1994) 'The politics of silence: the meaning of community and the uses of media in the new Europe', *New Formations*, 21, 80–102.

Roche, M. (2001) 'Citizenship, popular culture and Europe', in N. Stevenson (ed.), *Culture and Citizenship*, London: Sage, pp. 74–99.

Sassen, S. (2004) 'Local actors in global politics', *Current Sociology*, 52(4), 649–70.

Sassi, S. (2001) 'The transformation of the public sphere?', in B. Axford and R. Huggins (eds), *New Media and Politics*, London: Sage, pp. 89–109.

Schlesinger, P. (2004) 'The Babel of Europe? An essay on networks and communicative spaces', presented to the ESCUS conference 'Changing European Public Spheres', Sheffield, 23–24 September. Available at http://www.arena.uio.no/cidel/WorkshopStirling/PaperSchlesinger.pdf (last accessed January 2007).

Schmitter, P. and Streeck, M. (1991) 'From national corporatism to transnational pluralism: organised interests in the single European market', *Politics and Society*, 20(2), 133–64.

Shapiro, M. (1997) *Bowling Blind: Post-Liberal Society and the Worlds of Neo-Tocquevillian Social Theory*, Baltimore, MA: Johns Hopkins University Press.

Shaw, M. (2003) 'The global transformation of the social sciences', in H. Anheier, M. Glasius and M. Kaldor (eds), *The Global Civil Society Yearbook, Volume 3: Global Civil Society in an Era of Regressive Globalism*, Sage: London, pp. 35–44.

Splichal, S. (1999) *Public Opinion: Developments and Controversies in the 20th Century*, Boston, MA: Rowman and Littlefield.

Splichal, S. (2002) 'Publicity, democracy and public opinion', in S. Splichal (ed.), *Public Opinion and Democracy: Vox Populi – Vox Dei?*, Cresskill, NJ: Hampton Press, pp. 21–51.

Splichal, S. (2004) 'In search of the European public sphere: some critical observations on conceptualisations of publicness and the (European) public sphere', presented to the ESCUS conference 'Changing European Public Spheres', Sheffield, 23–24 September.

Street, J. (2005) 'Politics lost, politics transformed, politics colonised? Theories of the impact of mass media', *Political Studies Review*, 3(1), 17–36.

Thompson, J. (1995) *The Media and Modernity*, Cambridge: Polity Press.

Timmers, P. (2004) 'Agenda for eDemocracy – an EU perspective', presented at the conference 'The New Agenda for eDemocracy: Lessons from Initiatives Round the World', Oxford Internet Institute, 7 May.

Urry, J. (2003) *Global Complexity*, Cambridge: Polity Press.

Van der Steeg, M. (2002) 'Rethinking the conditions for a public sphere in the European Union', *European Journal of Social Theory*, 5(4), 499–519.

Venn, C. (2002) 'Altered states: post-Enlightenment cosmopolitanism and transmodern socialities', *Theory, Culture and Society*, 19(1–2), 65–80.

Warleigh, A. (2000) 'Beyond the functional–ideational gap: from network governance to network democracy in the European Union?', *Civic* (July).

Wellman, B. (2002) 'Little boxes, glocalization and networked individualism'. Available at http://www.chass.utoronto.ca/~wellman/publications/littleboxes/littlebox.PDF (last accessed January 2007).

White, H. (1995) 'Where do languages come from?', ISERP working paper pre-print series, Paul. F. Lazarsfeld Center for the Social Sciences, Columbia University.

CHAPTER 8

Cultural Europeanization and the 'Cosmopolitan Condition': European Union Regulation and European Sport

Maurice Roche

The concept of cosmopolitanism, and by derivation of 'Euro-cosmopolitanism', can be understood in a number of ways and can have a number of different referents and meanings. At the very least there is a basic distinction to be made between, on the one hand, theoretical and normative/ideal meanings mainly referring to the political sphere – pioneered in the Enlightenment period by Kant (1784) and revived in the contemporary period by, among others, David Held (1995) – and, on the other hand, more descriptive, *de facto* meanings, often referring mainly to the cultural sphere. The normative meanings refer to ideals of law and democracy beyond the level of the nation state and up to global level, which may (or may not) govern and be exemplified by existing international and trans-national political institutions, organizations and movements. The descriptive meanings refer to existing forms, processes and experiences of cultural diversity, coexistence, hybridization and communication within and between societies. The concept of a 'cosmopolitan condition' profiled in my chapter title refers particularly to the latter context and its dynamics, but also to the fateful motivational situation that this provides for the critical and political actions implied by the normative ideal.

The basic distinction in the concept of 'cosmopolitanism' between the normative and descriptive meanings generates a multiplicity of secondary and related meanings when it is applied and illustrated across global social space (that is, in relation to the range of world civilizations and world regions) and across the reach of historical time. This is particularly so in relation to Europe. The concepts of the 'cosmopolis' and 'cosmopolitanism' were born in Europe, in the classical period and the system of the Hellenic city states, which circled the Mediterranean and Aegean Seas from the eighth to the fourth centuries BC. Europe is the pre-eminent world region and civilization which, throughout the history of 'the West', recurrently developed globally influential examples of imperial cosmopolitan orders. Throughout recorded history European society and culture have been marked by the militarism, politics and economics involved in the war- and peace-making, and the rise and fall, of empires – regimes integrating large sections of the sub-continent, regimes based in Europe but dominating other world regions, and regimes bordering on and often threatening Europe. European empires and their particular kinds of cosmopolitan orders, particularly those based on the sub-continental mainland, often involved the encompassing and governing of multi-ethnic populations, the linking of widespread networks of trading cities, and the organization of multilingual cultural institutions and communication circuits for the purposes of trade, war, ideological transmission and hegemonic control (Davies 1997). In contemporary (twenty-first-century) perspective, in the form of the European Union (EU), arguably Europe can be said to be leading the world in the construction of a globally relevant regional international and trans-national order and governance system. The EU is an unprecedented system which, if it can be usefully compared with anything, can probably be more usefully compared with the regimes Europe is familiar with, from its (difference-organizing and cosmopolitan) imperial experiences, rather than with its (attempted identity-creating and cultural homogenizing) nation state experiences.

The EU's order can be sensibly referred to as being cosmopolitan in both the meanings outlined above. On the one hand, the EU is undoubtedly creating some (albeit unclear) kind of *de facto cosmopolitan order* within and between its member states, a new, historically unprecedented and dynamic *cosmopolitan condition* for Europe's peoples and states. On the other hand, the EU can also be claimed, albeit patchily and to variable and arguable degrees of adequacy, to be embodying *normative cosmopolitan ideals* in the course of its institution-building and integration processes. This is particularly so since the creation of the category of 'EU citizen' in the 1992 Maastricht Treaty, and the related inauguration of the policy dynamic that has led through to the current, albeit temporarily stalled, attempt to construct an EU constitution, including the Charter of Fundamental Rights.

De facto cosmopolitanism is accomplished in various ways in the contemporary social world – in official discourse, in the everyday life-world, and in the popular, public and interconnected cultural zones of consumer culture and media culture. Analytically we can collect these four zones together and conceptualize them as comprising a 'cosmopolitan condition'. This is comparable to the way in which the related notions of 'globalization' and 'postmodernity' have been addressed by some social analysts in recent times. For instance, in his notable analysis and critique of postmodernism, Harvey (1990) addresses himself to postmodernity as a phenomenon and as a 'condition' of the contemporary world (and thus of the theorist, and his or her 'fate'), not merely as a matter of theoretical position-taking (optional theoretical perceptions or the holding of optional normative/aesthetic ideals etc.). Something similar might be said about the way in which Held and his colleagues address the phenomenon of 'global transformations' as a condition of the contemporary world and a fateful condition of analysis of it (Held *et al.* 1999).

As a normative ideal, cosmopolitanism may appear not only as a touchstone to use to criticize (nation-state-oriented) social reality but, indeed, in some sense as a 'solution' to that reality's many problems, a new trans-national socio-political order to be striven for. My line of thought in this chapter, then, is that these normative and practical ambitions may be usefully understood as reflexive and critical responses to contemporary versions and aspects of the *de facto* cosmopolitan condition and the problems it involves and presents. The *de facto* cosmopolitan condition can be understood to be generated by volatile interconnections between, on the one hand, the important but weakening powers of formal governmental state authorities in nation state societies and, on the other hand, the strengthening challenges and dynamics of the globalizing capitalist economy and the new social formations it is calling into being.

In this perspective the cosmopolitan condition sets the scene, the fateful and motivational context, for the problem with identifications, idealizations and movements of normative cosmopolitanism, to render either formal authority or market power, or both, democratically legitimate, accountable and responsible, and thereby to create spaces for citizenship and civil society. It sets the scene for the actors – whether individual or collective, whether urban, national or international, whether governmental, non-governmental or corporate – who are moved by and who carry forward such cosmopolitan ideas and ideals.

So far I have suggested that, analytically, the *de facto* cosmopolitan condition in contemporary societies like those of the UK and other European countries can be understood to include experiential, official discursive, consumerist and mediatized aspects. In this chapter the aim is to illustrate some of these aspects, and some of their interconnections and sources, in the case of a particular field in which they can be most visibly encountered and instantiated, namely the field of sport, particularly professionalized and internationally oriented sport and, within this field, in the culture and social significance of professional football. Later the consumerist and mediatized aspects will be emphasized in considering European football as a cultural industry and as a media phenomenon. But a central concern in this chapter is with official discursive aspects of sport's *de facto* cosmopolitanism, in particular with the EU's regulatory role in sport and the media's presentation and use of sport. To address this first requires a general consideration of the EU as a regulatory order.

128

Understanding the EU in terms of 'regulation'

In the attempt to understand the EU, some recent sociological and political science studies of Europe have focused on the EU's regulatory role, including the thesis that the EU constitutes a 'regulatory state' (Bromley 2001; Majone 1996; Rumford 2002). Majone's 'regulatory state' thesis holds that the EU is mainly an agency, or set of agencies, concerned with regulating the operation of the Single Market, ensuring that it functions efficiently and effectively, and that it thereby delivers collective benefits to all the member states, which, in turn, keep them committed to participation in the Union. He conceives of the EU as being a basically technocratic rather than a political operation, and as capable of achieving 'legitimacy' in the eyes of Europe's publics and governments on this basis, rather than in more ambitious and contentious terms, such as operating as a democracy or being the expression of a common culture. Without engaging with this view further here, evidently, in terms of what we have said in this section so far, there are inadequacies with it. Firstly, the EU is not best conceived in analogy with any kind of 'state', regulatory or otherwise. Secondly, there is more to the EU than the market (notably 'political union', not to mention the aspirations to a 'common culture', on which see later). Thirdly, the Single Market remains a 'project', a building site in the early stages of construction, rather than a finished building to be 'regulated', a site characterized by market-changing and market-building processes, and thus by processes of construction of new regulations, rather than *only* by the implementation of regulations. Finally, even if, for the sake of argument, we agreed that the EU is in some basic sense 'only' a market, nevertheless it is a sociological commonplace to observe that, ultimately, modern markets and market economies need to be bounded around and supported by institutions of social policy, cultural communication and democratically grounded law-making. These social institutions themselves cannot be reduced wholly to markets and, indeed, they need in some respects to be protected from them, as being 'special' and 'in the public interest'. But without them markets cannot function properly or develop in the long term. If, for all of these reasons, the notion of the EU as a 'regulatory state' is not convincing, nevertheless the phenomenon of regulation is clearly central to understanding the EU, and the notion of the EU as being some kind of 'regulatory order' (Bromley 2001) is a useful one, particularly when conceived of in a dynamic market-building and institution-building way.

It seems to me that Europeanization is happening generally through processes involving regulation, through various mixtures of what can be called 'hard law' and 'soft law', and through the EU-licensed differentiation involved in 'subsidiarity'. Most of this 'Europeanization through regulation' is elite-driven and top-down 'official Europeanization', as it always has been in the EU. But regulation also creates new social spaces, particularly market spaces, and market-based demand and supply dynamics. So now, arguably, we can begin to see and analyse a significant element of 'bottom-up' Europeanization or 'creeping Europeanization' – a colonization of the new market spaces by 'Euro-consumers' and also by numerous Europe-wide cultural industries and producers. 'Euro-peanization through regulation', through market space creation and through consumer colonization can be seen to be occurring – in various ways and to various extents – in the three main dimensions of the emerging European social formation, namely the politico-legal, socio-economic and cultural dimensions. However, in this chapter, for substantive and space limitation reasons, the focus is on the cultural dimension, and on sport and its relations with the media as illustrations of this dimension.

In terms of 'regulation' and the related concept of 'governance' (Bromley 2001), contemporary Europeanization is both like and unlike the process of nation-building or 'nationalization' experienced by European nation states over the course of the modern period. Nationalization (in its differing forms in different nations' historical trajectories) typically developed through mixtures of what we can call 'substantive' and 'regulatory' forms of governance. 'Regulatory govern-ance' operates by control of non-state-based activities (i.e. both markets and civil society) through the authority and legitimacy of the law. It developed particularly from the mid-eighteenth century onwards. 'Substantive governance' operates through the resource mobilization and distribution activities of governments and the state, particularly taxation and spending programmes, and developed particularly from the mid-twentieth century.

In the field of 'substantive governance' the EU has relatively little presence or power when compared with the member states which comprise it. It has no real independent powers to tax and spend. Its income from levies on the member states is fixed at a low level (under 2 per cent) of their gross domestic products (GDPs) and also of EU aggregate GDP, and this is dwarfed by the 40–50 per cent or so GDP 'tax take' from national GDP which European nation states typically and traditionally claim to require in order to function. Nevertheless, there are significant EU spending programmes, and these do carry an echo of nation state spending programmes. In the politico-legal field we have seen the development of a 'rapid response force' (which might be argued to be the embryo of a future EU army), together with coordinated military technology spending and some coordinated police activities. In the socio-economic area there is the Common Agricultural Policy, a massive redistributive item in the EU's budget and a powerful influence on recipient countries, together with equally redistributive but smaller structural and regional funds. We will focus on aspects of the cultural sphere later.

Nevertheless, bearing all this in mind, it is clear that the EU operates mainly as a 'regulatory governance' system. In relation to this we can distinguish 'hard' and 'soft' regulatory strategies and approaches in each of the three societal sectors we have discussed above. In terms of the politico-legal sphere, the EU's 'hard regulation' is evidenced in the member states' international treaties with each other that constitute the EU (in particular the Treaty of European Union, which is periodically modified, as at Maastricht in 1992, Amsterdam in 1997 and Nice in 2001). This is also evidenced in the operations of the European Court of Justice, which enforces the treaties, and in the periodic enlargement processes which bring new nation states into the EU's treaty system. Some aspects of the EU's currently narrowly defined 'EU citizenship' status and its associated rights could be said to be part of its armoury of 'hard regulation' (Meehan 1993; Roche 1997).

The EU's 'soft regulation' is evidenced in the promotion and use of a common EU policy discourse among the major policy-making actors, in the notions of an 'EU social model' and other such alleged common policy models and 'common European values'. Also broad but vague notions of 'European (rather than EU) citizenship', which are often used in EU policy discourse, can be counted in the general panoply of 'soft regulation', as also, and relatedly, can the EU's Charter of Fundamental Rights. This was 'solemnly proclaimed' by the Council, the Commission and the Parliament and was incorporated into the presently stalled European constitution. It is indicative of the potential framework and character of the EU's aspiration to be a trans-national 'civil society' and community of citizens as well as a union of nation states.

In the socio-economic sphere, the EU's 'hard regulatory' approach is evidenced in its administration of the single currency and in its competition policy, while its 'soft regulatory' strategy is evidenced in the development of its 'open method of coordination' and the promotion of common EU discourses in the fields of member states' 'action plans', relating particularly to employment and social inclusion.

'Cultural Europeanization' through regulation

In the cultural field there is a combination of EU policy discourse about Europe's subsidiarity and diversity, with processes which enable both differentiation and standardization to be explored and reconfigured. Some of this stands in tension with the standardizing features promoted by competition policy, while other aspects are consistent with Europeanization as standardization, in the sense of the creation of common civil and cultural space (in which both traditional and new cultural identities may be reviewed and explored, and thus in which a cross-EU set of differences – albeit EU-sanctioned differences – may be developed). These tensions within cultural Europeanization produced by different types and aspects of regulation – 'hard' and 'soft' regulation, standardizing and differentiating regulation – are felt within the EU sport (and sport-related media) field to which we now turn.

'Substantive governance' has not been a notable characteristic of EU policy within the cultural sphere. Probably the most important of the EU's spending programmes in the general cultural sphere are its four-year 'Framework' programmes for the coordination and development of scientific research across the EU. The most recent of these, Framework 6 (2002–6), is valued at around €17 billion and aims to create a 'European Research Area'. In addition, and related to this, the EU's various higher-education student exchange programmes should also be noted. There are various small-scale programmes (e.g. related to the preservation of European heritage, the development of some aspects of the European media, the annual European City of Culture competition, etc.). Also there is spending on local cultural industries under the rubric of the structural and regional spending programmes (Guibernau 2001; Shore 2000).

However, it cannot be argued that sport and sport-related media have been areas of 'substantive governance' in the EU.[1] It is worth bearing in mind that this is unlike the situation in most of the EU's member states, where these cultural areas have been subjects of 'substantive governance' approaches in the course and in the cause of nation-building. European nations have traditionally developed government spending programmes to support such things as sport and physical education in their school systems, nationwide training systems for international-level sporting competitions, 'sport for all', locally financed sport stadiums and other facilities, and also national public service broadcasting of national sporting events.

In contrast, sport in the EU context has mainly been the subject of 'regulatory governance', of both a 'hard' and a 'soft' kind. 'Hard regulation' in the field is mainly represented by the EU's competition policy. This has had major impacts on sport and its media presentation in the EU member states since the mid-1990s and it has tended to promote a relatively standardized Single Market approach. 'Soft regulation' is represented by the ways in which the creation of the Single Market and the overarching unifying legal framework, as well as the 'civil society' processes and institutions related to it, also create a 'common EU space' in which individual and collective cultural choices, identities and differences can be expressed.

1 On the strategically important nexus which has developed between sport and the media in popular culture in the last decade or more see Boyle and Haynes (2000); Brookes (2002); Giulianotti (1999: ch. 5); King (2003); Roche (2000a: ch. 6, 2002, 2003); Roche and Harrison (2002); Sandvoss (2003).

Cultural Europeanization: sport in the EU

Addressing sport in the context of a book on theoretical issues in European studies could be said to be a risky business. Surely this is either a self-indulgent or an irrelevant activity? From the perspective adopted in this chapter, however, it is suggested that sport is a socio-culturally interesting and significant field of contemporary European cultural development, cultural politics and policy-making – a field needing more theoretical perspectives and debates to reflect on and engage with it.[2]

Since the mid-1980s the European Community/EU, in particular the European Commission, has sought to promote an awareness of a common 'European' cultural identity (notionally 'common' European heritages, 'values', 'models' and discourses) among the publics of the member states through various aspects of its cultural policy. This area of policy includes such symbols as the EU flag and policy towards such things as education, tourism, the media and even (arguably) the symbolic and cultural role of the euro (Fiddler 2003; Roche 2000b; Shore 2000). With the exception of the flag and the euro, however, the EU has had little real power to influence public opinions and attitudes. And certainly it has had little real impact as compared with the continuity and recent reanimation of public identification with nationhood and with national identities and differences in contemporary Europe.

In this context EU policy-makers have periodically acknowledged the potential cultural importance of sport as part of the process of EU integration and of the formation of a European collective identity. In 1985 the Adonnino report recommended the 'organization of European Community events such as cycle and running races through European countries', the 'creation of Community teams for some sports to compete against joint teams from geographical groupings with which the Community has special links' and 'inviting sporting teams to wear the Community emblem in addition to their national colours at major sporting events of regional or worldwide interest' (Adonnino 1985: 26 para 5.9.1). In the report sport was considered to have the potential to be an important and popular vehicle for the promotion of a positive European cultural identity, just as it has been, since the late nineteenth century, for the building of national identities. However, Europeans' sporting interests, loyalties and related cultural identities have remained stubbornly focused, for most sport, on their local clubs and national teams. With the notable exception of Ryder Cup golf, in which,

2 For EU policy statements and reports on sport see: European Commission (1998, 1999); European Council (2000); Monti (2000, 2001); Pons (1999); Reding (2000); Ungerer (2003). For an analysis of EU policy see: Foster (2000, 2003); Parrish (2003a, 2003b); Roche (2004); Roche and Harrison (2002).

every two years, a European team challenges a US one, there has never been any popular interest in the possibility of creating equivalent arrangements in other sports and events. The EU may attempt to intrude its flag and anthem into the cultural theatre of major sporting events held in EU territory, such as the 1992 Barcelona Olympics and the 2004 Athens Olympics, but national teams and national identities continue to reign supreme at global sporting mega-events such as the Olympics and World Cup in the twenty-first century, just as they always did throughout the twentieth century.

Nevertheless, the spirit of Adonnino appears to live on in the European Commission. In 2001, in an interview with the director of Commission President Romano Prodi's Forward Studies Unit, I was intrigued to discover that, as one way of promoting a common collective European identity, the Unit was giving some consideration to the creation of a major periodic athletic event in which a European team would challenge a US one. That said, nothing seems to have come of this 'bright idea'. So when we consider the topic of 'cultural Europeanization' in connection with sport, it appears, initially at least, that, the Ryder Cup apart, we have very little ground on which to stand, and very little of any substance to study.

However, such appearances are deceptive. Against this view we can observe that powerful cross-European social processes appear to be at work currently in the sport–cultural and media–sport systems in Europe's societies. In Germany and the UK, we witnessed the collapse in 2002 of the major media corporations Kirch and ITV Digital because of the debts they incurred in their desperation to possess the rights to broadcast football on television. And the loss of income that this entailed in turn threatened the very survival of long-established and world-class national football clubs and leagues in these two nations. We have also recently witnessed a major conflict between the EU, on the one hand, and, on the other, the long-term 'co-conspirators' of English football, the Premier League and Rupert Murdoch's Sky satellite television company. This was over the potentially anti-competitive character of the new 2003 television rights contract. Had this contract been legally voided by EU action, the resulting loss of income would have brought many major English clubs, and the Premier League along with it, household names and national institutions alike, to their financial knees. In the event the contract was marginally adjusted to provide coverage of a few live games to terrestrial television companies and to temper Sky's claim to absolute exclusivity. The EU made it very clear that exclusivity would be substantively banned in the renewal of this contract in 2007 and the implication is clear that the sooner the Premier League and Sky start adjusting to this new EU regulatory reality, the better it will be for them (Ungerer 2003). I suggest that these crises are just the tip of an iceberg of common structural problems afflicting the media–football systems across most European societies (Roche 2004).

This observation implies that when we consider the theme of 'cultural Euro-peanization' and people's potential collective identity as 'Europeans', it would make sense to lower our sights from grandiose and elite-driven ideals and dreams relating to the potential for sharing 'European values' through sport or for the development of EU teams competing in international sport. Perhaps a better approach would be to look for less direct and more practical, albeit more complex and ambiguous, forms of popular 'European awareness' and Euro-cosmopolitanism, such as those which have been loosed in the field of sports culture and sport-related media across Europe's societies.

Euro-cosmopolitanism in football

In one meaning or another of the concept 'cosmopolitan', English football can be argued to have become demonstrably and qualitatively cosmopolitanized in the last decade or more. The story of this cosmopolitanization – which is simultaneously a Europeanization, or a Euro-cosmopolitanization – is a familiar one. It coincided with and resulted from the new wave of commercialization and mediatization which flooded through professional football in all of the leading, mainly European, footballing countries in this period. The English Premier League was formed in 1990 and since that time the rights to transmit live games between Premier League clubs have been bought and controlled by Rupert Murdoch's Sky satellite television operation. Sky has been willing to pay unprecedented sums to the League and its clubs in auctions for the privilege of exclusive control of the rights to broadcast the games live. The resulting increase in club revenues enabled them to scour international and particularly European markets for players, thereby acquiring squads and fielding teams composed of wide mixtures of nationalities.

For over a century before the 1990s in 'the national game' Britain's football clubs were staffed by British players and managed by British managers. This presented the basis for recurrent intergenerational reaffirmations and recon-structions of cultural identities in relation to the local and national communities of fans and paying spectators, whose attendance sustained the game economic-ally and culturally. The *de facto* Euro-cosmopolitanization of the make-up of England's leading football teams, including their management, in the short period since the 1990s represents a historic and probably irreversible transforma-tion in the sport and in the popular culture surrounding it. The full meaning and future implications of this transformation are still being worked through and remain unclear.

The managers and star players at England's leading clubs more often than not now come from continental European countries, and not from Britain. The public, although perhaps unclear about this transformation at a reflexive level, nonetheless has appeared fairly rapidly to have become familiar with the new situation and with the disruption of the traditional sporting symbolization of national identity that this involves. Of course, we still have national teams with nationality eligibility requirements for players in football, as in all other sports, which enable traditional national identities to be reaffirmed. However, with the developing internationalization of the market for players and player mobility in football in particular, this situation is becoming increasingly subject to flexible interpretation, creative explorations of players' family backgrounds and reconstructions of nationalities and identities. Meanwhile the tension between (symbols of) the nation state and the market in sport, between the demands, on the one hand, of football clubs (which pay players' salaries and need to get a return for their money) and, on the other, of football's national governing bodies (which 'borrow' these 'club assets' to construct representative national teams), is growing inexorably around the world, but particularly in football's cultural heartland, Europe.

In addition, in this short period, in Britain and across European societies, we have also seen the transformation of fans' and clubs' aspirations, from the assumption that participation and success in national league and cup competitions represented the highest accomplishment, to the idea that participation and success in the main European competition, UEFA's Europe-wide 'Champions League', represented their highest ideal, the place to seek the contemporary version of 'authentic glory'. This not only implicitly relocates and downgrades 'national' football leagues and competitions but also presages the possibility of an evolution of a more substantially trans-national, European level of football club organization, namely what is sometimes referred to as a 'European Superleague'. This controversial possibility, which would give form and substance to the Euro-cosmopolitan dynamics currently under way in football within the European nations, has been pressed in recent years by the leading clubs and by media corporations (such as Italy's – Silvio Berlusconi's – Mediaset) and is currently being resisted by UEFA and Europe's national football authorities.

The rapid emergence of *de facto* Euro-cosmopolitanism in national football cultures such as that of Britain has interesting implications for popular politico-cultural discourse, particularly in the mediatized and sensationalized section of it led by the Europhobic British tabloid press, not only for football but also for general public attitudes to Europe in the form of the EU. It has always intrigued me that the British tabloids and their readers seem capable of a kind of politico-cultural schizophrenia in tolerating the apparent contradictions involved, on the one hand, in the often visceral anti-Europeanism periodically trumpeted on their front ('news') pages (in campaigns against the UK adopting the euro etc.), as against, on the other hand, the passionate pro-Europeanism of clubs' aspirations, which are regularly faithfully represented and trumpeted on their back ('sports') pages.

I take all this as substantial evidence (even if commonsensical and provisional, and as yet far too under-theorized as well as under-researched in social scientific and social theoretical terms) of a historically unprecedented, structurally based and practically irreversible process of Euro-cosmopolitanization of 'the British national game'. Our experience of this in Britain is only a local instance and manifestation of a Europe-wide phenomenon that affects all of the national football leagues involved in the emerging UEFA (or more accurately the emerging joint EU/UEFA) European football system (King 2003; Roche 2004).

Overall, then, it can be readily observed that there has been a Europeanization of the 'football industry' since the 1990s. This has implied the development of aspects of *de facto* Euro-cosmopolitanism in terms of European football's consumer cultural and mediatized dimensions. Europeanization is evident in the Europe-wide financial crises which have seemed to become endemic among Europe's football clubs and leagues, and to which the EU, together with European media corporations, have significantly contributed. It is also evident in the new institution-building promoted by these factors, in the shape of both UEFA's development of its role and also the increasing power of Europe's 'super clubs' and of G-14, their lobby organization. These new institutions are unstable and it is conceivable that they will be transitional, in the not too distant future transforming themselves into a more fully organized European-level football system, possibly culminating in some version of a 'European Super League'. This would no doubt have major implications for EU member states' national leagues, particularly those in the main football nations – Spain, Italy, Germany and England.

Of course, these Europeanization and *de facto* Euro-cosmopolitan dynamics have both positive and negative aspects, from new forms of cross-European cultural communication and exchange to new forms of racism and violence. The boost that Europeanization gives to local and fan cultures and identities in terms of new exclusionary, xenophobic and discriminatory attitudes and practices needs as much attention in research agendas as whatever more inclusionary, cosmopolitan and citizenship-affirming responses they may stimulate. Finally there are the European television 'football systems' and the emerging EU-driven regulatory system in relation to this (King 2003; Roche and Harrison 2002; Ungerer 2003). The impacts of these and other new EU-driven UEFA systems are unclear at present and they also call for monitoring and further research from the media/sport research and European studies communities, not least in view of the potential restructuring of the European football industry implied by the emergence of a 'European Super League' system, and the potential impacts of this on national and local fan cultures and identities.

Conclusion

Two main steps were taken in the discussion of Euro-cosmopolitanism and sport in this chapter. First, the concepts of 'cosmopolitanism', 'Europeanization' and 'regulation' were considered, together with some of their meanings and some of the perspectives necessary to apply them to the general sphere of EU cultural policy. Second, the case of European sport and sport-related media considered in order to provide a specific site in which the tensions within, and the challenges facing, EU cultural regulation could be seen at closer quarters and in which a sense of the consumerist dynamics of contemporary Euro-cosmopolitanization could be encountered.

The reconstruction of the field of sport and sport-related media currently observable in Europe indicates that partial and practical forms of 'cultural Europeanization' and *de facto* Euro-cosmopolitanization *can* be said to be occurring. 'Cultural Europeanization' was originally envisaged as a basically 'official discursive' form of Euro-cosmopolitanization and as a top-down policy process, as exemplified in the Adonnino report in 1985 and as still present in the thinking of the European Commission. This has been subject to much criticism for its elitism and ineffectiveness (e.g. Shore 2000). However, EU official discursive cosmopolitanism in the area of sport (and more specifically of football), and perhaps in some other popular cultural fields, has evolved from attempted visionary political agenda-setting into a style of regulatory policy-making which is simultaneously both more reactive and problem-solving and more interventionist and problem-creating for the industries, markets and civil society actors it seeks to influence. In relation to this, this chapter has suggested that EU policy and European social scientific research needs to be more aware of what can be called the 'creeping Europeanization', 'bottom-up' and 'unofficial' processes that are involved in the development of consumer culture across Europe's societies (Roche 2000b). The popular cultural forms and genres of sports and their media presentations are particularly influential in this development; they deserve further research, as indicated above, and also deserve to be taken more seriously in general social scientific analyses of European integration as a process and of 'Europe' as a social formation.

Studies in the field of European sport have the potential to connect with and throw light on broader sociological and policy-analytic aims and agendas. These include, for instance, a better understanding of the practical forms taken by the contemporary development of EU-level 'civil society', 'public spheres' and 'public interests', of Europe-wide collective cultural and political identities, and of both their event-oriented transience and their potential for persisting cross-national mobilization and institutionalization. In this context, the study of European sport and sport-related media can contribute to our understanding of the emerging 'cosmopolitan condition' in the EU, the distinctive mix of commonalities and differences which is beginning to mark the societies and peoples of 'new Europe'.

References

Adonnino, P. (1985) 'A people's Europe', *Bulletin of the European Communities*, supplement 7/85, Luxembourg: European Commission.

Boyle, R. and Haynes, R. (2000) *Power Play: Sport, Media and Popular Culture*, London: Longman.

Bromley, S. (ed.) (2001) *Governing the European Union*, London: Sage.

Brookes, R. (2002) *Representing Sport*, London: Arnold.

Davies, N. (1997) *Europe: A History*, London: Pimlico.

European Commission (1998) *The European Model of Sport*, consultation document of DG Culture, Brussels: European Commission.

European Commission (1999) *Safeguarding Current Sport Structures and Maintaining the Social Function of Sport Within the Community Framework*, report from the Commission to the European Council (the Helsinki report), Brussels: European Commission.

European Council (2000) 'Declaration on the specific characteristics of sport and its social function in Europe, of which account should be taken in implementing common policies' (the Nice declaration), Nice: European Council.

Fiddler, C. (2003) *British Attitudes to the Euro*, unpublished doctoral dissertation, Sheffield: Main Library, University of Sheffield.

Foster, K. (2000) 'European law and football: who's in charge?', *Soccer and Society*, 1.

Foster, K. (2003) 'Sport as a cultural commodity in the European Union', presented to the annual conference of the Universities Association for Contemporary European Studies, University of Newcastle.

Giulianotti, R. (1999) *Football: A Sociology of the Global Game*, Cambridge: Polity Press.

Guibernau, M. (ed.) (2001) *Governing European Diversity*, London: Sage.

Harvey, D. (1990) *The Condition of Postmodernity*, Oxford: Blackwell.

Held, D. (1995) *Democracy and the Global Order*, Cambridge: Polity Press.

Held, D., McGrew, A., Goldblatt, D. and Perraton, J. (1999) *Global Transformations*, Cambridge: Polity Press.

Kant, I. (1784) 'Idea for a universal history from a cosmopolitan point of view', in L. W. Beck (ed.), *Kant on History*, New York: Bobbs-Merrill, pp. 11–26.

King, A. (2003) *The European Ritual: Football in the New Europe*, Aldershot: Ashgate.

Majone, G. (1996) *Regulating Europe*, London: Routledge.

Meehan, E. (1993) *Citizenship in the European Union*, London: Sage.

Monti, M. (2000) 'Sport and competition', speech on behalf of European Commission DG Competition, presented to the conference 'Sport', organized by the European Commission, Brussels, April. Available at http://europa.eu/rapid/pressReleasesAction.do?reference= SPEECH/00/152&format=HTML&aged=0&language=EN&guiLanguage=en (last accessed January 2007).

Monti, M. (2001) 'Competition and sport – the rules of the game', speech on behalf of European Commission DG Competition, presented to the conference 'Governance in Sport', organized by the European Olympic Committee and the FIA, Brussels, February. Available at http://europa.eu/rapid/pressReleasesAction.do?reference=SPEECH/01/84&format=HTML&aged=1&language=EN&guiLanguage=en (last accessed January 2007).

Parrish, R. (2003a) 'The politics of sport regulation in the European Union', *European Public Policy*, 10(2), 246–62.

Parrish, R. (2003b) 'The European Convention and the future of EU sports policy', unpublished paper presented to the annual conference of the University Association for Contemporary European Studies, University of Newcastle.

Pons, J.-F. (1999) 'Sport and European competition policy', paper presented to the conference 'International Antitrust Law and Policy', New York, October. Available at http://ec.europa.eu/comm/competition/speeches/text/sp1999_019_en.pdf (last accessed January 2007).

Reding, V. (2000) 'The declaration on sport adopted in Nice defines a European model of sport which represents cultural diversity and has a strong social dimension', press release, 11 December. Available at http://europa.eu/rapid/pressReleasesAction.do?reference=IP/00/1439&format=HTML&aged=0&language=EN&guiLanguage=en (last accessed January 2007).

Reding, V. (2001) 'The reform of FIFA rules governing international transfers', statement to the European Parliament, Strasbourg, March.

Roche, M. (1997) 'Citizenship and exclusion: reconstructing the European Union', in M. Roche and R. van Berkel (eds), *European Citizenship and Social Exclusion*, Aldershot: Avebury.

Roche, M. (ed.) (1998) *Sport, Popular Culture and Identity* (2nd edition 2002). Aachen: Meyer and Meyer Verlag.

Roche, M. (2000a) *Mega-Events and Modernity: Olympics and Expos in the Growth of Global Culture*, London: Routledge.

Roche, M. (2000b) 'Citizenship, popular culture and Europe', in N. Stevenson (ed.), *Culture and Citizenship*, London: Sage, pp. 74–98.

Roche, M. (2002) 'Olympic and sport mega-events as media-events', in K. Walmsley, R. Barney and S. Martyn (eds), *The Global Nexus Engaged: Past, Present, Future Interdisciplinary Olympic Studies*, London: University of Western Ontario, pp. 1–12.

Roche, M. (2003) 'The Olympics and the development of global society', in M. de Moragas, C. Kennet and N. Puig (eds), *The Legacy of the Olympic Games 1984–2000*, Lausanne: International Olympic Committee, pp. 289–306,

Roche, M. (2004) 'Europe, the cosmopolitan condition and international sport: "cultural Europeanisation" and EU regulation in the case of European football', presented to the conference 'Europe and Cosmopolitanism', Royal Holloway College, London University. Available from the author (m.roche@shef.ac.uk).

Roche, M. and Harrison, J. (2002) 'Cultural Europeanisation through regulation? The case of media–sport in the EU', presented to the IAMCR annual conference, Barcelona. Available from the author (m.roche@shef.ac.uk).

Rumford, C. (2002) *The European Union: A Political Sociology*, Oxford: Blackwell.

Sandvoss, C. (2003) *A Game of Two Halves: Football, Television and Globalisation*, London: Routledge.

Shore, C. (2000) *Building Europe: The Cultural Politics of European Integration*, London: Routledge.

Ungerer, H. (2003) 'Commercialising sport: understanding the TV rights debate', conference paper, Barcelona, October 2003. Available at http://ec.europa.eu/comm/competition/speeches/text/sp2003_024_en.pdf (last accessed January 2007).

CHAPTER 9

The Language of Democracy: Vernacular or Esperanto? A Comparison of the Multiculturalist and Cosmopolitan Perspectives

Daniele Archibugi[1]

Citizens of the world, converse!

The Holy Roman Emperor Charles V, a man proud who reigned over a truly global empire, once said: 'I speak Spanish to God, French to men, Italian to women, and German to my horse'. Though he was no champion of democracy, it would have been interesting to ask Charles V what he thought the language of democracy was. Though we will never hear *his* answer, Will Kymlicka's has reached us loud and clear:

> Democratic politics is politics in the vernacular. The average citizen feels at ease only when he discusses political questions in his own language. As a general rule, only elites are fluent in more than one language and have the chance to maintain and develop their linguistic skills continuously and feel at ease discussing political questions in different languages in a multilingual atmosphere. Moreover, political communication has a large ritual component and these ritual forms of communication are characteristic of a language. Even if a person understands a foreign language in the technical sense, he may be incapable of understanding political debates, if he has no knowledge of these

1 This chapter is a shortened version of a paper published in *Political Studies* (vol. 53, 2005, pp. 537–55). I wish to thank Shilpi Banerjee, Neera Chandholke, Paola Ferretti, Mathias Koenig-Archibugi, Raffaele Marchetti, Eva Nag, Praveen Priyadarshi, Simone Roberti and Giorgio Ruffolo for the information they have provided and for their comments on an earlier draft. I also benefited from the comments made during two seminars held at the London School of Economics and Political Science, respectively at the Centre for Study of Global Governance (18 February 2004) and at the Political Philosophy Research Group (24 February 2004) and at the conference 'Cosmopolitanism and Europe', held at the University of London, Royal Holloway (22–23 April 2004).

ritual elements. For these and other reasons, we can believe, as a general rule, that the more the political debate takes place in the vernacular, the greater the participation. (Kymlicka 2001: 214)

If these affirmations are intended as a description of how democratic politics has evolved in the course of twenty-five centuries, it is hard to disagree: democracy developed in substantially restricted communities that managed to understand one another not only through the same language but also through a set of tacit codes shared among their members. From the descriptive point of view, no one denies that a monolingual community has considerable advantages for democratic practice: all citizens (with the sole exception of those with impaired hearing) are able to take part in political life, any institution (from parliament to a local residents' committee) can discuss and take resolutions without intermediaries, while government and all institutions can be controlled by citizens without any need for interpreters.

But in how many political communities does this ideal situation exist? Multi-cultural theorists have rightly described a real world that fails to comply with single-language or mono-ethnic states. Diversity of language and culture is a reality that is likely to increase inside each political community. I refer not only to the US, with its celebrated 'melting pot' and hundreds of ethnic and linguistic minorities. Even countries such as Sweden and Finland, whose languages remained the exclusive domain of natives for centuries, have found themselves addressing new problems as a result of recent immigration. At the same time, problems that transcend the competencies of single nationwide political communities are also bound to increase; for example, decisions on the agricultural and immigration policies of Sweden and Finland are increasingly taken in Brussels as opposed to Stockholm and Helsinki.

Nor is it possible to ignore the fact that, albeit with some difficulty, democracy has managed to solve problems of linguistic communication. The US has granted voting rights to immigrants from all over the world, and even if the President, the Congress and the Supreme Court have used exclusively English, political parties realize that, if they want to win elections, they need to attract the votes of millions of Hispanicos. India, too, has become a state with some democratic procedures, despite the diversity of its languages and income levels far below those of the US. In order to introduce democratic institutions, India had to adopt the English language of its colonizers as a lingua franca, along with Hindi, and this proved politically less controversial than the use of Hindi only, perceived as the language of some but not all Indians (Chandholke 2005). The same has happened in many other colonies, where the language of the colonizers has become the public language (often for restricted minorities), whereas vernaculars (often different from one another) have prevailed for private use. In other words, language is not historically independent from political community.

Yet the present era poses new problems and new demands, greater than the ones experienced in the past.[2] What can be done to address them? Neither the multiculturalist nor the cosmopolitan perspective intends to abandon the principles and values of democracy and tolerance. Despite the polemical fervour that has characterized the recent debate, the two perspectives have more points in common than is generally recognized. I wish to highlight four beliefs which, I assume, are shared by both multiculturalist and cosmopolitan theorists:

1 The building of nation states was an artificial process that involved the creation of an 'imaginary identity', in the sense clarified by Anderson (1991).
2 In all states, the effect of ongoing cultural homogenization is to destroy local cultures and languages. Directly or indirectly, even liberal states support this process of homogenization.
3 The diversity of the planet's languages deserves to be preserved. Once the speed with which old languages are disappearing in the contemporary world has been acknowledged,[3] it ought to be the job of governmental and inter-governmental institutions to preserve the linguistic variety, through special cultural policies.
4 Involving the highest number of citizens in the decision-making process is a constitutive value of democracy and it is the job of institutions to foster their participation (Beetham 2000).

On the basis of these premises, how must democratic practice be modified to deal with the existence of multilingual political communities? To think that democracy requires specific linguistic conditions (in order to survive) is to underestimate its versatility and its capacity to evolve. It is necessary, rather, to modify and extend democratic practice to enable it to live and prosper in environmental conditions – like the ones determined by multilingualism – different from those experienced to date. The fundamental difference between the multiculturalist and the cosmopolitan perspectives arguably transpires in the different answers they give to the following question:

How should political communities deal with problems that cut across different linguistic communities, while safeguarding individual liberties, maximizing participation and applying democratic procedures?

2 The essays collected by Kymlicka and Patten (2003) have the merit of discussing this relatively new area of political theory. See also Castiglione and Longman (2007).
3 For paradigmatic references on the disappearance of languages, see Nettle and Romaine (2000) and Crystal (2000).

Examples of problems that cut across different linguistic communities include: the supply of education or health care in a multilingual neighbourhood; the environmental management of a lake surrounded by two (or more) linguistically diverse states; and the appointment of a national or even an international parliament.

As far as the language problem is concerned, multiculturalism seeks to address common problems while conserving the linguistic identity of each community, thus enacting public policies which, *de facto*, separate communities by language. This is supposed to allow each community to conserve its own democratic procedure in the vernacular and to minimize exclusion *within* each community. In short, multiculturalism places the emphasis on the cohesion – linguistic cohesion included – of the community in question. Cosmopolitanism moves in the opposite direction. It has no intention of modifying the composition of the political community, even if, as a result of historical events, this community is made up of people who speak very different languages. In the face of common problems, cosmopolitanism seeks to apply democratic procedure, implementing public policies designed to remove linguistic barriers, even if this implies that some members of the population who are not fluent in the language used for public purposes might be somehow disadvantaged.

From a normative perspective, the thesis that democratic politics has to be carried out in the vernacular is dangerous. I refer to all the political groups in North America and Europe that oppose the integration of immigrants and races, often doing so not because they are driven by authoritarian motives but, rather, to preserve a high level of self-determination. Such political groups may, in good faith, think that minorities who do not speak their language could limit the democratic life of their community and that, to preserve their democracy, it is necessary to expel, isolate or naturalize those without the same knowledge of the language, and even to repress the use of languages other than the dominant one.[4] Kymlicka's thesis might thus lead to exactly the opposite effect to the one hoped for: instead of protecting the rights of minorities, it might even lead to their violation.

For these reasons, I oppose the idea that democratic politics is politics in the vernacular with the contrasting thesis that democratic politics *must* be in Esperanto. I argue against the *descriptive* thesis whereby democratic politics is carried on in the vernacular by adopting the following *normative* principle: democratic politics is not in Esperanto but, where necessary, it *can* and *must* be in Esperanto. This thesis refers not to all the problems of linguistic rights addressed so far, but solely and exclusively to the problem of the language necessary for political communication.

---

4 This is the case of the 'English only' movement in the US (Crawford 2000). More recently, similar concerns have been expressed in a provocative article by Huntington (2004).

Very regular and with a limited number of words, Esperanto was one of the sources of inspiration for the Newspeak of George Orwell's *Nineteen Eighty-Four*. It was invented by Ludwig Lejzer Zamenhof towards the end of the nineteenth century for instrumental reasons, namely to allow communication in multilingual communities (Zamenhof 1889). Zamenhof grew up in the city of Bialystok, in present-day Poland, then part of Tsarist Russia, where four different languages were spoken. Not surprisingly, practical misunderstandings arose among the four communities, and Zamenhof optimistically had the idea of solving them by creating a language that each community would be able to learn easily as a second language. His ambition for this Newspeak was, obviously, much greater than that: if it worked for a small town in Eastern Europe, it might have universal value. Note that the aim of Esperanto was not to replace existing languages but to supplement them. Since then, Esperanto has attracted few but fervent acolytes in every country, but has been supplanted as an international lingua franca first by French, then by English. Other idioms – Mandarin Chinese, Hindi, Spanish, Russian – have become lingua francas in various regions of the world. Esperanto can be seen as a positive Utopia, perfectly symmetrical to the dystopia of Orwell's Newspeak: whereas the ultimate aim of Newspeak was to repress thoughts against authority, the aim of Esperanto is to facilitate communication between individuals in the remote areas of the world. This is similar to how the introduction of universal weights and measures has sought to make economic and social life transparent, by breaking down informational asymmetries among individuals and social classes. When a linguistic medium is lacking, the prerequisite for institutions and individuals to take part in democratic life is to create one – if need be artificially. The universal language is thus the key to cosmopolitan citizenship.

What is democratic politics?

The language problem brings to the fore many aspects of the conceptions we have of democracy. If we espouse the 'aggregative' model – the conception of democracy that favours the aggregation of preferences (as opposed to their formation) – the problem of language is considerably reduced. The single members of the political community (electors) already have a definite set of choices before them, and if the political community is made up of individuals speaking different languages, it is sufficient and technically possible to make the various options available in all these languages.

In an aggregative model of democracy, a political community would be able to run elections easily by providing information in all the necessary languages. It ought to be the duty and in the interest of each political party to make its programme accessible to voters in the most appropriate linguistic medium. In this model, electors are expected to formulate their preferences and check that the political party that has won the election carries out its programme, while their direct participation in political life is reduced to a minimum. If citizens were granted access to administration and public services, language problems would obviously arise, but it is not impossible, as required by theorists of multiculturalism, to provide public services such as education and health in the languages most spoken by citizens. In many regions where two linguistic communities live side by side, public functionaries are already bilingual and the basic public services are provided in more than one language.

But both multiculturalists and cosmopolitans might hold the view that the aggregative model is not an accurate description of how democracies effectively operate, still less of how they *should* operate. Both approaches might favour a different model of democracy, which has been defined as 'deliberative' by Habermas (1998), as 'discursive' by Dryzek (2000) and as 'communicative' by Young (2000). In this model, the essence of democracy is to be found in communication, that is to say in the capacity to understand the reasons of others and to expound one's own. In many respects, the two models of aggregative and deliberative democracy are not opposed (as they are too often believed to be) but, rather, two phases of the same process. The first phase is that of the formation of parties and political programmes, in which dialogue and persuasion prevail. The second phase is that of choices and the aggregation of preferences at election time, during which the competitive arguments of political parties prevail.

If deliberation is an important part of the democratic process, the language issue becomes crucial. Patten (2003b: 379) argues that 'a common public language is not necessary for deliberative democracy'. This position is antithetical to that of Kymlicka, who, as we saw above, even goes as far as to argue that democratic politics can *only* be in the vernacular. Patten imagines the technical possibility of using translators and interpreters. In a national legislative assembly it is certainly possible to make use of simultaneous translations (examples already exist in this respect), but the more the level of politics narrows down, the more the possibility of resorting to linguistic intermediaries decreases. A 'strong' democracy (Barber 1984) stands out partly because of its more diffused, less formalized procedures: local residents' committees, parent–teacher–student associations, political parties and trade unions are all vital components of political life.

If, in short, we abandon the merely aggregative conception of democracy, the language problem emerges as a major practical hurdle. Yet I do not believe it is possible to generate democratic culture if the single components (be they neighbourhoods, schools, grass-roots associations, political parties, trade unions or local government) are not prepared to accept the principle of the inclusion of participants irrespective of their linguistic capability. It would certainly infringe all principles of democracy if the various groups were to be defined on the basis of religious, economic or cultural criteria. So why should we consider the creation of linguistic confines less atrocious? Where an obstacle to participation exists, it is up to democratic politics to seek to remove it.

To ask citizens to make an effort to understand each other is not a neutral act with respect to the conception of democracy preferred. Understanding others requires patience and an investment of time and resources in education, which might prove useless outside the political sphere. One example that comes to mind is that of the (few) Berliners who have learned the rudiments of Turkish to communicate with an essential part of their city's population. To ask citizens to make this effort is to opt for the freedom of the ancients, as opposed to that of the moderns – to use Benjamin Constant's (1819) terminology – insofar as it means asking members of the community to devote time and energy to overcoming existing barriers to communication, even if this serves only for democratic practice. A cultural cosmopolitan is inclined to see an intrinsic and not only instrumental value in the opportunity to speak an extra language.

Policy options: a comparison between multiculturalists and cosmopolitans

Arguably the best way to understand the differences between the multiculturalist and cosmopolitan positions is to consider specific cases. In this section, I discuss four paradigmatic cases: a neighbourhood school, a multilingual city, a great multi-ethnic country and a supranational parliament. We obviously find significant differences both among multiculturalist theorists[5] and among cosmopolitans (in particular between ethical and institutional cosmopolitans). Though I do not attempt to represent all the various positions faithfully, I do believe that it is useful to outline paradigmatic cases – even if forcing them somewhat – to identify the differences between the two approaches.

A state school in California

In a state school in a district of Pasadena, California, traditionally dominated by English-speaking pupils, demographic trends and waves of immigration are causing a sizeable growth in the number of Hispanic pupils. Since a certain demographic decline has been recorded among the 'Anglos', the school manages to assimilate the new 'Hispanicos' quite easily; indeed, their presence has saved

---

5 In particular between Kymlicka (1995) and Parekh (2002). For a variety of perspectives on multiculturalism, see Kelly (2002).

the school from being closed for lack of numbers. The problem is that the two communities differ in terms of income level, culture, religion and language.

The overall demographic data for Pasadena show that English is spoken at home by 55 per cent of the population only and that nearly 30 per cent speak Spanish. These facts are obviously reflected in schools: the Hispanic students do not speak good English and that of their parents is even worse. School meetings end in pandemonium, with the Anglo parents complaining that their children are starting to make a lot of spelling mistakes and the Hispanic parents protesting because their children are being bullied. At the end of one stormy meeting, an Anglo father, citing Samuel Huntington, invites the Hispanic community to dream in English. In return, he gets slapped in the face by an outraged Mexican![6]

The headmaster, a man with a fine sense of intuition, perceives that the Anglo parents are worried that the identity of their neighbourhood is going to be lost. The Hispanic parents also have identity problems, and they are worried because their children receive lower marks than the others. The Hispanicos are not even as good at sports as the Anglos, largely because the principal game played is American football. A number of the Hispanic parents were born and bred in the US but they still do not have a good command of English. Since many of them are cleaners in the homes of the Anglos, their aspiration is to enable their children to live in conditions that will avoid perpetuating the class division based on different ethnic groups.

The headmaster calls in a multiculturalist researcher and asks him to study the problem and to come up with a solution. After a few weeks, the researcher submits a prospectus in which he divides the pupils into different sections, A and H. Adopting an ingenious restructuring programme, he demonstrates that it is possible to teach in English in section A and Spanish in section H. The parents are free to choose the section they want for their children, although Anglos might be expected to enrol theirs in A and Hispanicos to enrol theirs in H. Without any extra costs, the project also envisages the teaching of the other language in both sections, allowing the Anglos to pick up some Spanish and Hispanicos to study English as a second language. The multiculturalist also notes that sport is a central element of group identity and that it would be wrong to prevent Hispanicos from playing the game they prefer and perform best at. Hence, while American football is to be played in section A, soccer will be introduced to section H.

The headmaster is puzzled. He wonders whether the project complies with the US constitution and, though California has been granted constitutional derogations, he decides to call in a cosmopolitan researcher for a second opinion.

---

6 Huntington (2004: 45): 'There is only the American dream created by an Anglo-Protestant society. Mexican Americans will share in that dream and in that society only if they dream in English'.

A few days later, the cosmopolitan submits her project. On the frontispiece is a quotation from Thomas Pogge (2003: 118): 'the best education for children is the education which is best for each child'. The plan envisages that all pupils receive the same education in English, since this is the dominant language in the country in which they live and also a worldwide lingua franca. Her report includes tables which show that US citizens with a good knowledge of English have: higher incomes; less risk of being unemployed; less risk of being imprisoned; and better hopes for a longer life. Another table shows how English is snowballing as a second language on every continent, and she asks whether it is the public school's job to condemn the pupil – at least in terms of statistical probability – to earning less, being unemployed, ending up in gaol and even living less long in order to preserve the language of his or her linguistic community. As regards sports, the study proposes the adoption of baseball, as it is popular in both the Caribbean and in North America.

Not content with demonstrating once and for all the advantages for the wellbeing of young pupils of teaching in English, the cosmopolitan also suggests introducing compulsory courses of Spanish language and culture for all, proposing as core subjects for a common identity the myth of Zorro, Ernest Hemingway and Isabel Allende. The avoidance of dividing the pupils into two sections makes it possible to save money, which the researcher suggests using for evening courses in English for the Hispanic parents. Pre-empting a predictable objection from the Anglos – namely that the parents of the other ethnic group will accumulate more resources – the cosmopolitan proposes evening courses in salsa and other Latin American dances for the Anglo parents. She also proposes setting up a tourist association to organize holidays in the Caribbean and Central America. After reading the project carefully, the headmaster is still perplexed.

The Bialystok problem

An emblematic case is that of Zamenhof's home town of Bialystok. As mentioned above, in the second half of the nineteenth century four linguistic communities lived in the town: Poles (3,000), Russians (4,000), Germans (5,000) and Jews (18,000). This created many practical problems for the commerce, education and basic public life that the Tsarist regime permitted in a territory that it had conquered only relatively recently. The most populous linguistic community, the Jews, did not have a large written corpus to rely upon in their own vernacular language, Yiddish, whereas two other linguistic communities, the Germans and the Russians, could count upon the consolidation of the language and culture of the two great bordering states, Germany and Russia.

Acknowledging the difference, a multiculturalist would probably have suggested setting up four ethnic councils, each endowed with broad autonomy over the provision of services such as education and health. He or she would also have set up a 'Chamber of Compensation' to help citizens exchange their homes if they wished, to make the city divisible into four homogeneous linguistic neighbourhoods. This would have greatly reduced problems of linguistic misunderstanding in commerce and facilitated education in the languages of the four communities. As we have seen, the ingenious solution of Zamenhof, a true champion of cosmopolitanism, was to create an artificial new language, Esperanto, designed to place the various communities on the same plane and, moreover, to enable them to communicate with all the citizens of the world. The fact that the solution was unworkable should not prevent us from admiring its grandiose ambition, whereby a local problem provided the thrust for a universal language. A less ingenious solution – but arguably likely to yield more tangible fruits – would have been to establish bilingualism for education and public communication in the main Slav language (Russian) and German (which bears many resemblances to Yiddish), allowing and developing the private use of other vernacular languages. Though constituting the absolute majority in the city, the Jewish community might have been concerned by this solution, but it would have taken into account the fact almost all the members of the community had a certain fluency in at least one other language. Zamenhof would probably have agreed with Van Parijs's proposal that each of the linguistic communities that were required to study the language of the others, in this case the Jews and Poles, would be entitled to tangible compensations from the communities not required to study other languages (Van Parijs 2003: 167).[7]

The case of India

India, unique for its large number of ethnic groups and languages, has the second largest population in the world (about a sixth of the world's inhabitants). Nonetheless, following independence, India managed to constitute a parliamentary democracy that has been relatively successful for a developing country (see Kohli 2000). This has been possible thanks, in part, to a national parliament whose members are elected in all the federal states. The best approach to the linguistic problem has proved to be pragmatism, accompanied by a healthy dose of flexibility and tolerance. Unlike in Italy, all attempts to create a unitary language as a means of fortifying national identity have so far failed (see Annamalai 2001). The desire to create an Indian identity on the basis of a common language, Hindi,

---

7 Van Parijs's proposal could be implemented at least in the academic community, where English has asserted itself unequivocally as a lingua franca, and where the most diffused, most read and most cited academic journals are Anglo-American. This offers English native speakers a notable advantage and all the rest a notable disadvantage. By way of compensation, it would not be a bad idea for academics from other countries to ask their privileged native English-speaking colleagues to correct their howlers.

different from that of the old English colonizers – supported by none other than Mohandas Gandhi, among others – has proved to be a factor of division rather than of union. To solve linguistic conflicts, it has thus been established that communication between central government and the single states may be in both Hindi and English. The country currently boasts as many as eighteen official languages, very few compared with the 1,650 languages actually spoken. A system has thus been created in which vernacular languages are used locally, one or other of the official languages is used for the political life of each state and the languages of communication for national politics are, *de facto*, Hindi and English (Chandholke 2005: 44).

A multiculturalist would notice immediately that Indian democracy is limited by the fact that the members of linguistic minorities have no possibility of controlling the acts of parliament and government. In the parliament itself, the variety of different idioms means that there is no certainty that the members of linguistic minorities are able to understand each other. For a multiculturalist, it might have been fitter if, in 1947, India had been separated into twenty independent states instead of just two. This would have allowed each community greater political participation in their vernacular languages, and even though none of the twenty independent states would have been linguistically homogeneous, it would have been possible to protect linguistic minorities by adopting the policies multiculturalists champion in countries such as Canada or Spain.

A cosmopolitan, on the contrary, would see the formation of a great nation in the wake of British colonization as a great advantage for the populations of the geographical area in question. In all likelihood, the formation of a federal state was in fact the best form of protection for the various ethnic, religious and linguistic minorities. Without it, conflicts would have broken out across the Indian peninsula as bloody as the ones that took place in the course of the subdivision of the Indian Union and Pakistan in 1947; nor can we rule out that interstate conflicts would have been generated analogous to those that have dominated African political life over the last sixty years. The fact that everyone can consider themselves Indian irrespective of language has reduced political violence, and the fact that individuals have been allowed to speak their own vernacular language has prevented traumatic changes of identity. Though Indians did not choose their colonizers, the fact that they spoke English rather than Dutch or Portuguese gave India a notable advantage insofar as the country has thus had direct access to the dominant contemporary idiom. Although this has so far favoured elites as opposed to the majority of the population,[8] today

8 Estimates provided by the International Corpus of English indicate that the portion of the Indian population able to speak English varies from 4 per cent to 20 per cent (see http://www.ucl.ac.uk/english-usage/ice/iceind.htm, last accessed January 2007).

suitable education policies are making English a notable competitive advantage for the development of India.

Looking to the future, a multiculturalist would probably seek to increase the number of official languages, and to establish local political autonomy and to preserve and teach the various vernacular languages. This would lead to a greater conservation of local languages but also more difficult economic, social and political integration, at both national and international levels. A cosmopolitan, on the contrary, would tend to invest more in education in English alongside local languages to make English the intra-national and international lingua franca. The consequences would be the opposite of those wished for by multiculturalists: many of the local languages would probably be lost, but India would gain in terms of both national and international integration.

The European Parliament

The European Parliament has twenty-three official languages; the number has increased together with that of the member states of the European Union. *De facto*, the official languages are those of the member states. There are no official languages for sub-state linguistic communities (the most significant claim for recognition being that of Catalan). The Members of Parliament rely on simultaneous translation and documents are translated into all the official languages. As the number of official languages has increased, so the translation procedure has grown more complex: there are currently $23 \times 22 = 506$ possible language communications ('into' and 'from') and finding interpreters capable of translating, for example, from Portuguese into Slovak or Lithuanian into Maltese and vice versa is often impossible, hence the recourse to 'double translations' (for example from Portuguese into French and from French into Slovak). Yet even this vast linguistic 'menu' fails to accommodate all the European languages and – albeit rarely – members of linguistic minorities sometimes speak their own mother tongues.

The problem has become greater with the expansion of member states of the European Union. Of the close on 5,000 employees of the European Parliament, 340 are translators and 238 interpreters, but the multiplication of languages could lead to a doubling of this figure. In a situation of this kind, the problem understandably arises of reducing the number of official languages of the European Parliament, although, politically speaking, it is a thorny one (see Mamadouh 2002; Phillipson 2003; Van Parijs 2007). The advantage would be more effective debating, whereas the disadvantage would be – *de facto* if not *de jure* – the limitation of the passive electorate to elites who speak foreign languages.

The Members of the European Parliament may express themselves in any official language (under article 117 of the Rules of Procedure of the European Parliament), although they generally speak in the language of their country.

Willy Brandt was one of the first Members to make a speech to the Parliament in a language that was not his mother tongue, speaking in English as opposed to German.[9] He opted for self-translation. His choice was justified by the fact that the number of Members who understood English was far higher than that of those who spoke German. The choice was welcomed with warm applause and a few whistles. Multiculturalists would probably have whistled him, since he would have been incomprehensible for electors in his own constituency, who were nevertheless entitled to exercise some control over their elected Member. Brandt also compelled his German colleagues who did not understand English (possibly because they were not members of an elite) to listen to the speech of a fellow countryman in translation. Cosmopolitans would have applauded him warmly, insofar as he was reducing the linguistic distance between Members of Parliament, hence promoting a common language for European politics.

Today, proposals are being made to reduce the official languages to two, three or four, and the organs of the European Parliament have also posed themselves the problem of limiting the extensive use of interpreters and translations. Multiculturalists are probably hostile to these proposals because they would reduce the number of candidates effectively eligible (only citizens with a good knowledge of at least one official language could perform their role as Members). Furthermore, although all parliamentary documents would continue to be available in the twenty-three official languages, there would always be the danger that an assembly working in only a few languages would distance itself from the electorate and ultimately turn into an oligarchy.

The cosmopolitans, on the contrary, believe that communication in one or a few languages would make parliamentary debate more authentic and direct (Van Parijs 2007). They would suggest leaving just two official languages, English and French, and placing all Members on the same plane, asking the English to speak in French and the French to speak in English. They would also point that, albeit elected in one country, Members of the European Parliament have to respond to the population of Europe, not only to their own constituency. Besides, to be able to work well in a legislative assembly it is necessary to be able to speak, informally if need be, with one's colleagues, and to do this it is necessary to have

---

9 For the sake of precision, it is worth adding that, perhaps ignorant of the proposal made 131 years earlier by Michel-Evariste-Népomucène Vincent, the extreme left-wing Italian Member Mario Capanna provocatively made a speech in Latin in the session of 13 November 1979, spreading panic among the interpreters' booths. One of the few Members to understand his speech perfectly was Otto of Hapsburg, a direct descendant of the royal house of the Austro-Hungarian Empire, and an elected Member for the right-wing Catholic Party (CSU) in Bavaria. His family lost Lombardy-Veneto in the 1860s and his Italian was rusty, so he congratulated his colleague in Latin. This was perhaps one of the last occasions in which, albeit at different ends of the political spectrum, European elites communicated in Latin.

knowledge of the most common languages. To avoid being escorted by a squad of interpreters, each Member of the Parliament should be able to communicate with colleagues in a common language. In short, the cosmopolitans would prefer an impoverished but directly understandable language to a myriad of more colourful yet non-accessible languages. A Parliament in which each Member speaks a language incomprehensible to others is not only ridiculous, but also useless.

For linguistic cosmopolitanism

The cosmopolitan position is founded on an assumption that needs to be made clear: namely, that nothing prevents human beings from mastering two or more languages.[10] Recent linguistic research clearly demonstrates that there is no obstacle to children learning two languages[11] and whole countries in the civilized world implement compulsory education programmes to enable students to learn properly not only their own mother tongue but also English. This is not necessarily to the detriment of the vernacular language, whose cultural value may be better understood (as an expression of the variety of humankind) precisely by individuals who speak more than one language. Polyglots are capable of appreciating the value of linguistic diversity much better than the illiterate.

To master a universal language is not to relinquish the language of one's own ethnic group. A more realistic solution than Esperanto was suggested by Aldous Huxley in his novel *Island* (1962), a utopian view of a small community in the Pacific, the imaginary island of Pala, as advanced as it is rooted in its own traditions. This community preserves its own local language, but all its members speak English, and this allows them access to technology, information and culture from the most advanced regions of the world. In the real world, the countries with the highest indices of human development – Norway, Sweden, the Netherlands – are very close to Huxley's ideal.

On a planet on which one-third of the population is still illiterate it is undoubtedly innovative to think in terms of institutionalizing a sort of bilingualism. It comes as a surprise to find out that two-thirds of the planet's inhabitants are already bilingual (Barker and Prys Jones 1998: section 1), but this still fails to

10 Multilingualism as a possible solution is strongly argued both by a multiculturalist such as May (2003) and by a cosmopolitan such as Van Parijs (2005). As far as education is concerned, and irrespective of the polemical fervour that has fuelled the debate so far, it seems possible to say that cosmopolitans want education to be carried out in the language of the majority for everybody and that the language of the minority be taught as a second language, whereas multiculturalists desire the opposite: that is, they want the principal language to be that of each community and the dominant language to be taught as a second language to the minority. See Patten (2003a, 2003b).
11 See Barker and Prys Jones (1998). The same case is argued on the multiculturalist front by May (2003).

bring the peoples of the world together, simply because no universal language of communication exists: in a word, what is lacking is a single language spoken by everyone as a second or third language. Yet, in the course of two or three generations, it may be possible to find a widely diffused linguistic medium. Rather than choose today between vernacular and Esperanto, it might be more useful to support investment in education to allow individuals to increase their language skills.

In India and Europe, multilingualism can already be seen in action (for Europe see Laitin 2000; Mamadouh 2002; Van Parijs 2007; and for India see Annamalai 2001; Chandholke 2005). The British in Europe and Hindis in India are among the privileged who can afford to speak a single language, whereas many others have to speak at least two (English as a lingua franca and their own vernacular language), and others still already speak three (like the Catalans who need to speak Spanish as the dominant language of their state, and English as the dominant European and international language). I do not intend to argue that linguistic access is open to all: as Kymlicka rightly points out, elites are still at an advantage and, in a globalized world, also enjoy a linguistic privilege. It is far too easy to make a society more egalitarian by making polyglots illiterate, but an enlightened social policy ought to attempt to make the illiterate polyglot.

References

Anderson, B. (1991) *Imagined Communities*, London: Verso.

Annamalai, E. (2001) *Managing Multilingualism in India: Political and Linguistic Manifestations*, London: Sage.

Barber, B. (1984) *Strong Democracy: Participatory Politics for a New Age*, Berkeley, CA: University of California Press.

Barker, C. and Prys Jones, S. (eds) (1998) *Encyclopaedia of Bilingualism and Bilingual Education*, Clevedon, PA: Multilingual Matters.

Beetham, D. (2000) *Democracy and Human Rights*, Cambridge: Polity Press.

Castiglione, D. and Longman, C. (eds) (2007) *The Language Question in Europe and Diverse Societies*, Oxford: Hart Publishing.

Chandholke, N. (2005) 'Negotiating linguistic diversity in democracies: a comparative study of the U.S.A. and India', manuscript, University of New Delhi.

Constant, B. (1819) 'The liberty of the ancients compared with that of the moderns', in B. Fontana (ed.) (1998), *Constant: Political Writings*, Cambridge: Cambridge University Press, pp. 308–28.

Crawford, J. (2000) *At War with Diversity: U.S. Language Policy in an Age of Anxiety*, Buffalo, NY: Multilingual Matters.

Crystal, D. (2000) *Language Death*, Cambridge: Cambridge University Press.

Dryzek, J. (2000) *Deliberative Democracy and Beyond: Liberals, Critics, Contestations*, New York: Oxford University Press.

Habermas, J. (1998) *The Inclusion of the Other: Studies in Political Theory*. Cambridge, MA: MIT Press.

Huntington, S. (2004) 'The Hispanic challenge', *Foreign Policy* (March–April), 30–45.

Kelly, P. (ed.) (2002) *Multiculturalism Reconsidered*, Cambridge: Polity Press.

Kohli, A. (ed.) (2000) *The Success of Indian Democracy*, Cambridge: Cambridge University Press.

Kymlicka, W. (1995) *Multicultural Citizenship*, Oxford: Oxford University Press.

Kymlicka, W. (2001) *Politics in the Vernacular*, Oxford: Oxford University Press.

Kymlicka, W. and Patten, A. (eds) (2003) *Language Rights and Political Theory*, Oxford: Oxford University Press.

Laitin, D. (2000) 'What is a language community?', *American Journal of Political Science*, 44(1), 142–55.

Mamadouh, V. (2002) 'Dealing with multilingualism in the European Union: cultural theory rationalities and language policies', *Journal of Comparative Policy Analysis*, 4, 327–45.

May, S. (2003) 'Misconceiving minority language rights: implications for liberal political theory', in W. Kymlicka and A. Patten (eds), *Political Theory and Language Policy*, Oxford: Oxford University Press, pp. 123–52.

Nettle, D. and Romaine, S. (2000) *Vanishing Voices: The Extinction of the World's Languages*, Oxford: Oxford University Press.

Parekh, B. (2002) *Rethinking Multiculturalism: Cultural Diversity and Political Theory*, Cambridge, MA: Harvard University Press.

Patten, A. (2003a) 'What kind of bilingualism?', in W. Kymlicka and A. Patten (eds), *Political Theory and Language Policy*, Oxford: Oxford University Press, pp. 296–321.

Patten, A. (2003b) 'Liberal neutrality and language policy', *Philosophy and Public Affairs*, 31(4), 356–86.

Phillipson, R. (2003) *English-Only Europe? Challenging Language Policy*, London: Routledge.

Pogge, T. (2003) 'Accommodation rights for Hispanics in the United States', in W. Kymlicka and A. Patten (eds), *Political Theory and Language Policy*, Oxford: Oxford University Press, pp. 105–21.

Van Parijs, P. (2003) 'Linguistic justice', in W. Kymlicka and A. Patten (eds), *Political Theory and Language Policy*, Oxford: Oxford University Press, pp. 153–68.

Van Parijs, P. (2007) 'Europe's three language problems', in D. Castiglione and C. Longman (eds), *The Language Question in Europe and Diverse Societies*, Oxford: Hart Publishing.

Young, I. M. (2000) *Inclusion and Democracy*, Oxford: Oxford University Press.

Zamenhof, L.L. (1889) *An Attempt Towards an International Language*, translated by Henry Phillips Jr, New York: H. Holt.

CHAPTER 10

Memories of Europe: Cosmopolitanism and Its Others

Daniel Levy and Natan Sznaider

Cosmopolitanism has recently become a political as well as a sociological topic in relation to the construction of a European identity. However, despite its declarative commitments to openness and diversity, underneath much of this European cosmopolitanism remains a thick veneer of European particularism hiding as universalism. As such, it stands in a long tradition of cosmopolitan thought in Europe, which has its origins with Kant (1795) and other Enlightenment thinkers, and which found renewed ideological and political attention in the aftermath of the Second World War. It is a tradition marked by a strong sense of universal mission that emanates from the centre of Europe and flows outward. Europeanism here essentially refers to a Western European model that took shape during the first post-war decade, in the context of Franco-German reconciliation and shared economic projects, and the emerging Cold War.

Against this narrow cultural, geographical and institutional focus, some theorists have suggested that Europeanization should be studied in a global context and with 'an awareness of the importance of cultural dynamics; the centrality of contestations generated by multiple perspectives on issues central to European transformation' (Delanty and Rumford 2005: 7). Ulrich Beck (2002) has proposed a 'methodological cosmopolitanism' that aims to include the 'otherness of the other', rather than projecting the European experience as a generalized model onto the rest of the world. Most scholars recognize that neither religion and culture nor political and economic integration alone can serve as a unifying foundation for Europeanness, let alone as a basis for 'thick' identification. Instead, much attention has been paid to an emerging set of shared memories, predicated on the need for historical consciousness and suitable for nation-transcending mnemonic practices. Revulsion with the horrors of the Second World War in general and the Holocaust in particular is frequently perceived as the constitutive element for this cosmopolitan outlook (Beck 2005; Fine 2003; Levy and Sznaider 2002). However, as this chapter will illustrate, common references to negative myths of European wars continue to produce a myriad of nation-specific reactions. Notwithstanding, or perhaps precisely because of the persistence of particular memories, universalism remains a salient feature of European cosmopolitanism, even if its proponents explicitly reject the type of homogenizing claims that characterized the Enlightenment thinkers. Our historical analysis exemplifies how a moral universalism continues to emanate from the European model, by generalizing its post-national aspirations and the centrality of human rights legislation as universal features, rather than in relation to particular West European experiences.

The problem with this universalistic account of cosmopolitanism is not only that it carries a Eurocentric bias and that it operates with 'thin' conceptions of identity (Delanty and Rumford 2005): its central shortcoming, politically and analytically, is that it operates with an ahistorical notion of history that seeks to mould particular memories of the past into universal standards for the future. In doing so, not only does it reduce what is essentially an ongoing process of cosmopolitanization to a status of cosmopolitanism (which is conceived as morally superior and legally anchored in human rights legislation) but it also fails to recognize the persistence of particularism and exclusion as central features of Europeanness. This misperception operates on both normative and analytical levels. This account of cosmopolitanism tends to privilege universalism as it emerged in a Western context and project it onto the rest of the world (Chakrabarty 2000). As such, it frequently becomes exclusionary, precisely by paying scant attention to the widespread persistence of particularism.[1]

Addressing some of these limitations, we propose to shift the attention from a normatively driven European cosmopolitanism to a historical–sociological analysis of the cosmopolitanization of Europe. The former is frequently employed in a categorical fashion, rather than in the context of changing cultural conditions and political contingencies. Cosmopolitanism is often perceived in a way that indicates that people have forgotten what the cosmopolitanization process consists of. Here we face the danger of reifying a phenomenon by rendering what is a process into a status (Levy 2004). This kind of process reduction is particularly salient when the deployment of normative terms (such as 'cosmopolitanism') implies the replacement of history with linearity, and the stipulation of a singular (or necessary) path towards development, rather than the coexistence of plural

---

1 These developments are reminiscent of the universalistic assumptions that guided modernization theories during the 1940s and 1950s. There was little (normative and conceptual) space to account for ethnic or religious particularities. They were treated as residual categories, and evidence for backward particularism standing in the way of progress.

forms of Europeanness. One objective of this chapter, then, is to elaborate on the need to historicize developments (of cosmopolitanization), rather than delineate categories (of cosmopolitanism). In contrast to the universalist Enlightenment view of cosmopolitanism, we refer to cosmopolitanization as a process in which universalism and particularism are no longer exclusive 'either/or' categories but instead a coexisting pair. Our historical approach revolves around the dynamic between the two.

In order to understand how the cosmopolitanization of Europe has taken shape, we propose thinking about the balance of universal and particular associations in terms of a 'continuum of changes' (Elias 1992: 46). This notion entails a transformative element, marked by a certain continuity. It suggests that meaningful political–cultural premises are informed by a significant past as well as by a present that is being transformed. On this view, collective modes of identification and the claims that are perceived as legitimate may change over time; however, the respective meanings those claims carry remain linked by a long 'continuum of changes'. Hence the persistence of older structures (e.g. national particularism) cannot be interpreted as a mere anachronism, as some cosmopolitans would have it (Kaldor 1996).

Accordingly, we focus on how the 'continuum of changes' that shapes the features of Europeanness is related to the emergence of cosmopolitan memories.[2] By cosmopolitan memories we are referring to a process that shifts attention away from the territorialized nation state framework that is commonly associated with the notion of collective memory. Rather than presuppose the congruity of nation, territory and polity, cosmopolitan memories are based on and contribute to nation-transcending idioms, spanning territorial and linguistic borders. The conventional concept of collective memory is nationally bounded. We argue that this 'national container' is slowly being cracked. Distinctive national and ethnic memories are not erased but transformed. They continue to exist, but globalization processes also imply that different national memories are subjected to a common patterning. Europeanization develops in accord with common rhythms and periodizations. But in each case, common elements combine with pre-existing idea(l)s to form something new.

More specifically, we are directing attention to a transition from 'history politics' (*Geschichtspolitik*),[3] which is characterized by a state-centric dynamic (through

---

2 For a detailed analysis of the concept of 'cosmopolitan memory' see Levy and Sznaider (2002).

3 Helmut Kohl's chancellorship of West Germany after 1982 provided a public arena for an attempted recovery of memory tropes from the post-war period, a time when the suffering of German victims dominated Germany's memory culture. These memories played an important part in what Kohl termed *Geschichtspolitik* (history politics), best captured in the words of his historical consultant Michael Stürmer, that 'whoever controls images of the past controls the future'.

official commemorations, textbooks etc.), to 'memory history' (*Erinnerungs-geschichte*), which corresponds to the fragmentation of memory and its privatiz-ation.[4] This transformation manifests itself in a changing relationship between memory and history. The difference between memory history and conventional historical narratives is instructive. History is a particularized idea of temporal sequences articulating some form of (national) development. Memory, on the other hand, represents a coexistence of simultaneous phenomena and a multi-tude of pasts. (National) history politics corresponds to the telos of modernity (as a kind of secularized religion, or civic religion). Memory can dissolve this sequence, which is a constitutive part of history. Memory history is a particular mnemonic mode which moves away from a state-supported (and state-supporting) national history.

The previous (attempted) monopoly by the state on the shaping of collective pasts has given way to a fragmentation of memories carried by private, individual, scientific, ethnic, religious and other mnemonic agents. To be sure, the state continues to exercise an important role in how we remember its history, but it is now sharing the field of meaning production with a host of other players. Modes of collective memory are being cosmopolitanized and also exist on supra- and sub-national levels. As we illustrate below, current attempts to Europeanize the memory (and historiography) of expulsions in the twentieth century exemplify this trend (Levy and Sznaider 2005a). The formation of cosmopolitan memories does not eliminate the national perspective, but renders nationhood into one of several options for collective identification. As the state loses its privileged command over the production of collective values (e.g. nationalism), the cosmo-politanization of memory becomes politically and culturally consequential.

'Memory history', then, is a process through which contemporary notions of Europeanness are being articulated and become a self-conscious project. It is, in other words, the kind of global process that Beck (2002) refers to as 'reflexive modernization'. 'As a constructive process, Europeanization can be seen as a form of reflexive creation in which the entire process produces its very own terms' and ... 'Europeanization [is a] particular response to globalization' (Delanty and Rumford 2005: 8, 12). Through memory, a political community validates, challenges and reproduces itself. Studying cosmopolitanized memories provides a diagnostic capacity that allows us to historicize the balance of particular and universal perceptions, rather than stipulate their mutual exclusiveness or a universal trajectory. Our historical analysis reveals how the cosmopolitanization of European memories entails both universalistic dimensions and processes of particularization.

---

4 Our distinction draws on a similar pairing proposed by Dan Diner, who distinguishes between *Erinnerungsgeschichte* (memory history) and *Nationalgeschichte* (national history) (Diner 2003).

The cosmopolitanization of the Holocaust: universal and particular interpretations

The balance of particularism and universal models can be located through the changing significance of Holocaust memories in Europe.[5] The choice of how the Holocaust is being remembered is not arbitrary, but serves as a paradigmatic case for the relation of memory to modernity. Modernity, still the primary analytical and normative framework for intellectual self-understanding, is itself questioned through memories of the Holocaust. It is precisely the abstract nature of 'good and evil' symbolizing the Holocaust that contributes to the cosmopolitanization of memories. Such memories of past injustices serve as a comparative frame of reference, against which the national is being reassessed and against which Europeanization unfolds.

In the past, memories of the Holocaust were organized around a dichotomy of universalism (the idea that it was an assault on humanity) and particularism (the recognition that it was primarily an attempt to exterminate European Jewry). Instead of reducing these terms to their ideological assumptions, we treat them as an important object in our investigation. We historicize notions of particularism and universalism, thereby demoralizing them, while retaining them as valuable sociological tools. Our objective is to disentangle these concepts from their conventional 'either/or' perspective and understand them in terms of 'as well as' options. Cultural and religious particularism can be justified with universal claims of difference, or what Beck (1999) refers to as 'contextual universalism'.

Consequently, speaking about the cosmopolitanization of Holocaust memory does not imply some progressive universalism subject to a unified interpretation. The Holocaust does not become one totallizing signifier containing the same meanings for everyone. Rather, its meanings evolve from the encounter between global interpretations and local sensibilities. The cosmopolitanization of Holocaust memories involves the formation of both nation-specific and nation-transcending commonalities. These cosmopolitanized memories refer to concrete social spaces that are characterized by a high degree of reflexivity and an ongoing encounter with different cultures. On this view, it is no longer the selection but the mutual constitution of particular and universal conceptions that determines the ways in which the Holocaust can be remembered. The cosmopolitanization of memory does not mean the end of national perspectives so much as their transformation into more complex entities, where different social groups have different relations to globalization.

In the following we examine how the balance between universal and particular articulations of Europeanness is shaped in the context of political contingencies

5 For a comparative historical analysis see Levy and Sznaider (2005b).

(domestic as well as exogenous) and historical junctures. While our examples draw primarily on Germany, the Europe-wide significance of Holocaust memories is apparent. The Intergovernmental Conference on the Holocaust that took place in Stockholm in January 2000 and the commemoration of the liberation of Auschwitz on 27 January are but two examples.[6] And in 2005, the United Nations adopted 27 January as an annual international day of commemoration of the Holocaust. Legal and political manifestations of this development are evident when we understand the diffusion of human rights norms during the last six decades as the distillation of changing modes of Holocaust memory (Levy and Sznaider 2004).

Our historical and conceptual point is that the Holocaust has been confronted by various forces, which have attempted to universalize, particularize and nationalize it. Examining this dynamic in the context of distinctive time periods, we demonstrate how post-war universalism is being articulated against the backdrop of Holocaust representations, which leaves little room to acknowledge the particular experience of the extermination of European Jewry. The Holocaust posed a challenge to the universal Enlightenment premises of reason and rationality. Paradoxically, it has functioned simultaneously as the source for a critique of Western universalism and the foundation for a cosmopolitan desire to propagate human rights universally.

The inscription of historical memories has become an integral part of public discourse and memories themselves are subject to self-conscious political appropriations. A central aspect of the politics of memory revolves around controversies about the validity of historical comparisons (Levy 1999). At first sight, comparisons might appear to be a neutral methodological device. However, they also set moral and political standards. Debates about the uniqueness or comparability of a historical phenomenon reveal a contest over whether the nation should articulate itself through universal criteria or a particularistic vocabulary. But there is more at stake. Comparisons can 'normalize' events, so that the significance of comparative historical approaches assumes a moral and political quality.

An important site for the organization of collective memory relates to debates about the perceived victim status of a group. The universal idea of victimhood begins with the idea that modern warfare made everyone victims. It does not matter if you start, win or lose the war, because war is a human tragedy. In the universalized discourse on victimhood, war is seen as a tragedy and as an aberration from the cosmopolitan path to peace. In universalized victimhood, there is no ultimate difference between victors and vanquished – the Second World

---

6 The Stockholm declaration can be found at http://www.Holocaustforum.gov.se (last accessed January 2007).

War made victims of them all – whereas in the consciousness of Jewish victims, there is an essential divide between victims and perpetrators. This duality is echoed in an ongoing historiographical debate about the origins of the Holocaust. One perspective explains the rise of Nazism in terms of Germany's exceptional national development (Eley 2000), whereas the other situates the Holocaust in a broader context of modernity. In this view, Germany ceases to be the exception to the standard path of European national development and becomes instead the exemplification of a common modernity (Bauman 1989). We now turn to a brief historical analysis of how the cosmopolitanization of Europe shapes the balance of universalism and particularism.

Cosmopolitanism and the spirit of Europe

A look at the post-war statements of the German philosopher Karl Jaspers is emblematic for the Eurocentric universalism that characterizes much of the core European post-national discourse of recent years. In the aftermath of the Second World War, Europeanization primarily implied the rebuilding of Western Europe with a pacified Germany in its midst, and the image of the US as a counterweight to Soviet influence in the East. Germany had to be 'Westernized' through its integration into a newly formed interdependent system of Western European states. Intellectual debates in Germany dealing with guilt and responsibility (spearheaded by Jaspers), and issues framed around the realization of Nazi atrocities before and during the war, would become paradigmatic European debates about the guilt of nations in general (Barkan 2000). Between the years 1945 and 1948, Jaspers was one of the most widely recognized thinkers in occupied Germany and the one the Allies trusted the most (Kirkbright 2004). He saw the post-war era (and the Nuremberg trials) as a world that needed to be based upon a universal Kantian cosmopolitanism, a world without 'others' and without borders. Early in 1946 he published a study that would subsequently become one of the foundational documents for the nascent Federal Republic: *Über die Schuldfrage* (*The Question of German Guilt*) sought to refute the notion that Germans were collectively guilty for the committed crimes (Jaspers 1946b). Distinguishing between criminal, political, moral and metaphysical guilt, Jaspers established his view that to condemn a people as a whole violates the claim of being human.[7]

Later in 1946, Jaspers participated in the 'Rencontres International' in Geneva, one of the first meetings of European intellectuals after the war. The theme of the conference, 'The European Spirit', was also the title of Jaspers' lecture. His views

---

7 Jaspers was not the only one to address the question of guilt in Germany, but since it seemed to absolve so many Germans from their collusion with the Nazi regime, the framework put forward by Jaspers would become the dominant trope then and the one remembered today (Olick 2005).

of a new cosmopolitan Europe were based on humanistic values that were found not only in Europe but also in China and India. The origin of such humanist values lay in a period he called the 'Axial Age', the years 800–200 BC. Jaspers viewed the 'Axial Age' as a new European common ground and a launching pad for a new cosmopolitan Europe based on freedom, history and science. He imagined the 'Axial Age' as a useable past for a new Germany and Europe, the latter consisting of references to the Bible, antiquity, Homer and most other iconic figures of European civilization (Jaspers 1946a: 238). At the same time, Jaspers perceived of the US and the USSR as being outside of this European civilization (Jaspers 1946a: 247–48), a theme that seems to unite much of recent core European discourse. Jaspers conceived of cosmopolitan Europe as the political antithesis to a nationalistic Europe, and the physical and moral devastation that had emerged from it. For him, Europe was to become a cultural project and, with it, European values of the Enlightenment were to be saved as well. A new world order would be based not on one super-power but on interdependent states subordinating themselves to core European values. At the same time it would be a religious Europe, not necessarily a Christian one, but one that believed in the transcendence of man, which for Jaspers also entailed a decisive sense of good and evil.

Another participant in these 1946 'Geneva talks', the socialist Hungarian philosopher Georg Lukács, objected to Jaspers' attempt to claim a universal heritage at the expense of socialism by putting it, at least implicitly, on a par with fascism. Lukács attacked Jaspers for his aristocratic and defeatist speech, portraying it as a bankrupt individualism (Kapferer 1993). Instead of the Western European conception propagated by Jaspers, Lukács suggested an alliance of all progressive and democratic forces in Europe with the USSR, which he saw as the embodiment of European democracy (Benda 1946: 211). The parameters of the nascent Cold War, with alternating claims to universalism and along with it the divisions in European memory, were put into play.

Attempts to universalize the experience of the Second World War are also evident in post-war legal deliberations about Nazi war criminals. The Nuremberg War Crimes Tribunal introduced a set of legal precedents addressing violations of human rights, and infringed on the state's sovereignty vis-à-vis its citizens. What today appears as normative was, during and before the trial, a highly charged and contested terrain on which various political and legal forces struggled to impose their vision of justice and international relations. The US understanding of the Holocaust, which framed the Nuremberg trials, was originally universalistic: Nazi war crimes happened to 60 million people, among them 6 million Jews. The crimes against the Jews took up a tiny percentage of the total Nuremberg indictment, and the Jews themselves remained abstract victims. Even though, or perhaps precisely because, the Holocaust and the fate of the Jews remained a neglected aspect of the

Nuremberg trial, they formed the backdrop for its universalistic message. The struggle at Nuremberg was conceived as one between civilization and barbarism. Civilization was the victim, Nazi barbarism the perpetrator. The Jews were there, but they were standing in for 'humanity as a whole'.

The horrors of the Holocaust also formed the background against which human rights norms and a host of United Nations (UN) conventions initially established their legitimacy (Morsink 1999). The Nuremberg trials are remembered for establishing the legal notion of crimes against humanity, thus providing a precedent that has structured public and legal debate about genocide ever since. This understanding was also echoed when the UN declared 'genocide' a crime and asserted that human beings had universal rights. A telling example of how the Holocaust served as the background for the incipient implementation of universal values during the late 1940s, and yet itself was not explicitly referred to, involves the Convention on the Prevention and Punishment of the Crime of Genocide, which was adopted by the UN General Assembly on 9 December 1948. The term 'genocide' was coined in 1946 by Raphael Lemkin, a Polish Jew. No doubt the example of the Holocaust was the trigger for Lemkin's efforts to warn the world about systematic attempts to annihilate specific groups. He justified his project with references to genocidal activities that took place before and after the Holocaust, including references to the population transfers (since the 1990s referred to as 'ethnic cleansing') that were part of Europe's post-war reconfiguration during the 1940s. He was eager, as were so many others, not to present the Holocaust as an exclusive threat to European Jewry:

> The Nazi leaders had stated very bluntly their intent to wipe out the Poles, the Russians; to destroy demographically and culturally the French element in Alsace-Lorraine, the Slavonians in Carniola and Carinthia. They almost achieved their goal in exterminating the Jews and Gypsies in Europe. (Lemkin 1946: 227)

The particular experience of the Holocaust was perceived in the context of the brutality of modern warfare.

Ultimately, it was the memory of the Second World War and not the Holocaust that stood at the centre of both the Nuremberg trials and the nascent idea of a European Community. Today the Nuremberg precedent is largely remembered for its seminal influence on international law and persecutions of 'crimes against humanity'. However, during the Nuremberg trials the primary impulse was to create a legal order that would outlaw 'aggressive' war itself. Article 6a of the Nuremberg charter[8] introduced the notion of crimes against peace, 'namely,

---

8 Formally, the London Charter of the International Military Tribunal, the decree issued on 8 August 1945 that established the procedures for the Nuremberg trials.

planning, preparation, initiation or waging of a war of aggression, or a war in violation of international treaties, agreements or assurances, or participation in a Common Plan or Conspiracy for the accomplishment of any of the foregoing'. Article 6b focused on 'violations of the laws or customs of war'. Much of this was premised on the notion that all nation states would subscribe to the same international premises.

Underlying this vision was not only the creation of a universal jurisdiction but also the idea that economic interdependencies would yield peace and stability. Economic failures preceding the First World War and the hyperinflation that beset the Weimar Republic were perceived as the central reasons for the outbreak of both world wars. It was this premise that drew Germany and France together in their original understandings of a European Community. The lessons of Nuremberg thus contributed to the rescue and reordering of a new (Western) European system of interdependent states (Milward 1992).

Europeanization and the spirit of cosmopolitanism in the post-Cold-War period

The post-war period was followed by a shift away from universal ideologies and towards the individualization of memories in the context of identity politics during the 1970s. The Eichmann trial in Israel serves as a reminder that the Holocaust is a Jewish tragedy. The *Sonderweg* (special path) approach, emphasizing Germany's responsibility for the Second World War and the Holocaust, became the official historical narrative of the Bonn Republic. With the end of the Cold War, these particularized forms of memory are increasingly cosmopolitanized. By the late 1990s, the Holocaust had been reconfigured as a decontextualized event. It is now a concept that has been dislocated from space and time precisely because it can be used to dramatize any act of injustice. This is particularly salient in the context of what can be addressed as a kind of Western European civil religion.[9] We observe a return to the provincializing post-war universalism that pays scant attention to extra-European realities and the political–cultural salience of particularism.

Since the end of the Cold War the Holocaust has become an official part of European memory and is a new founding moment for the idea of a European civilization. The aforementioned commemoration on 27 January, as a reminder of the liberation of Auschwitz, has become the first (official) Western European commemoration of the third millennium. The future of the Holocaust (and not

---

9 This choice of terminology is not merely metaphorical. Alexander (2002) has pointed to the Holocaust as a source of moral universalism.

the past) is now considered in universal terms: it can happen to anyone and at any time, and everyone is responsible. The Holocaust is no longer about the Jews being exterminated by the Germans. Rather, it is about human beings and the most extreme violation of their human rights. The Holocaust is turned into a holocaust and becomes a decontextualized symbol. Genocide, ethnic cleansing and the Holocaust are blurred into an apolitical and ahistorical event circumscribed by human rights as the positive force and nationalism as the negative one.

The end of the Cold War and the aftermath of reunification also compelled Germany to find a new political and cultural place in Europe. It did so by pursuing a dual strategy, centring the Holocaust as an integral part of national history (e.g., the decade-long debate regarding the Memorial to the Murdered Jews of Europe in Berlin) and simultaneously decentring it by turning the Holocaust into a European event (e.g., using it as justification for humanitarian intervention in Kosovo). The Holocaust remains a specific event but also spans a universalizing human rights discourse that conceals the magnitude of the Holocaust as a particular historical occurrence. The Europeanization of the Holocaust in Germany reveals a double bind. On the one hand, memories of the Holocaust remain central to retaining the *Sonderweg* perspective, implying Germany's unique trajectory to and responsibility for the Holocaust. On the other hand, Europeanization serves as a mechanism to depart from this *Sonderweg* and, paradoxically, leads to a renationalization of Germany through the discourse of Europeanization. Those who wish to understand the Holocaust in a comparative perspective often regard the widespread claim of its singularity as constraining the return to a self-confident German nation. The revisionist right seeks to reverse this by situating the German experience in a comparative framework that revives the Cold War vocabulary of totalitarianism, aiming to shift attention from the Holocaust as a unique event that led to the discrediting of the nation of Germany to one amenable to comparisons.

Examining recent political and public debates on how expulsions of ethnic Germans, for instance, are politicized and remembered reveals how comparisons to other incidents of state-sanctioned violence shape the balance of universal and particular modes of commemoration. Expulsions are no longer treated with historical specificity but are being reframed as a universal evil called 'ethnic cleansing'. The new understanding of ethnic cleansing, including Germans as victims and attempts to memorialize their victimhood, is part of that dynamic. Much of this relates to a broader debate about modernity and the idea of the ethnically homogeneous nation state. In this view, the Holocaust loses its German specificity and is reset in the context of modernity. Germany ceases to be the exception to the standard path of European national development, and the

Third Reich is distinctive because of its extremity but is not unique. It is the ethnic nation state that is now perceived as the quintessential evil in history. The Holocaust is subsumed under the broader category of the 'century of expulsions' and, as such, is merely another, even if more extreme, incident of ethnic cleansing or genocide. Here the Second World War becomes an encompassing 'European civil war', a term that ignited the German 'historians' dispute' during the 1980s but that now barely registers as something extraordinary. Depending on the particular political–cultural and geo-political context, Holocaust representations become a source for both cosmopolitan and particularistic national outlooks.

Europeanism and its others

Many of the aforementioned post-war tropes articulated by Karl Jaspers shape contemporary debates about the nature of Europeanness, and influence the precarious balance of universal and particular modes of remembrance. Overall, European cosmopolitanism retains a strong universalistic penchant, but draws on a narrow Western European experience. Jaspers' post-war call for a core Europe propelled by France, Germany and the Benelux countries, the rejection of nation-centric politics, the commitment to spread Enlightenment values, the cultivation of a particular social model and, above all, the 'lessons' of the Second World War circumscribe the contours of this European cosmopolitanism. For the most part, it is still predicated on a sense of universalism and a missionary vision that brackets particularisms by seeking to homogenize what is essentially a Europe of plural and contentious voices.

A telling example of this trajectory is the 'manifesto' Jürgen Habermas and Jacques Derrida published in May of 2003, aimed to consolidate a European public sphere.[10] They write:

> Contemporary Europe has been shaped by the experience of the totalitarian regimes of the twentieth century and by the Holocaust – the persecution and the annihilation of European Jews in which the National Socialist regime made the societies of the conquered countries complicit as well. Self-critical controversies about this past remind us of the moral basis of politics.... A bellicose past once entangled all European nations in bloody conflicts. They drew a conclusion from that military and spiritual mobilization against one another: the imperative of developing new, supranational forms of cooperation after the Second World War. The successful history of the European Union may have confirmed Europeans in their belief that the domestication of state

10 For the manifesto and the ensuing debate see Levy *et al.* (2005). See also Chapter 1 of the present volume.

power demands a mutual limitation of sovereignty, on the global as well as the national-state level. (Habermas and Derrida 2005: 11–12)

The manifesto also invoked the notion of a 'core' Europe, relegating both the UK as well as the countries in the process of joining the EU to a secondary status. Membership, so the argument implied, should primarily rely on secular European Enlightenment values and social democratic traditions. The underlying idea was to generalize the experiences of France, Germany and the Benelux countries and posit them as the standard-bearer for European integration. For Habermas and Derrida:

> [the] EU already offers itself as a form of 'governance beyond the nation state', which could set a precedent in the post-national constellation. And for decades, European social welfare systems served as a model. Certainly, they have now been thrown on the defensive at the level of the national-state. Yet future political efforts at the domestication of global capitalism must not fall below the standards of social justice that they established. If Europe has solved two problems of this magnitude, why shouldn't it issue a further challenge: to defend and promote a cosmopolitan order on the basis of international law, against competing visions? (Habermas and Derrida 2005: 7–8)[11]

However, a closer look shows that much of the post-national universalism that informs this European vision clashes with a polyvocal Europe and cannot be resolved by recourse to 'unity in diversity' slogans. We are not engaging in a substantial argument about the virtues of a specific social model, the historical centrality of the Second World War, the critical assessment of public religiosity[12] or a particular understanding of globalization. The point is that this core European version of cosmopolitanism seeks to flatten the continuous divisions in Europe, rather than acknowledge particular otherness as key features of European diversity. In many ways, as the immediate reactions to the manifesto showed, talk about European integration has become a barometer for disagreement in Europe, especially pertinent in the context of European expansion. Here the divergent

---

11 Parodying this European cosmopolitanism, the Hungarian writer Peter Esterhazy replied to the manifesto. 'Once, I was an Eastern European; then I was promoted to the rank of Central European. Then a few months ago, I became a New European. But before I had the chance to get used to this status – even before I could have even refused it – I have now become a non-Core European. It's like someone who has always lived in Munkács, and has never left Munkács in his entire life and who is, nevertheless, a one-time Hungarian, one-time Czech, one-time citizen of the Soviet Union, then a citizen of the Ukraine. In our town, this is how we become cosmopolitans' (Esterhazy 2005: 74).

12 To quote the manifesto: 'For us, a president who opens his daily business with open prayer, and associates his significant political decisions with a divine mission, is hard to imagine' (Habermas and Derrida 2005: 10).

historical memories of existing (and prospective) EU member states are largely ignored. Faced with this non-recognition, many of the new member states from the East seek to garner legitimacy for their particular experiences and memories. Most notably, they disavow the centrality of the Holocaust at the expense of their own victimhood under Stalin (Judt 2005; Krzeminski 2005a).

This 'clash of memories' is especially marked when we consider how the West perceives the East, how the East looks at how the West views the East, and how the East itself is reconfiguring its historical memories in the context of European integration. Most Western conceptualizations of Europe tend to neglect the contributions of Central, Eastern and non-European pasts (Delanty 2003). Western perceptions of the East at times resonate with an older, Orientalizing discourse, in which the East simply represents the uncivilized other. The German historian Hans-Ulrich Wehler wrote:

> White Russia, the Ukraine ... Moldova, Russia itself, and Turkey in particular have never been part of a historic Europe. They do not live off the legacy of Judaic, Greek or Roman antiquity that is present in Europe to this day. They have not fought their way through the far-reaching separation of state and church, or they even return, as they did after the Bolshevist or Kemalist intermezzo, to a symbiotic relationship between the two. They have not experienced any Reformation and, even more importantly, hardly any Enlightenment. They have produced no European bourgeoisie, no autonomous European bourgeois cities, no European nobility, and no European peasantry. They have not participated in the greatest achievement of European political culture since the late nineteenth century: the construction of the social welfare state. (Wehler 2005: 121)

Less blatant, but in line with a generalized perception of Europe and its civilizing mission, are the post-national visions that characterize the 'core' European states' expectations. 'And the central and eastern European countries, while certainly working hard for their admission into the EU, are nevertheless not yet ready to place limits on the sovereignty that they have so recently regained' (Habermas and Derrida 2005: 5). If Hans Kohn's classical dichotomy of civic Western and primordial Eastern nationalism set the tone for the first half of the twentieth century, a new binary discourse has emerged that celebrates Western post-nationalism and condemns the persistence or return of ethnic, religious and/or national particularism in the East (or anywhere else for that matter).

The civilizational undertones and Western superiority that are common to most of these statements correspond to the heated discussions about and restrictive policies related to European enlargement. Eastern European intellectuals (and politicians) responding to the idea of a 'core' Europe resented both the assumed superiority of the West and the way it perceived (let alone treated) the East. Having to fulfil a long list of political and economic conditions to join the EU, as well as negotiations over full freedom for labour to move across Europe, and the failure of the European constitution in 2005, contributed to a sense of Eastern Europeans being second-class citizens in the European project. Adam Krzeminski, an important public intellectual and publisher in Poland, in an essay entitled 'First Kant, now Habermas', wrote as follows:

> Whereas the USA was organized democratically from the very beginning, Europe seems to maintain its feudal framework. Over centuries, it had been built according to the principle of seniority. And even now, frightened that the barbarians have captured the outer walls of the EU. After all, the economic and spiritual warriors of the Occident are attempting to retreat into the redoubt of 'Core Europe,' probably in the hope that hosts of angels will provide for relief. Politically, they wish to remain among themselves as *'avant-garde'*; economically, they think of tightening the Maastricht criteria for the Euro-zone so that none of the poor can intrude. And finally, the latter are also deliberately excluded from a philosophical dispute concerning Europe's spirit. (Krzeminski 2005b: 147)

This sense of exclusion is also evident in Eastern Europe's looking-glass self, that is, how those in the East think they are perceived by the West. Andrzej Stasiuk, a Polish writer, describing 'the map of the territory of two hundred million future Europeans', writes sarcastically:

> The plan for the coming decades looks more or less like this: the Sinti will arrive with their wagons and will set up camp in the middle of the Champs-Elysées; Bulgarian bears will perform their tricks on Berlin's Kudamm; half-wild Ukrainians will encamp their misogynistic Cossack troops on the plain of the Po before the gates of Milan; drunken Poles rapt in prayer will ravage the vineyards of the Rhine and Mosel and will plant bushes that bear fruit full of pure denatured alcohol and then move on; they will sing their litanies and will not stop until they reach the edge of the continent in the arch-Catholic Santiago de Compostela famous for its miracles. It is difficult to say what the Romanians will do with their millions of sheep. They are a people known especially for their sheep breeding, but also for their unpredictability. Serbs, Croatians and Bosnians will cross the English Channel in Dalmatian dug-out canoes and balkanize Britain, which will finally be divided as God commanded it, into Scotland, England and Wales. (Stasiuk 2005: 103–4)

This caricature is not merely a sardonic comment but also a stark reminder of the salience of 'otherness', along with ethnic, religious and national inflections, complicating cosmopolitan imageries.

Nowhere is this more apparent than in the mnemonic divide that is emblematic for East–West relations and in the fact that the cosmopolitanization of Europe is a work in progress, rather than a progressive vision based on set universalistic principles. In his work on post-war European memory, Tony Judt points out that the Holocaust and the murder of European Jewry play a marginal role in post-communist Eastern Europe, mirroring the bracketing of Jewish victimhood in the post-war period. Much of it is the product of how communist regimes in the post-war era, not unlike their Western counterparts, excluded references to Jews, preferring to remember the Second World War as an epic struggle against fascism.

> There were national categories ('Hungarians') and above all social categories ('workers'), but ethnic and religious tags were studiously avoided. The Second World War was labeled and taught as an anti-fascist war; its racist dimension was ignored ... but if East Europeans paid less attention in retrospect to the plight of the Jews it was not just because they were indifferent at the time or preoccupied with their own survival. It is because the Communists imposed enough suffering and injustice of their own to forge a whole new layer of resentments and memories. (Judt 2005: 823)

State-imposed commemorative practices themselves became the subject of fiery debates in the aftermath of communism, contributing to the renationalization of memories and a challenge to the Holocaust-centric narrative of the West. It was a development compounded by post-communist memories of Stalinism and corresponding forms of *Vergangenheitsbewältigung* (coming to terms with the past). As Judt pointed out, overcoming communism was accomplished by inverting it.

> What had once been official truth was now discredited root and branch – becoming, as it were, officially false. But this sort of taboo-breaking carries its own risks. Before 1989 every anti-Communist had been tarred with the 'Fascist' brush. But if 'anti-Fascism' had been just another Communist lie, it was very tempting now to look with retrospective sympathy and even favor upon *all* hitherto discredited anti-Communists, Fascists included. Nationalist writers of the 1930s returned to fashion. (Judt 2005: 824)

In short, Eastern Europeans have rediscovered long delegitimized forms of nationalism. This renationalization was matched by a growing resentment towards the West for privileging memories of the Holocaust and paying little attention to the suffering in the Stalinist Gulag.

With this post-Communist reordering of memory in Eastern Europe, the taboo on comparing Communism with Nazism began to crumble. Indeed politicians and scholars started to insist upon such comparisons. In the West this juxtaposition remained controversial.... To many Western European intellectuals Communism was a failed variant of a common progressive heritage. But to their Central and East European counterparts it was an all too successful local application of the criminal pathologies of authoritarianism and should be remembered thus. Europe might be united, but European memory remained deeply asymmetrical. (Judt 2005: 826)

This transformation and pluralization of memory regimes renders any singular and unifying notion of European cosmopolitanism highly controversial.

Underlying this debate is a continuous balancing of competing conceptions of victimhood. National memories tend to privilege their own victims. However, owing to the aforementioned transformations, cosmopolitanized memories complicate matters, insofar as they contribute to an emerging duality, because nations have to engage with both their status as victims and their role as perpetrators. Competing conceptions of victimhood are thrust into a dynamic that oscillates between denationalization and renationalization, comparable to the tension between universal human rights and specific privileges. On the one hand, the European gaze rejects clear-cut perpetrator/victim distinctions and any hierarchy of victimhood, and instead stresses the virtues of dialogue among the different parties. On the other hand, it is precisely this absence of a hierarchy of victims that decontextualizes (and at times dehistoricizes) the actual deeds of past injustices. We are not supposed to distinguish between the respective sufferings of groups and every attempt to privilege one group over another is met with strong resistance. Levelling the field of suffering also has unintended consequences, as it challenges existing beliefs about who the perpetrators and who the victims are.

The central problem with this vision is not merely that it limits cosmopolitanism to a particular Western European experience, but that it tends to denigrate the particularism of others in its post-national vision of politics. Despite its declaration to recognize otherness, core European cosmopolitanism is falling back into established patterns of 'othering'. Operating with old antinomies of cosmopolitanism versus nationalism, the aforementioned Eastern European resurgence of national narratives is one relationship onto which core Europeans project this new universalism. As such, an imagined East 'has been cut loose from its geographical point of reference and has become a generalised social marker in European identity formation' (Neumann 1999: 207). And it is not the sole manifestation of alterity that serves as a means for the consolidation of a core European cosmopolitanism.

The aforementioned European values – manifested in the social model, post-nationalism, human rights and limited state sovereignty – have been contrasted with US society (said to be characterized by religiosity, limited welfare and unabashed patriotism) and politics (for example privileging national interest over international law and bellicose policies). The disjuncture between valuable suggestions to theorize Europe in the context of global processes (Beck and Grande 2004; Delanty and Rumford 2005) and the rejection of globalization because of its association with Americanization (Beck *et al.* 2003) could not be starker. Core Europeans continue to 'Orientalize' the other and 'are still caught in the trap of a binary moral geography. To varying degrees, their polarising ideological narrative seeks to freeze authoritatively the meaning of "Europe" by expurgating its Other, which is now "America"' (Heins 2006: 433).

The transatlantic rift as well as the East–West divide are complemented by the widespread rejection of Europe's 'domestic' others, namely its Muslim population. Inverting previous multicultural ideas and policies celebrating particularism, many European states and intellectuals are now frequently rejecting Islamic traditions by portraying them in their most particularistic extremes. Only if we recognize that particular attachments of various sorts remain an integral part of political cultures can we rescue the cosmopolitanization of Europe and a corresponding theoretical toolkit.

We are, of course, aware that all of these developments – European integration, transatlantic relations, multicultural societies – are complex issues that resist easy solutions. It is precisely because of these complexities and the importance of new interdependent figurations that this chapter has taken issue with the universalist fundamentalism that continues to be at the root of (much) cosmopolitan thinking. It is not only analytically misleading, but politically unpersuasive. While the cosmopolitanization of Europe continues to dissolve physical borders, European cosmopolitanism is, if not intentionally then in effect, redrawing moral boundaries.

References

Alexander, J. (2002) 'On the social construction of moral universals: the "Holocaust" from war crime to trauma drama', *European Journal of Social Theory*, 5(1), 5–85.

Barkan, E. (2000) *The Guilt of Nations*, New York: Norton.

Bauman, Z. (1989) *Modernity and the Holocaust*, Ithaca, NY: Cornell University Press.

Beck, U. (1999) *What is Globalization?*, Cambridge: Polity Press.

Beck, U. (2002) 'The cosmopolitan society and its enemies', *Theory, Culture and Society*, 19(1–2), 17–44.

Beck, U. (2005) *Power in the Global Age: A New Global Political Economy*, Cambridge: Polity Press.

Beck, U. and Grande, E. (2004) *Das kosmopolitische Europa*, Frankfurt: Suhrkamp.

Beck, U., Sznaider, N. and Winter, R. (eds) (2003) *Global America: The Cultural Consequences of Globalization*, Liverpool: Liverpool University Press.

Benda, J. (1946) 'L'esprit Européen. Textes des conferences et des entretiens organisés par les Rencontres Internationales de Genève, Neuchâtel: Editions de la Baconnière.

Chakrabarty, D. (2000) *Provincializing Europe: Postcolonial Thought and Historical Difference*, Princeton, NJ: Princeton University Press.

Delanty, G. (2003) 'The making of a post-Western Europe: a civilizational analysis', *Thesis Eleven*, 72, 8–25.

Delanty, G. and Rumford, C. (2005) *Rethinking Europe: Social Theory and the Implications of Europeanization*, London: Routledge.

Diner, D. (2003) *Gedächtniszeiten: Über Jüdische und andere Geschichten*, Munich: Beck.

Eley, G. (ed.) (2000) *The 'Goldhagen Effect': History, Memory, Nazism – Facing the German Past*, Ann Arbor, MI: University of Michigan Press.

Elias, N. (1992) *Time: An Essay*, London: Blackwell.

Esterhazy, P. (2005) 'How big is the European dwarf?', in D. Levy, M. Pensky and J. Torpey (eds), *Old Europe, New Europe, Core Europe: Transatlantic Relations After the Iraq War*, London: Verso, pp. 74–79.

Fine, R. (2003) 'Taking the "ism" out of cosmopolitanism: an essay in reconstruction', *European Journal of Social Theory*, 6(4), 451–70.

Habermas, J. and Derrida, J. (2005) 'February 15, or, what binds Europeans together: please for a common foreign policy, beginning in core Europe', in D. Levy, M. Pensky and J. Torpey (eds), *Old Europe, New Europe, Core Europe: Transatlantic Relations After the Iraq War*, London: Verso, pp. 3–13.

Heins, V. (2006) 'Orientalising America? Continental intellectuals and the search for Europe's identity', *Millennium*, 34(2), 433–48.

Jaspers, K. (1946a) 'Vom Europäischen Geist', in *Rechenschaft und Ausblick. Reden und Aufsätze*, Munich: Piper (1951), pp. 233–64.

Jaspers, K. (1946b) *Über die Schuldfrage*, Munich: Piper (1963).

Judt, T. (2005) *Postwar: A History Europe Since 1945*, New York: Penguin.

Kaldor, M. (1996) 'Cosmopolitanism versus nationalism: the new divide?', in R. Caplan and J. Feffer (eds), *Europe's New Nationalism: States and Minorities in Conflict*, Oxford: Oxford University Press, pp. 42–58.

Kant, I. (1795) *On Perpetual Peace*, Indianapolis, IN: Hackett (1982).

Kapferer, N. (1993) 'Das philosophische Vorspiel zum Kalten Krieg. Die Jaspers-Lukacs Kontroverse in Genf 1946', in *Jahrbuch der Österreichischen Karl-Jaspers Gesellschaft*, vol. 6, Innsbruck: Studien Verlag, pp. 79–106.

Kirkbright, S. (2004) *Karl Jaspers: A Biography. Navigations in Truth*, New Haven, CT: Yale University Press.

Krzeminski, A. (2005a) 'As many wars as nations. The myths and truths of World War II', *Polityka*, 23 March. Available at http://www.signandsight.com/features/96.html (last accessed January 2007).

Krzeminski, A. (2005b) 'First Kant, now Habermas: a Polish perspective on "core" Europe', in D. Levy, M. Pensky and J. Torpey (eds), *Old Europe, New Europe, Core Europe: Transatlantic Relations After the Iraq War*, London: Verso, pp. 146–52.

Lemkin, R. (1946) 'Genocide', *American Scholar*, 15(2), 227–30.

Levy, D. (1999) 'The future of the past: historical disputes and competing memories in Germany and Israel', *History and Theory*, 38(1), 51–66.

Levy, D. (2004) 'The cosmopolitan figuration: historicizing reflexive modernization', in A. Poferl and N. Sznaider (eds), *Ulrich Becks kosmopolitisches Projekt*, Baden-Baden: Nomos Verlagsgesellschaft, pp. 177–87.

Levy, D. and Sznaider, N. (2002) 'Memory unbound: the Holocaust and the formation of cosmopolitan memory', *European Journal of Social Theory*, 5(1), 87–106.

Levy, D. and Sznaider, N. (2004) 'The institutionalization of cosmopolitan morality: the Holocaust and human rights', *Journal of Human Rights*, 3(2), 143–57.

Levy, D. and Sznaider, N. (2005a) 'Memories of universal victimhood: the case of ethnic German expellees', *German Politics and Society*, 23(2), 1–27.

Levy, D. and Sznaider, N. (2005b) *Memory and the Holocaust in a Global Age*, Philadelphia, PA: Temple University Press.

Levy, D., Pensky, M. and Torpey, J. (eds) (2005) *Old Europe, New Europe, Core Europe: Transatlantic Relations After the Iraq War*, London: Verso.

Milward, A. (1992) *The European Rescue of the Nation-State*, Berkeley, CA: University of California Press.

Morsink, J. (1999) *The Universal Declaration of Human Rights: Origins, Drafting, and Intent*, Philadelphia, PA: University of Pennsylvania Press.

Neumann, I. (1999) *Uses of the Other: 'The East' in European Identity Formation*, Manchester: Manchester University Press.

Olick, J. (2005) *In the House of the Hangman: The Agonies of German Defeat, 1943–1949*, Chicago, IL: Chicago University Press.

Stasiuk, A. (2005) 'Wild, cunning, exotic: the East will completely shake up Europe', in D. Levy, M. Pensky and J. Torpey (eds), *Old Europe, New Europe, Core Europe: Transatlantic Relations After the Iraq War*, London: Verso, pp. 103–6.

Wehler, H.-U. (2005) 'Let the United States be strong', in D. Levy, M. Pensky and J. Torpey (eds), *Old Europe, New Europe, Core Europe: Transatlantic Relations After the Iraq War*, London: Verso, pp. 120–27.

Part III
Europe, Trans-nationalism and Cosmopolitan Mobilities

Social Indicators of Cosmopolitanism and Localism in Eastern and Western Europe: An Exploratory Analysis

Victor Roudometof and William Haller

Ever since Beck's (1999) cosmopolitan manifesto, a heated debate has erupted among academics and other intellectuals about the vision for a twenty-first-century society. Thus far, several varieties of cosmopolitan projects have been proposed and each carries with it highly important practical consequences for twenty-first-century Europe. An analysis of the alternative pathways of political, economic and social development and their consequent scenarios for European societies leads Beck (2000) to raise the call 'Cosmopolitans of the world unite!'

While this call is addressed to the 'world', a significant aspect of the emerging literature on cosmopolitanism concerns Europe. Beck (2000) is certainly aware of this geographical dimension of his analysis – for his work is designed to address the possibility that a future united Europe will mirror Brazil or the US, which would encompass the collapse of the welfare state and, indeed, the entire structure of society and lifestyles associated with Europe since the end of the Second World War. Thus conceived, the cosmopolitan project provides an ideological infrastructure for a strategy to construct a Europe that will not be a passive recipient of US-sponsored neo-liberalism. Without being uttered, the cosmopolitan state of the future is the future European state, a state that can exist only by opposing both the influence of US economic liberalism and local 'national' protectionism. 'Nationalism has now become the enemy of Europe's nations', Beck and Giddens (2005) proclaim, in an attempt to convince the European public of the need to find a solution to the impasse brought about in the European scene in the aftermath of the failed referendums on the constitution for the European Union (EU) in France and the Netherlands in 2005.

Attempting to walk the very fine line of populist cosmopolitanism is difficult enough. But to make such an ambition even more problematic there is no specific or uniform definition of cosmopolitanism itself (see Delanty and Rumford 2005;

Featherstone 2002; Rumford 2005; Vertovec and Cohen 2002). Vivienne Boon and Gerard Delanty (Chapter 2 in this volume) distinguish three different avenues for discussing cosmopolitanism: moral cosmopolitanism; political cosmopolitanism or cosmopolitan governance; and cultural cosmopolitanism. Our chapter is an attempt to confront this third aspect of the emerging cosmopolitan agenda.

For social scientists this presents the challenge of unpacking and operationalizing cosmopolitanism as a concept and ensuring it is not confused with other, related concepts. Cultural cosmopolitanism warrants an additional differentiation between observable tendencies on the part of the public, on the one hand, and processes or ongoing trends transforming cultural reality in society at large, on the other. That is, within cultural cosmopolitanism we draw a distinction between: the notion of cosmopolitanism as a frame of mind, manifested in people's attitudes and orientations; and cosmopolitanism as a process or project, or what Beck (2002) refers to as 'cosmopolitanization' (for further discussion see Roudometof 2005a). This chapter is concerned with the first interpretation of cosmopolitanism – the notion of cosmopolitanism as frame of mind, manifested in people's attitudes and orientations. Robbins (1998: 3) refers to this notion as 'actually existing cosmopolitanism' – that is, the *reality* of cosmopolitan attitudes as manifested in people's opinions, attitudes, values and orientation. There has been no attempt before now at empirical – comparative or cross-national – study of this phenomenon reported in the literature.

A conceptualization for cross-national research: data and methods

Living in a trans-national world, individuals can adopt an open, encompassing attitude or a closed, defensive one. In the first case, individuals are labelled *cosmopolitans*, while in the second case they are labelled *locals* (Hannerz 1996). Research on cosmopolitanism has stressed the contextual foundations of the concept and its reliance on a particular setting or locale (see Szerszynski and Urry 2002: 471–73; Urry 2002: 133–38). While the concept can be interpreted in this fashion, it is also true that Hannerz's (1990) stress on situational 'openness' does contain a methodological bias in favour of a 'context', to produce a concept of cosmopolitanism that is capable of producing meaning independently of relations or associations with the 'outside world' (for an alternative formulation, see Merton 1968: 387–420). If it is not to be solely context-bound, 'openness' requires a more rigorous operationalization. In such a case, the features of cosmopolitans and locals are clusters of attitudes or predispositions, rather than sheer contextual or situational 'openness' (see Turner 2002). Underlying this approach is the issue of attachment to specific places, institutions, locales, traditions and so on. Thus, the cosmopolitan (or local) is the person whose attitudes to the world are more (or less) 'open'; that is, she or he is less (or more) bound by territorial attachments and ethnic particularism. The continuum generated by this simultaneous definition of the twin concepts of cosmopolitan and local is what Roudometof (2005a) has referred to as 'the cosmopolitan–local continuum'. Recent research has actually yielded results that suggest that attachment to locality is consequential in terms of openness to outsiders.[1]

The operationalization of these two concepts requires the development of indicators that are capable of measuring the dimensions of the continuum. Roudometof (2005a) has proposed that the dimensions of the cosmopolitan–local continuum take the form of different degrees of attachment to specific locales, countries, local cultures and communities, and, finally, to the 'national economy'. These concepts dovetail nicely with questions included in the National Identity Module of the International Social Survey Programme (ISSP 1995). We therefore used exploratory factor analysis with a broad set of plausible indicators from the National Identity Module of the 1995 ISSP for Eastern and Western European countries to examine whether and to what degree the two ends of this conceptual continuum are present in the attitudes of Western and Eastern Europeans. These indicators are presented in Table 11.1.

Factor analysis determines the extent to which a set of measured variables reflects an underlying factor, or factors. These factors may also be interpreted as latent variables. In the appendix to this chapter, the factor analyses are organized by country and then combined to give aggregate summaries by Western and Eastern European regions. Western Europe is represented by Germany (Eastern and Western presented separately), Austria, Sweden, Norway, Spain, Italy, the UK, Ireland and the Netherlands. Eastern Europe is represented by Russia, Poland, Latvia, Hungary, the Czech Republic, the Slovak Republic, Slovenia and Bulgaria. We acknowledge that presenting the factors by nation state runs the risk of promoting a naïve view of nation states as concrete, discrete entities, as Glick Schiller and Wimmer (2003) state in their critique of methodological nationalism.[2] If the populations within nation states view the nation state as their accepted or natural boundary this is not a problem. However, the sweep of recent

---

1 In his analysis of data from the Australian census, Phillips (2002: 614) found that divergent modes of geographic identification are associated with significantly different levels of acceptance of outsider groups ('locals' were far less accepting). Even Szerszynski and Urry (2002: 469), who advocate a nationalized or context-specific model of cosmopolitanism, admit the presence of the 'thin' or 'cool' version of cosmopolitanism in their research results ('a widespread if rather general cosmopolitanism') (Szerszynski and Urry 2002: 472).

2 'Methodological nationalism is the naturalization of the global regime of nation-states by the social sciences. Scholars who share this intellectual orientation assume that national borders are the natural unit of study, equate society with the nation-state, and conflate national interests with the purposes of social science' (Glick Schiller and Wimmer 2003: 576).

Table 11.1. Indicators of cosmopolitanism/localism from the ISSP 1995

Variable in ISSP*	Indicator
4	How close respondent feels to neighbourhood
5	How close respondent feels to town/city
7	How close respondent feels to country
12	Improve conditions of other countries (*cosmopolitan measure*)
15	Important to be born in respondent's country
16	Important to have citizenship in respondent's country
17	Important to spend most of life in respondent's country
19	Important to be a member of respondent's religion
21	Important to feel a member of respondent's country
22	Rather be a citizen of respondent's country
23	Things about respondent's country to feel ashamed of (*cosmopolitan measure*)
24	World would be a better place if it was more like respondent's country
25	Respondent's country better than others
38	Limit imports of foreign products
39	International bodies should enforce solutions (*cosmopolitan measure*)
40	Schools should teach more foreign languages (*cosmopolitan measure*)
41	Follow own interests even in conflicts
42	Foreigners should not be allowed to buy land
43	Preference for respondent's country's television films and programmes
44	Share traditions; become fully a member

*Only variables conceptually relevant to the cosmopolitan–local continuum are included in the table. The variables' numbers given correspond to the numbers assigned by the ISSP.

and past European history belies this viewpoint. The pace of territorial redistribution among European governments and governing bodies is more appropriately measured in terms of decades, not centuries. Thus, we would prefer to use data with greater geographical detail so that micro-regional differences, or differences between spaces defined for example by linguistic characteristics, could be examined. Nevertheless, the ISSP is organized by nation state and it is therefore impossible to specify more refined sets of geographical units using these data. Although the ISSP data-sets are based on sampling schemes to achieve national representativeness, we still urge caution in interpreting the following analyses, and in particular the avoidance of the ecological fallacy.[3] As a case in point, note

3 According to Babbie (2004: 100), the ecological fallacy is defined as 'erroneously drawing conclusions about individuals based solely on the observation of groups'. For more details, readers unfamiliar with this term can consult the entry 'ecological fallacy' in the online encyclopaedia Wikipedia (http://en.wikipedia.org/wiki/Ecological_fallacy, last accessed January 2007).

the differences in factor loading between the Czech and Slovak Republics in the appendix. But because national identification is addressed by several of the variables we use as potential indicators of localism versus cosmopolitanism it seems appropriate to view popular national identification as an empirical question, even though we take the critique of methodological nationalism seriously.

In the appendix, up to three factors are reported for each country. Consistent with common practice, factors with eigenvalues less than one are not reported. High factor loadings show strong contributions from that particular indicator to the corresponding factor. Thus, indicators that strongly reflect the underlying factor have high loadings.

As can be seen in the appendix, this set of indicators yielded not one but two factors for most of the countries in the analysis. Ireland, the Netherlands and Norway exhibit one factor, while Poland and Russia exhibit three.

Interpretation of factor analyses is always a subjective process. While there is a common convention that factors with eigenvalues less than one should not be regarded as genuinely meaningful, some researchers take exception to applying such an arbitrary rule. Likewise, interpreting how strong factor loadings have to be for an indicator to make a real contribution to a given factor is also subjective. To provide some guideline, the STATA manual states that 'Values over 0.6 are definitely high' (Statacorp 2003: 378). Because variability from country to country is to be expected, and because of the exploratory nature of this research, our view is that imposing any explicit and universal cut-off point for which indicators should be regarded as meaningful is necessarily arbitrary and would stand to conceal more than it reveals.

Results and discussion

Our *a priori* expectation was to find a single factor running along the localism–cosmopolitanism continuum. The fact that our exploratory factor analysis resulted in not one but two factors for most countries (and in Russia and Poland *three* factors) reveals that our theoretical expectations were too simplistic to accommodate the messy realities of these attitudinal configurations. Thus it is appropriate to work inductively, moving from observation to theoretical refinement.

First, a general pattern that holds in the case of most of the Western and Eastern European countries is a relatively high loading of factors for variables 4 and 5, and often also variable 7 (respondent's closeness to neighbourhood, town/city and country, respectively). Thus we do find an underlying factor that reflects attachment to *place* (or lack of it). This is the *place-based variant of localism/cosmopolitanism*. This variant confirms the centrality of these variables as described in the literature (Rosenau 2003; Roudometof 2005a; Turner 2002). Here we might be able to juxtapose locals (those who have high levels of attachment to neighbourhood, city, country) to cosmopolitans (those who have low levels of attachment to neighbourhood, city, country).

Norway, Italy, Ireland and the Netherlands are the only countries in which this factor is not observed. Though this might be expected of the Netherlands, such lack of attachment to place among the other two countries appears to contradict popular stereotypes. Furthermore, some countries have strong negative loadings (for example, Spain, Russia and the Czech Republic). While this finding suggests disenchantment with local identification, it is equally important to stress that in all likelihood this is the result of regional specificity.

Second, there is a factor that consists of variables 15–17 and sometimes 21 (relating to the importance attached to being born in, having citizenship in, spending most of one's life in, and feeling a member of the respondent's country). This factor reflects attachment to specific European national societies or nation states. We use the label of state-centred or *nation-based variant of localism/cosmopolitanism* for it. Its existence complicates the analysis, for, contrary to cultural theorists' predictions, the 'national' does not seem to have faded away, only to be replaced by the 'local' and the 'global'. To make sense of the results, we follow Rosenau's (2003: 81) suggestion and treat national worlds as local phenomena, that is, interpret current forms of attachment to national societies as a reaction to globalization, in the form of an endorsement of the older types of community. In this case, European cosmopolitanism might be viewed as the very antithesis of attachment to European national societies – precisely the interpretation Beck and Giddens (2005) suggest. It is from within these frameworks, then, that we would consider the nation-based variant of localism (nationalism)/cosmopolitanism. It is worth pointing out that in no instance do we see negative loadings on this factor.

Finally, when we compare the aggregate factor loadings of Eastern and Western Europe (see appendix) it is important to recognize that we do not see the place-based variant (variables 4, 5 and 7) when viewing Western Europe as a whole, while it nevertheless remains strong in Eastern Europe (including Eastern Germany) at the aggregate level. Thus, it is possible to generalize that, at least for the mid-1990s – when these data were collected – *Western Europeans did not display a significant attachment to place, while, on the contrary, Eastern Europeans did*. But, contrary to the place-based variant, *the nation-based variant of localism/ cosmopolitanism is present throughout Europe*. In itself, this finding might offer a clue as to why societies that appear to be much more 'open' to the world may also manifest strong forms of exclusionary sentiments (as registered in the failed EU constitutional referendums in the Netherlands and France).

While both place-based and nation-based variants of localism/cosmopolitanism are the focus of the remainder of this chapter, it is important to note that the results do not confirm Roudometof's (2005a) prediction that support for local culture and against or in favour of specific forms of economic, cultural and political protectionism would be able to define 'locals' and 'cosmopolitans'. While some countries – such as the Slovak Republic – show strong support for cultural protectionism (with positive loadings on variables 22, 24, 25, 43 and 44), there is no general pattern that can be observed throughout Europe. Poland also seems to share some of these indicators with the Slovak Republic, except that being a member of one's religion (variable 19) is connected to the Slovakian-like profile of nationalism, while preferring to be a citizen of one's own country seems to be tied to the localism factor. Additionally, with its commonness and high factor loadings, the 'standard' nationalism factor (variables 15–17) appears stronger in Poland than in any of the other countries.

Consequently, support for forms of cultural protectionism can be attributed to regionally specific factors. For example, consider Russia's unique inclusion of limiting imports of foreign products (variable 38). Although this might seem a vestige of nostalgia for the relative security of a state-run economy, it should also be noted that variable 38 appears to be connected with variable 43 (a preference for respondent's own country's television films and programmes). This seems to suggest the possibility that Russian protectionist attitudes are not strictly based on economics but that a cultural component is at work as well. Even in the 1990s, market penetration of Russia by foreign interests was occurring on an unprecedented scale, in combination with a widespread importation of the signs, symbols and icons of global corporate capitalism. Even so, these were hard times for the majority of the Russian population, as the redistribution of economic resources was moving primarily in one direction: upwards. Linkage of distaste for the cultural content of global capitalism with attitudes of economic protectionism should therefore not come as a huge surprise.

Identifying profiles of cosmopolitans and locals

Theoretically, cosmopolitans and locals are defined in terms of clusters of attitudes or predispositions. It is a foregone conclusion that very few would display a complete set of particular characteristics, but what is important is whether such characteristics correlate with each other and whether individual attitudes are indeed clustered around the ideal types at the two ends of the continuum. Because all the relevant questions used in our data for cosmopolitanism/localism follow a Likert format, our method of determining the existence of profiles of cosmopolitans and locals is the following. For each of the variables that make up the two factors, we isolate the cases with the most extreme scores at either end of the response categories of the variables comprising each factor.

For example, for the place-based variant of the continuum, 'local' profile is based on the cases where variables 4, 5 and 7 are all coded 1 (respondent feels 'very close' to neighbourhood, town/city and country), while the 'cosmopolitan' profile is based on respondents who 'do not feel close at all' to any of these places. Hence, from each variable (for example, variable 4) two new variables are created (4L and 4C respectively, for locals and cosmopolitans). If 4C (and 4L) correlates with 5C (5L) and 7C (7L), then individual attitudes are clustered around the two ends of the continuum. It is then possible to suggest that the public's attitudes are polarized, and that the concepts of local and cosmopolitan can be defined cross-nationally, that is, independently of a specific national or regional context. If there is no correlation among 4C, 5C and 7C (or 4L, 5L and 7L), then individual attitudes are not clustered around the two ends of the continuum. In the latter case, there are no consistent cross-national profiles of local and cosmopolitan, and this means that the two terms cannot be meaningfully defined outside a specific context. We apply a similar analysis to the nation-based variant of the continuum.

As Table 11.2 shows, there are correlations between the extreme scores at both ends of the cosmopolitan–local continuum and all correlations are significant at the alpha = 0.001 level. However, the correlations are somewhat higher among those extreme scores that indicate localism. Thus, cosmopolitanism is, as one may reasonably expect, somewhat more diffuse than localism in its concrete manifestations. There is greater heterogeneity among cosmopolitans than among locals.

Table 11.2. Results of the place-based variant of the continuum: correlation of extreme scores for variables 4, 5 and 7

	Cosmopolitanism: ratings on variables of 'Not close at all'				*Localism: ratings on variables of 'Very close'*		
	4C	5C	7C		4L	5L	7L
4C	1.00			4L	1.00		
5C	0.41***	1.00		5L	0.52***	1.00	
7C	0.17***	0.26***	1.00	7L	0.35***	0.42***	1.00

$*p < 0.05, **p < 0.01, ***p < 0.001.$

Within the place-based variant of the continuum, we can make some generalizations about cosmopolitans versus locals on the basis of the information shown in Table 11.3. Locals are far more numerous than cosmopolitans, as can be seen in the relative sample sizes of those indicating that they had strong attachments to their neighbourhoods, towns/cities and countries versus those whose attachments were weak or non-existent. It appears that locals outnumber cosmopolitans by roughly thirty to one across both Western and Eastern Europe.

Cosmopolitans were younger, less likely to be married, better educated, much more likely to be students and more likely to be employed full time than locals, and they were less likely to supervise the work of others. As one might readily expect, cosmopolitans were far more urbanized in their residential patterns than were locals (nearly 76 per urban as opposed to merely 55 per cent). Suburban cosmopolitans, according to our operational definition of the concept, were quite rare indeed (only 3.3 per cent compared with 12.3 per cent, and out of a sample of merely 119 persons as compared with the sample of 3,415 persons for the locals).

Religiosity separates cosmopolitans from locals. There were more atheists and Protestants among cosmopolitans, whereas locals included more Catholics and Orthodox Christians. Similarly, attendance at religious services was less frequent among cosmopolitans than among locals. In particular, 56 per cent of cosmopolitans reported that they never attended religious services, compared with 26 per cent of locals. Only about 14 per cent of cosmopolitans attended religious services once a week or more, compared with nearly 20 per cent of locals. Rates of attendance once or a few times a month were similar but locals attended several times a year or less frequently than yearly at twice the rate of cosmopolitans (approximately 21 per cent as opposed to 10 per cent).

Subjective perceptions of social class were similar between locals and cosmopolitans, except that locals seemed to perceive themselves a little bit higher in social class. Cosmopolitans were less likely to be members of trade unions than locals. With regard to party political affiliation, cosmopolitans tended to be farther to the right and were also more likely to have no affiliations or preferences.

Consistent with the lower marriage rates of cosmopolitans, cosmopolitans lived alone more frequently than locals, but they were less likely to be single parents. However, the pattern of two-parent households may belie expectations: cosmopolitans had higher rates of traditional two-adult households with children (28 per cent versus 20 per cent), while locals were more likely to be in two-adult households without children (26 per cent versus 15 per cent). Because they had fewer children, it is possible that couples who were locals tended to view social change as more threatening and were less open than cosmopolitans to the idea of raising children in a less predictable world. This interpretation is consistent with our theoretical expectation that locals are less open than cosmopolitans to the outside world.

Our next step is to perform the same analysis on the nation-based variant of the cosmopolitan–local continuum. In this case, our strategy is to split the sample, according to variables 15–17, into nation-based cosmopolitans (15C, 16C, 17C)

Table 11.3. Profiles of place-based locals and cosmopolitans

	Locals (n = 3,415)	Cosmopolitans (n = 119)
Demographic characteristics		
Male (%)	46.4	49.2
Ever married (%)	85.5	61.3
Mean age (years)	52	38
Urban/rural residence (suburban includes towns) (%)		
Urban	54.9	75.8
Suburban	12.3	3.3
Rural	32.8	20.9
Years of education (excluding the UK)		
Mean	10.3	13.7
Median	10.0	11.0
Mode	8.0	12.0
Employment (%)		
Full time	35.1	41.3
Part time	4.8	4.2
Unemployed	6.5	8.6
Help family	0.3	0.0
Student	2.9	12.1
Retired	35.6	15.5
Housewife	10.0	9.4
Disabled	3.4	4.1
Not in labour force (excluding disabled)	1.4	4.9
Employment status (%)		
Self-employed	11.6	9.4
Working for someone else	88.4	89.3
Both	0.0	1.3
Work status (%)		
Supervisor	25.5	18.2
Non-supervisor	74.5	81.8
Religion (%)		
Catholic	51.8	30.2
Protestant	11.8	15.7
Orthodox	17.1	5.4
Other Christian	1.5	2.0
Jewish	0.2	0.0
Muslim	2.2	1.9
Atheist	14.5	49.1
Other	0.3	1.0

Religious service attendance (%)

Once a week or more	19.8	14.3
Two to three times per month	7.1	5.2
Once a month	4.7	4.6
Several times a year	21.3	10.0
Less frequently than yearly	20.8	10.4
Never	26.4	55.6

Subjective social class (1 = lower, 2 = working, 3 = lower middle, 4 = middle, 5 = upper middle, 6 = upper)

Mean	2.8	2.7
Median	3.0	2.0
Mode	2.0	2.0
Standard deviation	1.2	1.3

Trade union membership (%)

Member	27.6	21.5
Not a member	72.4	78.5

Party political affiliation (%)

Far left, etc.	7.5	2.2
Left, centre left	27.7	22.1
Centre, liberal	20.1	16.4
Right, conservative	24.9	24.1
Far right, etc.	3.5	5.0
Other, no specific	1.1	5.8
No party, no preference	15.3	24.4

Household (%)

Single-person household	16.4	37.5
Single-parent household	13.5	4.4
Two adults, no child	26.2	15.1
Two adults, with child(ren)	19.8	27.7
Three or more adults, no child	13.4	4.3
Three or more adults, with child(ren)	9.8	6.9
Other	1.1	4.1

Table 11.4. Results of the nation-based variant of the continuum: correlation of extreme scores for variables 15–17

	Cosmopolitanism: ratings on variables of 'Not close at all'				Localism: ratings on variables of 'Very close'		
	15C	16C	17C		15L	16L	17L
15C	1.00			15L	1.00		
16C	0.42***	1.00		16L	0.55***	1.00	
17C	0.38***	0.38***	1.00	17L	0.51***	0.50***	1.00

$*p < 0.05, **p < 0.01, ***p < 0.001.$

Table 11.5. Profiles of nation-based locals and cosmopolitans

	Locals *(n = 5,355)*	*Cosmopolitans* *(n = 367)*
Demographic characteristics		
Male (%)	46.1	53.7
Ever married (%)	83.3	70.9
Mean age (years)	50	40
Urban/rural residence (suburban includes towns) (%)		
Urban	51.0	61.8
Suburban	10.4	10.6
Rural	38.6	27.6
Years of education (excluding the UK)		
Mean	12.0	15.9
Median	10.0	12.0
Mode	8.0	12.0
Employment (%)		
Full time	37.0	54.1
Part time	6.0	11.1
Unemployed	7.2	7.4
Help family	0.3	0.9
Student	2.9	8.1
Retired	31.2	9.5
Housewife	10.7	6.2
Disabled	3.3	0.6
Not in labour force (excluding disabled)	1.3	2.1
Employment status (%)		
Self-employed	12.7	8.7
Working for someone else	87.2	91.0
Both	0.1	0.04
Work status (%)		
Supervisor	27.1	35.6
Non-supervisor	72.9	64.4
Religion (%)		
Catholic	50.5	33.0
Protestant	19.9	17.3
Orthodox	10.2	7.1
Other Christian	1.3	2.1
Jewish	0.1	0.0
Muslim	0.6	0.7
Atheist	16.9	37.8
Other	0.3	1.1

Religious service attendance (%)		
Once a week or more	23.2	8.1
Two to three times per month	7.6	5.0
Once a month	4.5	3.8
Several times a year	18.6	12.2
Less frequently than yearly	21.3	23.6
Never	24.9	47.3
Subjective social class (1 = lower, 2 = working, 3 = lower middle, 4 = middle, 5 = upper middle, 6 = upper)		
Mean	3.0	3.3
Median	3.0	4.0
Mode	2.0	4.0
Standard deviation	1.2	1.2
Trade union membership (%)		
Member	32.1	34.9
Not a member	67.9	65.1
Party political affiliation (%)		
Far left, etc.	5.9	10.6
Left, centre left	28.7	36.9
Centre, liberal	19.6	14.4
Right, conservative	26.5	23.2
Far right, etc.	3.2	4.9
Other, no specific	1.2	1.6
No party, no preference	14.8	8.4
Household (%)		
Single-person household	16.9	17.9
Single-parent household	9.0	17.0
Two adults, no child	28.5	13.6
Two adults, with child(ren)	21.2	31.2
Three or more adults, no child	12.9	7.4
Three or more adults, with child(ren)	10.9	11.5
Other	0.5	0.5

and nation-based locals (15L, 16L, 17L), and to determine whether correlations exist within each group. The results are shown in Table 11.4. Just as with the place-based variant of the continuum, significant correlations are located among the set responses most associated with identification with country (nationalism) and among those with the least such identification. Just like the place-based cosmopolitans, nation-based cosmopolitans are a more diffuse, varied group than the nation-based locals. Another similarity, observed in Table 11.5, is that nation-based locals are far more common than the corresponding cosmopolitans on the nationally oriented continuum (at a rate of approximately fifteen to one).

The profiles of the nation-based cosmopolitans and locals are shown in Table 11.5. Nation-based locals were less likely to be male, more likely to be married and more likely to be a bit older than those who reported no such attachments. Their corresponding cosmopolitans tend to be somewhat more likely to live in cities but equally likely to live in suburbs. As with the cosmopolitans derived from the place-based continuum, educational attainment was higher among these cosmopolitans. The mean of nearly 16 years versus merely 12 years shows that pursuit of higher education has a significant effect in ameliorating feelings of nationalistic attachment. This is further supported by median values of 12 versus 10 years of education, and modal values of 12 versus only 8 years of education.

These cosmopolitans were more likely to be employed either full time or part time or to be students, and were less likely to be retired or to be housewives or disabled. They were also less likely to be self-employed than nation-based locals but were more likely to supervise the work of others. Just as with the place-based locals and cosmopolitans, religiosity separates nation-based locals from cosmopolitans. Nation-based locals were more likely to be Catholic and Orthodox and much less likely to be atheists. Differences in religious service attendance were also apparent. Approximately three times as many nation-based locals attended religious services once a week or more (23 per cent) than their corresponding cosmopolitans (8 per cent) and only a quarter of nation-based locals reported that they never attended church while nearly half of these cosmopolitans said they never attended.

The nation-based cosmopolitans tended to rate their social class membership a bit higher than nation-based locals, an important difference from place-based locals and cosmopolitans. The mean difference of 3.3 versus 3.0 (with medians of 4 versus 3, and modal responses of 4 versus 2) may not appear so great but this must be viewed in the wider research context that nearly everyone in modern industrial societies rate themselves as middle class. Trade union membership was marginally higher among nation-based cosmopolitans and, whereas those who were place-based cosmopolitans were skewed to the right politically, those who were nation-based cosmopolitans were skewed to the left (although they also appeared to include more people on the far right than did nation-based locals). The proportion of nation-based locals stating no party and no political preference was also somewhat higher (15 per cent) than the proportion among nation-based cosmopolitans (8 per cent).

Regarding household composition, nation-based locals were less likely to be parents than their cosmopolitan counterparts (both singly and in couples). Single-parent households among nation-based locals ran at a rate of only 9 per cent, whereas among their cosmopolitan counterparts the rate was 17 per cent. Two-parent households had a prevalence of 31 per cent among nation-based cosmopolitans as opposed to 21 per cent among nation-based locals. And the dual-income no-child category was twice as large among nation-based locals as among cosmopolitans (29 per cent as opposed to just 14 per cent).

Conclusion

In this chapter, we sought to uncover the extent to which cosmopolitan and local attitudes among the European public display uniformity across national contexts. We also pursued a strategy of testing a minimalist definition of cosmopolitanism and localism, basically as a function of attachment. Our central finding is that the simultaneous definition of cosmopolitans and locals as those who are more or less 'bound' to place and nation produces clusters of people that are observed cross-nationally. Therefore, the cosmopolitan–local continuum does provide a valid and meaningful analytical framework for these twin concepts. Past discussion of these concepts in the literature has been based on theory and speculation. The work presented here shows evidence of these concepts among the opinions and attitudes of ordinary people within national populations. Further research on these concepts on a cross-national basis is required because our exploratory analysis has not addressed the critical issue of European regional specificity (for example in comparison with US or Asian contexts). In any event, the results of this research offer some empirical basis for further regional or national studies of cosmopolitanism and localism.

Contrary to our expectations, we uncovered two different variants of the cosmopolitan–local continuum, a placed-based variant and a nation-based variant. We also determined that support for or opposition to strategies of cultural, economic and political protectionism is not a valid indicator for either localism or cosmopolitanism. On the contrary, it is likely that this type of support is the result of complex interactions among local and global forces.

The existence of two distinct variants of the cosmopolitan–local continuum suggests that our theories have to differentiate between 'openness' with regard to place and the declining significance of the nation state as a reference point for the European public. Western Europeans appear more 'open' in terms of place, but – as events concerning the EU constitution and Turkey's bid for EU membership illustrate – that does not necessarily make them less attached to their nation state or less willing to attribute great importance to a person's membership of their own national society. In terms of political leanings, place-based and nation-based locals and cosmopolitans display markedly different profiles. For example, the place-based cosmopolitans lean more towards the right than do place-based locals, while the nation-based cosmopolitans lean more towards the left (or centre left) than the nation-based locals. Religion emerges as a key variable that separates locals from cosmopolitans in both variants. This feature suggests that a unifying factor for both variants of locals and cosmopolitans is their attitudes regarding secularization. Normative cosmopolitanism is a profoundly secular orientation – it might even be suggested that it represents a vision for addressing the dilemmas of globality in a manner that mirrors the religious responses to globality (see Roudometof 2005b). Moreover, in both variants locals are far more numerous than cosmopolitans.

Our results have corroborated other survey data (reported by Delanty and Rumford 2005: 73) that point out the limited nature of post-national or pan-European identification. It is fair to say that the cosmopolitan agenda as championed by Beck and Giddens (2005) requires further revisions in order to specify both the meaning of normative or ethical cosmopolitanism and the public that is the carrier of such a normative ideal. Perhaps many academics have been too willing to accept that the declining significance of 'place' will carry with it repercussions for the nation state. But our results suggest that this is not the case. On the contrary, we find two types of cosmopolitans, those on a place-based and those on a nation-based continuum with locals. These two types may overlap to some extent, but not completely. The assumption that one is going to lead to the other is not valid and our theories need to develop the required complexity to address this divergence. In terms of developing a European cosmopolitanism, or a pan-European ideology that would prevent Europe from turning into another 'Guatemala' (Eco 2005) it is fair to say that the majority of the European public remains steadfastly localist – and, more importantly, it is only the cosmopolitans along the nation-based continuum who can be the motor of such a pan-European cosmopolitanism. If, indeed, 'nationalism is now the enemy of Europe's nations', as Beck and Giddens (2005) argue, then the future of Europe is rather bleak. We hope, however, that such inferences are more hyperbole than substance and that any implications for Europe's future will be mild in comparison with those suggested by Europe's past.

Cosmopolitans on the place-based continuum might be predisposed to a different agenda, an agenda that views the EU as a new North American Free Trade Agreement or perhaps as something else that needs to be imagined. Delanty and Rumford (2005: 23), for example, propose that we 'conceive of European identity as a cosmopolitan identity embodied in the pluralized cultural models of a societal identity, rather than as a supra-national identity or an official EU identity that is in a relation of tension with national identities'. Given the results presented in this chapter, this suggestion may actually be the *only* viable strategy for making empirically and meaningfully connections between cosmopolitanism and a European identity. Place-based cosmopolitans and locals certainly can be viewed along these lines, especially in terms of the varied degrees of attachment to town, region and nation state. This type of cosmopolitanism is certainly a 'thin' – as opposed to a 'thick' – form of attachment, but 'this does not preclude the possibility of viable "thin" kinds of loyalty to emerge in European public discourse' (Delanty and Rumford 2005: 85).

References

Babbie, E. (2004) *The Practice of Social Research* (10th edition), Belmont, CA: Wadsworth/ Thompson Learning.

Beck, U. (1999) *World Risk Society*, Malden, MA: Polity Press.

Beck, U. (2000) *The Brave New World of Work*, Cambridge: Polity Press.

Beck, U. (2002) 'The cosmopolitan society and its enemies', *Theory, Culture and Society*, 19(1–2), 17–44.

Beck, U. and Giddens, A. (2005) 'Nationalism has now become the enemy of Europe's nations', *The Guardian*, 4 October.

Delanty, G. and Rumford, C. (2005) *Rethinking Europe: Social Theory and the Implications of Europeanization*, London: Routledge.

Eco, U. (2005) 'An uncertain Europe between rebirth and decline', in D. Levy, M. Pensky and J. Tropey (eds), *Old Europe, New Europe, Core Europe: Transatlantic Relations After the Iraq War*, London: Verso, pp. 14–20.

Featherstone, M. (ed.) (2002) *Cosmopolis*, Durham, NC: Duke University Press (special issue, *Theory, Culture and Society*, 19(1–2)).

Glick Schiller, N. and Wimmer, A. (2003) 'Methodological nationalism, the social sciences and the study of migration: an essay in historical epistemology', *International Migration Review*, 37(3), 576–610.

Hannerz, U. (1990) 'Cosmopolitans and locals in world culture', in M. Featherstone (ed.), *Global Culture: Nationalism, Globalisation, and Modernity*, London: Sage, pp. 237–52.

Hannerz, U. (1996) *Transnational Connections: Culture, People, Places*, London: Routledge.

ISSP (International Social Survey Programme) (1995) *National Identity Codebook*, Kohl: Zentralarchiv für Emporische Sozialforschung.

Merton, R. (1968) *Social Theory and Social Structure*, New York: Free Press.

Phillips, T. (2002) 'Imagined communities and self-identity: an exploratory quantitative study', *Sociology*, 36(3), 597–617.

Robbins, B. (1998) 'Introduction. Part I: Actually existing cosmopolitanism', in P. Cheah and B. Robbins (eds), *Cosmopolitics: Thinking and Feeling Beyond the Nation*, Minneapolis, MN: University of Minnesota Press, pp. 1–19.

Rosenau, J. N. (2003) *Distant Proximities: Dynamics Beyond Globalisation*, Princeton, NJ: Princeton University Press.

Roudometof, V. (2005a) 'Transnationalism, cosmopolitanism and glocalization', *Current Sociology*, 53(1), 113–35.

Roudometof, V. (2005b) 'Morality and globality: a comparison of secular and religious globalization projects', presented to the 2005 annual meeting of the American Sociological Association, Philadelphia, PA.

Rumford, C. (ed.) (2005) *Cosmopolitanism and Europe*, London: Taylor and Francis (special issue, *Innovation: The European Journal of Social Science Research*, 18(1)).

Statacorp (2003) *Stata Statistical Software: Release 8*, College Station, TX: StataCorp LP.

Szerszynski, B. and Urry, J. (2002) 'Cultures of cosmopolitanism', *Sociological Review*, 50(4), 461–81.

Tomlinson, J. (1999) *Globalisation and Culture*, Chicago, IL: University of Chicago Press.

Turner, B. S. (2002) 'Cosmopolitan virtue, globalisation and patriotism', *Theory, Culture and Society*, 19(1–2), 45–63.

Urry, J. (2002) *Global Complexity*, Cambridge: Polity Press.

Vertovec, S. and Cohen, R. (eds) (2002) *Conceiving Cosmopolitanism: Theory, Context, Practice*, Oxford: Oxford University Press.

Appendix. Results of the factor analysis of the ISSP (1995) results

Note that higher values indicate greater cosmopolitanism. Variables marked * are reverse coded for consistency. The factor numbers (1, 2 and 3) refer to the rank-order strength of each factor, as indicated by their respective eigenvalues.

Country	Variable																				Eigen-value
	4	5	7	12*	15	16	17	19	21	22	23*	24	25	38	39*	40*	41	42	43	44	
Western Germany																					
Factor 1	0.315	0.361	0.546	0.551	0.652	0.663	0.595	0.488	0.588	0.722	0.274	0.628	0.560	0.484	0.100	0.130	0.495	0.658	0.641	0.662	5.724
Factor 2	0.645	0.616	0.220	0.165	-0.042	-0.077	-0.030	0.113	-0.050	0.021	-0.070	-0.175	-0.079	-0.068	-0.063	-0.173	-0.133	-0.166	-0.054	-0.208	1.067
Eastern Germany																					
Factor 1	0.345	0.313	0.500	0.452	0.648	0.602	0.628	0.406	0.559	0.701	0.192	0.669	0.624	0.479	0.077	0.094	0.582	0.539	0.503	0.548	5.072
Factor 2	0.580	0.591	0.510	0.293	-0.134	0.008	-0.070	-0.046	0.115	0.140	-0.219	-0.303	-0.177	-0.184	-0.035	-0.168	-0.284	-0.201	-0.025	-0.084	1.453
Austria																					
Factor 1	0.539	0.523	0.591	0.575	0.605	0.655	0.714	0.520	0.623	0.615	0.273	0.515	0.448	0.427	-0.019	-0.013	0.380	0.489	0.486	0.470	5.148
Factor 2	-0.545	-0.602	-0.290	-0.066	0.199	0.042	0.021	0.129	-0.031	-0.048	0.038	0.151	0.106	0.241	-0.001	-0.110	0.235	0.224	0.168	0.246	1.109
Sweden																					
Factor 1	0.190	0.150	0.215	0.422	0.660	0.489	0.605	0.485	0.401	0.541	0.170	0.588	0.517	0.516	0.013	0.142	0.442	0.465	0.394	0.551	3.811
Factor 2	0.602	0.623	0.403	0.120	-0.199	0.018	-0.162	-0.094	0.042	0.209	-0.078	-0.121	0.024	-0.057	-0.112	-0.048	-0.038	-0.058	-0.057	-0.063	1.100
Norway																					
Factor 1	0.310	0.320	0.465	0.559	0.612	0.524	0.599	0.531	0.394	0.664	0.112	0.555	0.492	0.484	0.154	0.199	0.387	0.504	0.276	0.522	4.226
Spain																					
Factor 1	0.403	0.425	0.643	0.223	0.764	0.769	0.627	0.483	0.650	0.532	0.196	0.511	0.531	0.191	0.048	-0.012	0.180	0.206	0.399	0.242	4.228
Factor 2	-0.544	-0.585	-0.237	-0.092	0.053	0.045	0.079	0.159	0.035	0.036	-0.184	0.270	0.212	0.171	-0.093	0.087	0.236	0.283	0.042	0.155	1.101
Italy																					
Factor 1	0.316	0.309	0.306	0.429	0.603	0.576	0.557	0.540	0.434	0.598	0.078	0.584	0.487	0.333	0.030	0.036	0.308	0.403	0.407	0.262	3.504
Factor 2	-0.130	-0.199	-0.229	-0.062	-0.246	-0.346	-0.239	0.020	-0.347	0.077	-0.070	0.270	0.117	0.255	0.160	0.163	0.315	0.435	0.304	0.280	1.145
UK																					
Factor 1	0.324	0.304	0.387	0.396	0.642	0.576	0.610	0.540	0.552	0.641	0.125	0.648	0.620	0.417	0.114	0.019	0.443	0.525	0.425	0.461	4.501
Factor 2	0.481	0.562	0.419	0.048	-0.020	0.132	0.009	0.063	0.152	0.054	0.150	-0.093	-0.033	-0.338	0.057	-0.154	-0.259	-0.380	-0.214	-0.271	1.276

Victor Roudometof & William Haller

Appendix continued

Country	4	5	7	12*	15	16	17	19	21	22	23*	24	25	38	39*	40*	41	42	43	44	Eigen-value
Ireland																					
Factor 1	0.398	0.383	0.403	0.412	0.593	0.608	0.623	0.536	0.509	0.555	0.020	0.413	0.431	0.337	0.006	0.017	0.304	0.318	0.399	0.314	3.522
Netherlands																					
Factor 1	0.261	0.193	0.287	0.330	0.633	0.566	0.571	0.363	0.373	0.619	-0.227	0.493	0.382	0.430	0.055	-0.038	0.411	0.476	0.446	0.554	3.529
Russia																					
Factor 1	0.456	0.412	0.336	0.356	0.479	0.405	0.429	0.323	0.250	0.508	-0.163	0.392	0.416	0.506	0.011	0.150	0.299	0.406	0.495	0.314	2.849
Factor 2	0.332	0.381	0.159	-0.145	0.327	0.336	0.276	0.074	0.087	-0.018	0.055	-0.174	-0.289	-0.324	0.064	0.031	-0.317	-0.286	-0.280	0.102	1.143
Factor 3	-0.407	-0.525	-0.346	-0.051	0.327	0.298	0.366	0.196	0.079	-0.023	0.056	0.009	-0.052	-0.048	-0.023	-0.021	0.010	0.060	-0.046	0.259	1.020
Poland																					
Factor 1	0.488	0.389	0.409	0.309	0.608	0.637	0.538	0.609	0.192	0.612	0.016	0.541	0.620	0.254	0.011	-0.017	0.233	0.283	0.463	0.347	3.711
Factor 2	0.464	0.514	0.431	0.313	-0.413	-0.367	-0.293	-0.126	-0.027	0.138	-0.019	-0.098	-0.045	0.053	-0.081	-0.119	0.016	0.043	0.000	-0.024	1.229
Factor 3	-0.096	-0.181	-0.187	-0.108	-0.265	-0.311	-0.324	0.130	-0.370	-0.100	0.062	0.415	0.308	0.200	-0.009	0.109	0.304	0.243	0.306	0.196	1.129
Latvia																					
Factor 1	0.170	0.217	0.293	0.318	0.525	0.568	0.446	0.410	0.369	0.488	0.054	0.400	0.384	0.419	-0.134	-0.087	0.388	0.346	0.469	0.555	2.915
Factor 2	0.554	0.660	0.483	0.233	-0.339	-0.307	-0.229	-0.158	0.054	-0.024	-0.114	-0.132	-0.056	0.037	-0.115	-0.173	0.070	0.115	-0.010	0.057	1.420
Hungary																					
Factor 1	0.438	0.440	0.378	0.427	0.519	0.610	0.565	0.436	0.159	0.558	0.118	0.447	0.514	0.315	-0.182	0.039	0.274	0.313	0.396	0.335	3.251
Factor 2	0.524	0.570	0.347	0.291	-0.316	0.343	-0.243	0.228	0.005	0.234	0.049	-0.110	-0.092	-0.078	0.119	0.048	-0.175	-0.053	-0.064	-0.093	1.280
Czech Republic																					
Factor 1	0.375	0.342	0.368	0.480	0.653	0.680	0.658	0.287	0.497	0.652	-0.030	0.393	0.485	0.383	0.001	-0.012	0.205	0.207	0.426	0.314	3.600
Factor 2	-0.385	-0.549	-0.387	-0.189	0.115	0.039	0.072	0.104	-0.135	-0.076	-0.194	0.177	0.198	0.273	0.065	0.122	0.249	0.213	0.181	0.181	1.065
Slovak Republic																					
Factor 1	0.462	0.412	0.620	0.559	0.439	0.471	0.544	0.315	0.433	0.737	0.257	0.526	0.577	0.437	0.134	0.159	0.345	0.241	0.572	0.607	4.404
Factor 2	-0.488	-0.550	-0.218	-0.133	-0.095	-0.072	-0.045	0.078	-0.028	0.002	0.085	0.317	0.303	0.092	0.085	0.198	0.269	0.024	0.197	0.148	1.016

Appendix *continued*

Country	| Variable																				Eigen-value
	4	5	7	12*	15	16	17	19	21	22	23*	24	25	38	39*	40*	41	42	43	44	
Slovenia																					
Factor 1	0.436	0.370	0.356	0.399	0.601	0.517	0.520	0.505	0.370	0.594	0.112	0.581	0.529	0.421	-0.109	-0.129	0.408	0.317	0.438	0.410	3.719
Factor 2	0.498	0.608	0.279	0.165	-0.281	-0.280	-0.302	-0.131	-0.139	0.016	0.062	0.018	0.120	-0.028	0.064	0.054	-0.009	-0.032	-0.031	-0.138	1.060
Bulgaria																					
Factor 1	0.519	0.514	0.559	0.519	0.459	0.522	0.488	0.400	0.319	0.605	0.232	0.449	0.530	0.382	-0.037	0.040	0.362	0.312	0.577	0.390	3.864
Factor 2	-0.429	-0.405	-0.164	-0.183	0.450	0.416	0.385	0.245	0.201	-0.042	-0.053	-0.118	-0.079	-0.089	-0.096	0.010	-0.089	-0.066	0.031	0.107	1.099
Western Europe																					
Factor 1	0.340	0.339	0.414	0.430	0.655	0.587	0.621	0.545	0.487	0.624	0.029	0.573	0.492	0.454	0.053	-0.074	0.421	0.455	0.475	0.366	4.197
Eastern Europe																					
Factor 1	0.428	0.406	0.444	0.368	0.548	0.504	0.532	0.471	0.376	0.609	0.100	0.485	0.526	0.436	-0.059	0.016	0.405	0.366	0.502	0.462	3.731
Factor 2	0.536	0.609	0.362	0.177	-0.189	-0.140	-0.150	-0.172	0.016	0.053	0.077	-0.149	-0.139	-0.080	0.030	-0.024	-0.189	-0.085	-0.122	-0.135	1.062
All countries pooled																					
Factor 1	0.390	0.388	0.442	0.415	0.609	0.536	0.592	0.518	0.467	0.625	0.028	0.506	0.444	0.464	-0.012	-0.098	0.404	0.441	0.507	0.408	4.018

CHAPTER 12

Cosmopolitanism, Collective Belonging and the Borders of the European Union

Maria Rovisco[1]

Cosmopolitan ideas and sensibilities offer a valuable response to the demands of managing increasing cultural diversity in the European Union (EU). The great challenge for the 'new Europe' is how to deal with the stranger, the foreign and our sense of the otherness of the other. In a more culturally diverse EU, this involves the ways in which people interact and engage with established immigrant communities and people with non-European backgrounds in the political space of the EU. Furthermore, if we agree that electronic media facilitate the creation of trans-national representations and the imagination of trans-national spaces, how much and how easily Europeans engage with images, symbols and narratives about cultures and values deemed non-European are questions of the foremost importance for the accomplishment of a truly cosmopolitan Europe. Arguably, then, cosmopolitan attitudes and dispositions open up the prospect of cultural change within an enlarged EU. Some recent literature on cosmopolitanism emphasizes cosmopolitanism as an ethos of 'solidarity among strangers', which is consistent with the view of Europe as a space of open cultural boundaries.

I shall argue in this chapter that while cosmopolitan ideas and principles – such as peace, social justice, human rights, tolerance and social solidarity – thrive as distinctively European qualities, racism, xenophobia and intolerance are viewed as polluting elements (see Douglas 1966) and a threat against which European societies must be defended. I will do so by critically engaging with the report *The Spiritual and Cultural Dimension of Europe – Concluding Remarks* published by the European Commission (Biedenkopf *et al.* 2004). I shall explore the implications of

1 I would like to thank Chris Rumford for his helpful comments and suggestions on previous versions of this chapter. I am also grateful to Magdalena Nowicka for her comments on an earlier draft. The research was funded by a grant (SFRH/BPD/14522/2003) awarded by the Fundação para a Ciência e Tecnologia (Portugal).

the new idea of Europe for questions of space and identity in the context of recent EU enlargements. I will first discuss how cosmopolitan ideas and sensibilities are being nurtured to convey the view of Europe as a space of tolerance and inclusion. I will then show how cosmopolitan ideas and values are being used to further a European polity. Finally, I will demonstrate that the logic of openness underlying the narrative of Europe as a space of tolerance and inclusion conflicts with the narrative of Europe as a space of peace and security, which defines new boundaries of exclusion. More generally, my aim is to show how the Commission's 2004 report reflects a struggle over the meaning of Europe in view of the novel demands of EU enlargement and the growing cultural diversity within the EU.

Europe, cultural diversity and cosmopolitan solidarity

Social theorists such as Beck (2002a, 2002b), Turner (2002a) and Habermas (2001) have suggested that the idea of cosmopolitan solidarity, as a form of 'solidarity among strangers', is gaining significance in the contemporary world. For Beck, 'in the second age of modernity, therefore, the question to be asked is not how to revive solidarity, but how *solidarity with strangers*, among non-equals can be made possible' (Beck 2002b: 75, emphasis added). Habermas raises a similar question:

> precisely the artificial conditions in which national consciousness arose argue against the defeatist assumption that a form of civic *solidarity among strangers* can only be generated within the confines of the nation. If this form of collective identity was due to a highly abstractive leap from the local and dynastic to the national and then to democratic consciousness, why shouldn't this learning process be able to continue? (Habermas 2001: 102, emphasis added)

The possibility of 'solidarity among strangers' is seen as an upshot of the process of individualization, which is characteristic of our contemporary condition. Individualization suggests that the individual, in becoming increasingly reflexive, is able to design and shape the course of his or her own autobiography (Beck 2002a; Giddens 1991; Stevenson 2002). In the literature, this cultural process is understood as a *sine qua non* for the emergence of cosmopolitan solidarity. The boundaries of nation states are becoming increasingly porous in a world where mobility and globalization, in its multiple manifestations, expose individuals to a whole new set of experiences and 'other' peoples, cultures and values. The alleged decline of communal solidarities based on face-to-face relationships, and the loosening of social bonds, in particular those tied to ascriptive categories of race or nationality, open up the prospect for cosmopolitan solidarity – a form of solidarity capable of connecting individuals, both mentally and experientially, to far-flung places and local cultures. That is to say, people are more and more able to develop cosmopolitan sensibilities, which are generally manifested in a willingness to comprehend and embrace otherness. This proclivity is stronger in a world of increasingly interconnected political communities (Held 2002) and where individuals embody complex repertoires of allegiance, identity and interest in multiple cultural and political contexts (Vertovec and Cohen 2002). Individualization implies flexible lifestyle choices of the 'disembedded' individual and these choices are profoundly open to the influence of the other, both 'here' and 'there'. Attachments to the local are compatible with cosmopolitan dispositions and find expression, for instance, in the notion of 'rooted cosmopolitanism' (Beck 2003), a perspective which opposes the parochialism of exclusive localism (Calhoun 2002). There is here a sense that neither localism nor nationalism constitutes an obstacle to the cosmopolitan's willingness to get to know and embrace other peoples and their cultures. For Turner (2002a), cosmopolitan dispositions appeal to 'thin' collective attachments, based on an ironic detachment from one's own local or national culture.

This cosmopolitan outlook resonates with the approach of the EU's governments and institutions to questions of culture and identity in the European space, particularly in view of the challenges posed by enlargement. In redefining its concrete outer borders through the process of enlargement, the EU has been also compelled to reconsider its own cultural boundaries, that is, the idea of a European cultural space. In public discourse, particularly at the level of EU rhetoric, the narrative of Europe as a space of common cultural roots and core values is being abandoned in favour of a conception of Europe based upon a commitment to cosmopolitan values and ideas of peace, human rights, social justice and social solidarity.[2] This is, in part, a response to the need to encourage greater conviviality and solidarity among 'traditional' European peoples and the 'newcomers', those Eastern European peoples who have recently joined the EU, within a more multicultural and multi-ethnic EU. But the framing of cosmopolitan values and principles as universal (i.e. not uniquely European) is also part of an attempt to redefine Europe's position in the world within a normative framework that is embedded in European experiences and traditions of trade and law (Therborn 2002). In this context, the consolidation of a European public sphere is seen as a crucial step towards an emergent global civil society constituted by various social movements, communication networks and informal organizations that aim to build a 'better world' (Habermas 2001).

2 There is evidence of this cosmopolitan view of Europe in the report considered at length later in this chapter (Biedenkopf *et al*. 2004), as well as in the report *Building a Political Europe: 50 Proposals for Tomorrow's Europe* (Strauss-Kahn 2004).

The new idea of Europe: *The Spiritual and Cultural Dimension of Europe*

The new idea of Europe is readily apparent in the report by Biedenkopf, Geremek and Michalski *The Spiritual and Cultural Dimension of Europe – Concluding Remarks* (Biedenkopf *et al.* 2004; referred to hereafter simply as 'the report'). This was drafted by a reflection group set up by the then President of the European Commission, Romano Prodi, to discuss the cultural dimension of the EU in the process of enlargement.[3] The group consisted of independent academics, intellectuals and politicians from several EU member states. The report, which explicitly states that it does not necessarily reflect the views of the European Commission, was also published in several daily newspapers in various EU countries.

By drawing on the tools of cultural sociology (Alexander 2003), I will argue here that, in the discourse of Europe, cosmopolitan ideas and values have recently emerged as a symbol of Europeanness to answer the demands of a more culturally and ethnically diverse EU. In contrast, racism, xenophobia and, more generally, an unwillingness to engage with other cultures and values emerge as its negative opposites. Europe is discursively constructed around a complex set of symbolic codes, themselves structured around the binary forms of the sacred and the profane, which possess mutually exclusive opposing qualities (Alexander and Smith 1993). It is implied here that even societies and peoples (e.g. the French, British, Italians) who have been symbolically represented as quintessentially European embody negative, profane or polluting elements, in relation to which Europeans must be protected. The widely accessible symbolic patterns or codes through which individuals more or less consciously interpret 'what is Europe' are embedded in a variety of public narratives, rituals and images (Geertz 1973). Competing claims about the meaning of Europe linger in public narratives and are powerfully shaped by the concrete historical, organizational and institutional settings in which they are formulated, articulated and enforced. Ultimately, the discourse of Europe is constituted by a set of logically arranged symbols, which provide a vocabulary, a universe of shared understandings, which people selectively use to make sense of Europe. Furthermore, just as the idea of Europe has been translated, through history, into different cultural configurations (e.g. medieval Europe, Christian Europe, Oceanic Europe), so there have been many

---

3 It is useful to distinguish here between 'Europe' and the 'European Union', even though the two notions are often conflated in EU public documentation (Sassatelli 2002: 446). Europe is an idea, a symbolic construct, which has persisted through time and over space, and which has assumed distinct cultural configurations. The EU is an instance of supranational governance, which currently includes twenty-seven member states under the umbrella of four main institutions: the European Commission, the Council of Europe, the European Parliament and the European Court of Justice. The EU is also a political project – initiated by the 1992 Maastricht Treaty – devised to create a European polity which emphasizes a shared democratic political culture while fostering new forms of collective belonging and civic participation.

different ways of relating to it, depending on particular political and historical circumstances (Kumar 2003a).

Europe as a space of tolerance and inclusion: building European solidarity

The narrative of Europe as a space of tolerance and inclusion is predicated on the development of European solidarity. This is required to bring Europeans together, so as to enable greater social cohesion and a shared political culture within the EU. Cosmopolitanism, conceived as a form of solidarity among strangers, is here captured in the notion of European solidarity. Against the backdrop of EU enlargement, the report appeals for European solidarity so that Europeans, irrespective of their particularistic identities, will be able to develop solidaristic ties with fellow EU citizens, as well as with individuals from non-European countries. One can thus have a strong sense of national identity and still be open to engage with the stranger, the foreign. This new kind of solidarity, while sensitive to collective identities, such as those drawn along the lines of religion or the nation, nurtures conviviality and mutuality among both EU citizens and people of non-European background. This notion of solidarity resonates with Habermas's theorization of solidarity as an ethical principle with universal validity, which centres on reciprocal concern for one another.[4] This concern with the welfare of others is part of an intersubjective way of life (*Lebensform*), with the implication of reciprocity (Stjernø 2005: 302). In this sense, European solidarity comes close to the idea of cosmopolitan solidarity among strangers, as it facilitates mutual understanding between geographically and socially 'distant' groups and individuals. Reciprocal engagement with others in public is itself a form of social solidarity, as communication in the public sphere also informs the sharing of social imaginaries (Calhoun 2003: 259).

The notion of 'stranger' involves here a notion of 'other', whose presence invokes sympathy and hospitality and emphasizes alterity beyond sameness (Kearney 2002; see also Derrida 2001). As suggested by Amin (2004: 3), 'empathy/engagement with the stranger could become the essence of what it is to be "European"'. Cosmopolitan solidarity among strangers posits encounters between different world views, lifestyles and contrasting value systems within and beyond the social space of the EU. In this sense, trans-national affiliations and identities are facilitated not only by geographical mobility and new migration patterns but also by people's increasing exposure, via the mass media, to non-Western values, images and narratives. New forms of collective belonging make it easy to accept

4 Note that, in the context of European political affairs, the notion of solidarity is often used in a rather more restricted sense, to refer to specific social policies designed to reduce inequalities between different EU member states or social groups. This is usually a top-down and technocratic approach to solidarity. See Calhoun (2003: 274).

perceived cultural differences between self and other, 'us' and 'them', while fostering new modes of dealing with otherness.

Interestingly, the report does not explicitly refer to Europeans as cosmopolitans (this is in fact generally the case in EU public documentation – see Rumford 2005 and also Chapter 1 of the present volume). This may be explained in part by the fact that cosmopolitanism, in being commonly associated with an allegiance to universally grounded values regardless of any particularistic attachments, could be seen as hindering the EU's efforts to foster a sense of Europeanness among EU citizens while preserving a desirable cultural diversity across discrete nation states. As clearly stated in the report: 'the common European cultural space cannot be defined in opposition to national cultures. Polish farmers and British workers should not see "European culture" as something foreign or even threatening' (Biedenkopf *et al.* 2004: 9). Arguably, then, the nation state is too important as a cultural referent and a form of collective self-understanding for the report – again, drawn under the auspices of the President of the European Commission – to consider Europeans as cosmopolitans holding multiple thin and cool loyalties.

Yet it is hard to deny that globalization involves an increasing mobility of individuals, ideas, narratives, images and symbols, which 'travel' irrespectively of territorial boundaries. Hence, in a world where social distance is becoming less conceived as physical distance (Shamir 2005: 200), the phenomena of globalization and Europeanization bring new dangers and opportunities, cultural change and contestation, into the political space of the EU. On the one hand, European solidarity can be seen as an opportunity to further a European citizenship and new ways of feeling European; on the other, intolerance and xenophobia arising from the social nearness of the 'other' constitute 'polluting' elements, dangers, which EU institutions, governments and citizens must resist to be able to live in a 'new Europe' that is more culturally diverse.

It is important to note that the narrative of Europe as a space of inclusion and tolerance does not necessarily correspond to an extant empirical reality. It is, rather, a cultural form, a new cultural idea, which aims to explain new ways of being European. As such, it competes with the narrative of Europe as a space of peace and security, which, as we shall see, tells a very different story about this new Europe.

The vast majority of these new EU citizens, many of whom endured decades of subjugation to Communist regimes, hold thoughts and values indelibly marked by experiences unfamiliar to long-time EU citizens.... If the countries of Europe are to grow together into a viable political union, the people of Europe must be prepared for a European solidarity.... European solidarity – the readiness to open one's wallet and to commit one's life to others because they, too, are Europeans – is not something that can be imposed from above. It must be more than institutional solidarity. It must be felt by Europeans as individuals. (Biedenkopf *et al.* 2004: 5, 10)

European solidarity is adamantly opposed to the view of Europe as a self-contained space grounded in common cultural roots and essential European values. Its underlying foundation is a European cultural space of open and negotiable boundaries: 'the common European cultural space cannot be firmly defined and delimited; its borders are necessarily open, not because of our ignorance, but in principle – because European culture, indeed Europe itself, is not a "fact". It is a task and a process' (Biedenkopf *et al.* 2004: 8).

The vision of Europe as a space of open cultural boundaries comes close to Habermas's conception of an expanding European public sphere with a shared and homogeneous political culture (Habermas 2001). However, unlike Habermas and, more generally, the advocates of a European citizenship founded on shared political rights and duties, the report goes on to define the 'European cultural space' as a 'community of values' that offers the basis for a truly European solidarity. This view of Europe appeals to a recognition of difference (Honneth 1996) across Europe's diverse communities while emphasizing the ever-changing character of European culture. It follows that aspects of cultural diversity, such as ethno-cultural elements, have to be reconciled with demands for greater political and social cohesion within the EU. The narrative of Europe as a space of tolerance and inclusion reflects, to a great degree, the cultural relativism of some recent approaches to cultural diversity and the idea that the unity of Europe derives from its diversity (Delanty 2003a). But, more importantly, the report explicitly sets out to oppose the idea of a market-based Europe, which is now seen as a 'polluting' element, as it recognizably fails to fulfil universal ideals of social justice, social solidarity and peace:

The original expectation, that the political unity of the EU would be a consequence of the European common market has proven to be illusory. Indeed, the current debate over the reform of the Union's Growth and Stability Pact shows once again that economic integration … can only continue as the basis of Europe's peaceful order if it is followed by a deeper political integration within the Union.… So Europe's political union demands political cohesion, a politically grounded community bound by the ties of solidarity. (Biedenkopf *et al.* 2004: 6–7)

What is being contested in this narrative of Europe is the metaphor of the 'space economy', which conveys the idea of a European space with thick outer boundaries and based on the notion of a legally regulated market with a common currency (Entrikin 2003: 58). This finds expression, for instance, in the notion of the Single Market and, arguably, also in unfair trade agreements imposed on developing countries, which contribute to growing world poverty and inequality. This self-limited space of highly porous internal boundaries is ultimately embodied in the individualistic ethos of the 'citizen consumer', who holds thin collective attachments and freely chooses where to purchase, live and work.

In contrast, Europe conceived – both internally and externally – as a space of open cultural boundaries emerges as a space where individuals are able to develop cosmopolitan sensibilities and dispositions in the process of engaging with others. This conception of Europe as a space able to accommodate increasing cultural diversity prepares the ground for envisaging the EU as an emerging cosmopolitan political order. Here, individuals would be morally, and increasingly legally, bound to universally grounded values of peace, equality and human rights, rather than to the imperatives of the market or of the rational individual. Not surprisingly, the emergence of a European civil society is seen as crucial for the development of European solidarity, which is expected to foster people's active involvement in issues of European governance.

Strikingly, Europe, in being discursively constructed as a 'community of values' and a 'common cultural space', is conceptualized in the absence of any essential European values; no list or catalogue of European values can be defined *a priori* because Europe, as a cultural space, is being permanently redesigned in view of new cultural and political demands. There is here a rejection of Europe as an expression of cultural unity built upon a common European heritage and core values. This view converges, to some degree, with some scholarship sustaining the idea of Europe as an open, discursive form (Malmborg and Stråth 2001; Stråth 2002). Here, Europe is seen as a pure invention, a discourse open to multiple meanings and conflicting claims, which draws on symbols and narratives from diverse philosophical and religious traditions for specific political and ideological purposes. Europe is thus refracted within different traditions of national imagination and in concrete historical settings, drawing on a variety of ideas, values and traditions.

> What is European culture? What is Europe? These are questions that must be constantly posed anew. So long as Europe is of the present, and not simply the past, they can never be conclusively answered. Europe's identity is something that must be negotiated by its peoples and institutions. Europeans can and must adapt themselves and their institutions, so that European values, traditions, and conceptions of life can live on and be effective. (Biedenkopf *et al.* 2004: 8)

What is implied in the new idea of Europe is some notion of cultural change that is missing from earlier interpretations of Europe: individuals and institutions are now expected to change and adapt to the shifting social and political conditions of an expanding EU. It is interesting, moreover, that the report lacks an account of *how* and *where* people find the cultural resources, if not the European values, they require to engage with this new kind of solidarity (i.e. European solidarity). The narrative of Europe as a space of tolerance and inclusion is imbued with a 'presentist spirit' that appears to ignore the fact that Europe, as a public narrative, can be largely understood in terms of earlier temporal and spatial manifestations, which give it the status of a historical as well as of a cultural object (cf. Somers 1995: 237). In fact, it remains remarkably indifferent to the way collective memories shape a sense of shared pasts by providing a narrative frame, that is, stories which help individuals to make sense of who they are and where they come from. Such narratives are passed on, and transformed generationally, through traditions, rituals, ceremonies, films, novels and public performances (Connerton 1989; Eyerman 2004; Halbwachs 1992). Collective memories therefore play an important role in the constitution of the collective identities of ethnic groups and national communities. In this context, it is feasible to argue that European experiences and memories also help individuals to make sense of themselves as being Europeans, or not. Representations of Europe are part of the collective imaginary of many generations of people who have learnt to think of themselves as being Europeans. There is, indeed, a universe of collectively shared meanings about Europe which is powerfully shaped by different traditions of national imagination, education systems, the mass media, oral traditions and post-colonial world views, which both enable and constrain people's understanding of 'what Europe is' and of where it starts and ends. That is, the possibility of dialogical understanding and conviviality among 'old' EU citizens, the EU 'newcomers' and non-EU citizens, in the current historical circumstances, depends on diverse, and often conflicting, cultural understandings of Europe. Levy and Sznaider (2002) have argued, for instance, that the Holocaust provides the foundations for a new cosmopolitan memory, which is also a European memory transcending ethnic and national boundaries, based on a mutual recognition of the history of the other (see also Chapter 10).

A European solidarity within a more culturally diverse EU could, then, benefit from people's ability to remember, and to learn, how the history of European peoples and nation states is entangled with the history of other peoples and civilizations (Delanty 2003b; Eisenstadt 2001; Therborn 2002).

The EU as a cosmopolitan project

The development of a global legal order came to be seen as the institutional embodiment of cosmopolitan ideas and values as well as the expression of a universal political consensus (Archibugi *et al.* 1998; Beck 2002a). Some aspects of this legal cosmopolitanism are already visible in the conversion of human rights conventions into international laws, and in the implementation of international criminal tribunals to stop humanitarian crises and crimes against humanity (Fine and Chernilo 2004).

The idea of a cosmopolitan legal order enforced by international law is consistent with the political project of the EU. This can already be found in the outlines of an emerging supranational public sphere embedded in a shared political culture enforced by European integration. As a communicative network, this European-wide public sphere is based on a civil society that consists of different interest groups, non-governmental organizations and private initiatives (Llobera 2003: 167). EU institutions seek to uphold a robust European public sphere by encouraging deliberative procedures, so that Europeans become more deeply involved in processes of decision-making in EU affairs. This stance is, for instance, clearly apparent in the 2001 white paper on European governance, which explicitly suggests that democracy depends on people being able to take part in public debate (European Commission 2001).

Surprisingly, cosmopolitanism is not part of the self-identity of the EU and there is in fact no mention of Europeans as cosmopolitans in EU public documentation (see Chapter 1). Yet EU institutions have been, more or less explicitly, making use of cosmopolitan ideas to further the EU as an instance of supranational governance (Rumford 2005). This is particularly apparent in the way EU institutions and governments have grounded the idea of a European polity in universal ideals of peace, human rights and democracy.

The 2000 EU Charter of Fundamental Rights[5] is the most explicit commitment to a rights-based political union founded on the universal values of democracy and human rights (Eriksen 2004). Interestingly, the Charter protects the rights of Europeans not as national citizens but as individuals and, as such, it shifts the responsibility from the polity to the person (see Berezin 2003: 23–24). Thus the EU, in being portrayed as a supranational polity, can hardly be thought of as resting on thick loyalties to place, ethnicity or territory. As an instance of supranational governance, the EU has been conceived as a homogeneous social space of the public sphere, a space which emphasizes common citizenship and equally shared duties and responsibilities (Entrikin 2003: 60–61). This civic view of the European space resonates with Habermas's views on European citizenship. For Habermas (2001: 99), there is an emerging Europe-wide civil society, which is fostered by a legally constructed cosmopolitan solidarity, which is in turn based upon the moral universalism of human rights and is supported by supranational institutions. The underlying assumption here is that although collective

---

5 Available at http://www.europarl.europa.eu/charter/default_en.htm (last accessed January 2007).

identities constitute an important source of collective self-understanding and civic solidarity at the level of the nation state, they are not expected to constitute an obstacle to an expanding European public sphere founded on the deliberative procedures of communicative rationality. In this context, cultural and political boundaries are seen as largely permeable and even transient. The emergence of 'cosmopolitan consciousness' across European societies will progressively encourage the expansion of the European public sphere until this embraces the 'world society' of individual citizens (Habermas 2001: 112). The report endorses such a view:

> To the extent that Europe acknowledges the values inherent in the rules that constitute the European identity, those very same values will make it impossible for Europeans not to acknowledge the duty of solidarity toward non-Europeans. This globally defined solidarity imposes on Europe an obligation to contribute, in accordance with its ability, to the securing of world peace and the fight against poverty. But despite this global calling there can be no justification for attempting to impose, perhaps with the help of the institutions of a common European foreign and defence policy, any specific catalogue of values on other peoples. (Biedenkopf *et al.* 2004: 12)

The new cultural idea of Europe – embedded in the narratives of Europe as a space of inclusion and tolerance and Europe as a space of peace and security – sets out to define a normative framework based upon the human rights regime. In fact, since the nineteenth century the idea of human rights has provided the meta-narrative for a better Europe; now, however, the notion has been extended to the status of an ethic of global responsibility (Eder and Giesen 2001: 258). With its cosmopolitan underpinnings, the global human rights narrative developed from European traditions of trade and law (Therborn 2002; see also Pagden 2003). Not surprisingly, the report calls for more political legitimacy at the supranational level of governance, so that the EU will be able to answer the challenges of the global order and thus seek to assure the accomplishment of equality and peace on a worldwide scale.

Europe as a space of peace and security: new boundaries of exclusion

The European project – which started with the 1957 Treaty of Rome – represents, to a great degree, an answer to the atrocities of the Second World War and the experiences of totalitarianism embodied by fascism and communism. As a political project, the EU aims to achieve a 'lasting European peace', which has to be preserved in opposition to the continent's past of war, division and conflict.

The principle of peace is part of Europe's self-understanding – 'Europe sees itself as a zone of peace and a community of values' (Biedenkopf *et al.* 2004: 12) – and as such it has, paradoxically, helped to create new boundaries of exclusion. EU governments and some popular media attempt to justify the exclusion from the EU political space of particular social categories (e.g. illegal immigrants, asylum seekers, low-skilled immigrants, some Muslims) by invoking the narrative of Europe as a space of peace and security. The underlying assumption here is the need to protect an allegedly peaceful and secure European space from infiltration by particular social groups deemed dangerous (cf. Shamir 2005). The metaphor of 'fortress Europe' does justice to the attempts of EU institutions and national governments to harden and close the EU's outer boundaries in the process of dealing with the fear of the 'other' (Zielonka 2003).

> The Union also needs freedom of political action because it confronts a myriad of new tasks: overcoming the consequences of Europe's aging population; managing, both politically and legally, the desire of people from around the globe to immigrate into the Union; dealing with the increasing inequality that is the direct result of increased immigration as well as the Union's expansion; preserving peace in a globalised world. (Biedenkopf *et al.* 2004: 7–8)

The narrative of Europe as a space of peace and security is thus animated by a logic of closure of the European space, but this is not consistent with the narrative of Europe as a space of tolerance and inclusion. While the logic of closure underlying the design of immigration policies and the negotiation of the accession terms to the EU defines new boundaries of exclusion, the logic of 'opening' that underlies the idea of the 'European cultural space' calls for more 'open' and inclusive cultural communities within the EU. Hence, under the logic of closure of the European space, the prospective immigrant and the asylum seeker embody the figure of the 'alien' – a stranger associated with suspicion, discrimination and scapegoating (Kearney 2002) – who is symbolically constituted as a 'problem'. This needs to be politically managed so as to avoid conflict and xenophobia arising from the dangers of increasing social nearness. It is implied here that only by regulating immigration flows into the EU – by deciding who is worthy or not worthy of working and living within the EU – does it become possible to assure a more peaceful, equal and secure EU. In contrast, the idea of the 'European cultural space' is predicated on the development of cosmopolitan sensibilities and dispositions so as to assure peaceful relations and mutuality among EU citizens and non-EU citizens. Here, under the logic of opening the European space, the immigrant symbolizes the figure of the 'other' – who invokes sympathy and hospitality (Kearney 2002) – and constitutes an opportunity for intercultural understanding and social cohesion while taming, for example, the dangers of xenophobia and virulent nationalism.

The fall of communism, the attacks on the US on 11 September 2001 and the subsequent 'war on terror' intensified old and new divisions in the international arena, which affected the relations between EU member states, the US and other parts of the world, especially the Islamic world (see Turner 2002b; Wallace 2001). As noted by Turner (2002b: 109), 'Islam, and in particular fundamentalist Islam, has been constructed as the unambiguous enemy of western civilization'. Islam is increasingly associated with global terrorism while ethnic and ideological concerns are woven together to create an even more powerful image of the 'enemy' (Shamir 2005: 202). In this context, a new interpretation of Europe's 'others' took shape in public narratives of Europe and started to crystallize in the public imaginary.

It is important to note that the forces of globalization and Europeanization, which set the stage for the consolidation of European solidarity, are also at the heart of populist and xenophobic responses to immigration and the process of European integration, as these forces have ultimately resulted in a reassertion of the national (Berezin 2003). Racism and xenophobia are becoming widespread European phenomena, which find renewed expression in cultural fundamentalism (Stolke 1995) and fears pertaining to 'mixed loyalties'. In Amin's words, 'the new phenomenon expresses anxieties about the negative implications – both for "us" and "them" – of "having them in our midst"' (Amin 2004: 12). This is the case in a time when new right-wing parties as well as some elements within the popular press and television fuel fears of social unrest provoked by permissive immigration policies. Many Europeans appear to experience a feeling of being 'swamped' by people from non-European countries, even though official figures show that the numbers of immigrants and asylum seekers are actually declining in some European countries,[6] as a result of more restrictive policies.

The European idea and the 'Islamic threat'

It is against this background that the narrative of Europe as a space of peace and security casts a particular group – Muslim immigrants – as a threat to the European idea. This stance sits uneasily with the narrative of Europe as a space of tolerance and inclusion, particularly the claim that Europeans are able to embrace the 'otherness of others', irrespective of their particularistic attachments.

6 The International Organization for Migration (2005) reported that international migration is indeed decreasing. North America and the former USSR are the only regions of the world that have seen an increase in their migrant stock.

The narrative of Europe as a space of peace and security draws new boundaries of exclusion, based upon respect for religious pluralism, which now thrives as a quintessential European quality alongside secularism and modernity. The report clearly states: 'European culture cannot be defined in opposition to a particular religion (such as Islam)' (Biedenkopf *et al.* 2004: 9). But, in the current circumstances of world politics, Islam, in being equated with the dangers of religious fundamentalism – or, more specifically, with ethnic conflict drawn along religious lines – is being discursively constructed as a threat to Europe's peaceful order. If religious pluralism is now held as a symbol of the 'new Europe' and, thus, a necessary condition for intercultural understanding and peace in the EU, the pollution of this European space by Islam invokes long-term historical divisions and tensions regarding the symbolic boundary separating Christian Europe and the Muslim world (Delanty 1996). Nonetheless, while for centuries Islam represented for Europe an 'external other', it is now increasingly perceived as an 'internal other'. This claim is substantiated by the increased presence of Muslim communities of faith in many EU countries. As noted by Turner (2002b: 116), 'the modern global economy has produced the development of an Islamic diaspora, and as a result it is difficult to sustain the myth of Islam as an external Other'.

The cosmopolitan values which are currently held as symbols of Europe – such as human rights, solidarity, democracy, religious pluralism – hinder any attempts to exclude Muslim immigrants from the EU on the basis of religious particularism. Yet the report, despite its cosmopolitan underpinnings, clearly identifies 'Muslim immigration into Europe' and 'the prospect of Turkey's becoming an EU member' (Biedenkopf *et al.* 2004: 11–12) as concrete menaces to the European idea. These threats involve 'a possible invasion of the public sphere by religious institutions, as well as the threat that religion may be used to justify ethnic conflicts' (Biedenkopf *et al.* 2004: 11). These claims have important consequences for the accomplishment of European citizenship:

> It is, to be sure, hard to deny that the increasing presence of the various forms of Islam in Europe's public space poses both new opportunities and new dangers for European integration. It potentially calls into question the prevailing current ideas about Europe's public space.... But the only feasible path toward a solution of the problems posed by Islam in Europe consists in understanding the consequences of transplanting Islam into a European context, not in a frontal confrontation between the abstractions of 'Christian Europe' and 'Islam'. (Biedenkopf *et al.* 2004: 12)

The concrete representation of Muslim immigration as a threat to the European idea is explained, in part, by the fact that fundamentalist Islam, in being increasingly tied to global terrorism in the mass media, fuels fears of ethnic conflict and xenophobia, in part because it is believed that institutional Islam blocks the observance of rights consecrated by the 2000 European Charter of Fundamental Rights.[7] For example, the ritualistic killing in November 2004 of the Dutch filmmaker Theo Van Gogh, an outspoken public figure highly critical of Islam, by an extremist Muslim sent shockwaves across the Netherlands. As Dutch citizens appeared to awaken to the reality of the Islamic presence, freedom of expression and opinion, a right protected by article 11 of the 2000 Charter and a cornerstone of liberal democracies, was collectively understood to be severely endangered. But equally important is the way in which Islam is publicly perceived as a highly institutionalized religion with a strong influence on the conduct of and collective identity demands on European Muslims, and which has, therefore, a strong presence in the public sphere. The use of the headscarf, for instance, makes the assertion of Muslim identity more visible in the public sphere. This is so in a context in which Christian religions, particularly Protestantism and Catholicism, have become less institutionalized and have had a diminishing role in civil society. Throughout the EU, Christian churches are losing members and in no other part of the world has religion become more 'invisible' (Luckman 2003). In many EU member states religion has become an increasingly a private matter.[8]

The 'Islamic threat' is all the more problematic because the rights to freedom of religion and to manifest religious belief in public or private are protected by articles 10 and 12 of the 2000 Charter. Furthermore, the perceived 'invasion' of nationally defined public spheres by 'institutional Islam' results from the growing visibility of Muslim identity. It is the public visibility of this 'other' that is seen as potentially fuelling xenophobia and ethnic conflict in many EU countries. In other words, it is the perceived dangerous social proximity of this 'other within' that appears to justify the report's plea to understand 'the consequences of transplanting Islam into a European context'. Despite the emphasis on religious pluralism as a symbol of the 'new Europe', there is here little sense of how the civilizational encounters between Islamic and Christian peoples have shaped and informed European memories and experiences (Kumar 2003b; Mazower 2000).

The prospect of Turkey's membership raises similar concerns for EU institutions and governments. As long as Turkey can fulfil the institutional, economic and legal requirements for membership, all of which are necessary to meet other

---

7 For example, article 11 of the Charter refers to 'Freedom of Expression and Information' and article 23 to 'Equality between Men and Women'.

8 Note that this is not to say that religious diversity is declining in the EU. On the contrary, Protestant, Catholic, Orthodox, Jewish and Muslim religious traditions coexist with the proliferation of the so-called 'New Age' religious beliefs and practices. What is declining is the role that official and institutional religion plays in civil society. See Luckman (2003).

conditions, including those relating to human rights, Turkey is not in principle excluded from the political space of the EU, which has been shaped by EU institutions, civic values and law (Mayer and Palmowski 2004: 593). In fact, no cultural criteria have been set as a condition for membership. Yet Europe-wide polling shows that public opinion in existing member states, notably France, Germany, the Netherlands and Austria, is fiercely opposed to Turkish membership (Ash 2005; Freedland 2005).

Conclusion

By discussing the 2004 report *The Spiritual and Cultural Dimension of Europe*, I have shown that there is a tension between the narrative of Europe as a space of tolerance and inclusion and the narrative of Europe as a space of peace and security (which retains much of the spirit of the metaphor of 'fortress Europe') that cannot be easily resolved. Arguably, while the former serves to explain how a European citizenship beyond the nation state would be possible (Eder and Giesen 2001: 266–67), the latter explains the need to adjust nationally defined labour markets and public spheres to the conditions of globalization, Europeanization and 'global terrorism'. Ultimately, each narrative seeks to offer a distinctive explanation for how the cosmopolitan values and principles that make up the idea of Europe translate new ways of being European in the context of a more culturally diverse and expanding EU.

The paradox underlying current interpretations of Europe is that cosmopolitan values of solidarity, peace and human rights, in becoming part of Europe's self-understanding, can be used to justify the exclusion from the political space of the EU of social categories – such as Muslim immigrants – who seemingly do not embrace such values. Yet cosmopolitan ideas and dispositions are believed to cement the new idea of Europe as a space of intercultural understanding, where people are willing to engage, both mentally and experientially, with fellow European citizens and with other people and cultures, regardless of their particularistic loyalties. This contradiction reflects a struggle over the meaning of Europe at a time when the EU is challenged by the need to cope with the increasing proximity and interpenetration of cultures, with the normative conditions of globalization and with complex forms of collective belonging.

References

Alexander, J. C. (2003) *The Meanings of Social Life: A Cultural Sociology*, New York: Oxford University Press.

Alexander, J. C. and Smith, P. (1993) 'The discourse of American civil society: a new proposal for cultural studies', *Theory and Society*, 22(2), 151–207.

Amin, A. (2004) 'Multi-ethnicity and the idea of Europe', *Theory, Culture and Society*, 21(2), 1–24.

Archibugi, D., Held, D. and Kohler, M. (eds) (1998) *Re-imagining Political Community: Studies in Cosmopolitan Democracy*, Cambridge: Polity Press.

Ash, T. G. (2005) 'How the dreaded superstate became a commonwealth', *The Guardian*, 5 October.

Beck, U. (2002a) 'The cosmopolitan society and its enemies', *Theory, Culture and Society*, 19(1–2), 17–44.

Beck, U. (2002b) 'The cosmopolitan perspective: sociology in the second age of modernity', in S. Vertovec and R. Cohen (eds), *Conceiving Cosmopolitanism: Theory, Context, and Practice*, Oxford: Oxford University Press, pp. 61–85.

Beck, U. (2003) 'Rooted cosmopolitanism: emerging from a rivalry of distinctions', in U. Beck, N. Sznaider and R. Winter (eds), *Global America? The Cultural Consequences of Globalization*, Liverpool: Liverpool University Press, pp. 15–30.

Berezin, M. (2003) 'Introduction: territory, emotion, and identity', in M. Berezin and M. Schain (eds), *Europe Without Borders: Remapping Territory, Citizenship, and Identity in a Transnational Age*, Baltimore, MD: Johns Hopkins University Press, pp. 1–30.

Biedenkopf, K., Geremek, B. and Michalski, K. (2004) *The Spiritual and Cultural Dimension of Europe – Concluding Remarks*, Brussels: European Commission. Available at http://ec.europa.eu/archives/commission_1999_2004/prodi/pdf/michalski_281004_final_report_en.pdf (last accessed January 2007).

Calhoun, C. (2002) 'The class consciousness of frequent travellers: towards a critique of actually existing cosmopolitanism', in S. Vertovec and R. Cohen (eds), *Conceiving Cosmopolitanism: Theory, Context, and Practice*, Oxford: Oxford University Press, pp. 86–109.

Calhoun, C. (2003) 'The democratic integration of Europe: interests, identity and the public sphere', in M. Berezin and M. Schain (eds), *Europe Without Borders: Remapping Territory, Citizenship and Identity in a Transnational Age*, Baltimore, MD: Johns Hopkins University Press, pp. 243–74.

Connerton, P. (1989) *How Societies Remember*, Cambridge: Cambridge University Press.

Delanty, G. (1996) 'The frontier and identities of exclusion in European history', *History of European Ideas*, 22(2), 93–103.

Delanty, G. (2003a) 'Europe and the idea of "unity in diversity"', in R. Lindahl (ed.), *Whither Europe? Borders, Boundaries, Frontiers in a Changing World*, Goteborg: CERGU, pp. 25–39.

Delanty, G. (2003b) 'The making of a post-Western Europe: a civilizational analysis', *Thesis Eleven*, 72, 8–25.

Derrida, J. (2001) *On Cosmopolitanism and Forgiveness*, London: Routledge.

Douglas, M. (1966) *Purity and Danger*, London: Routledge and Kegan Paul.

Eder, K. and Giesen, B. (2001) 'Citizenship and the making of a European society: from the political to the social integration of Europe', in K. Eder and B. Giesen (eds), *European Citizenship Between National Legacies and Postnational Projects*, Oxford: Oxford University Press, pp. 245–69.

Eisenstadt, S. N. (2001) 'The civilizational dimension of modernity – modernity as a distinct civilization', *International Sociology*, 16(3), 320–40.

Entrikin, N. (2003) 'Political community, identity, and cosmopolitan place', in M. Berezin and M. Schain (eds), *Europe Without Borders: Remapping Territory, Citizenship, and Identity in a Transnational Age*, Baltimore, MD: Johns Hopkins University Press, pp. 51–63.

Eriksen, E. O. (2004) 'Reflexive integration in Europe', in E. O. Eriksen and J. E. Fossum (eds), *Making the European Polity: Reflexive Integration in the EU*, London: Routledge, pp. 9–29.

European Commission (2001) *European Governance: A White Paper*, COM(2001) 428 final, Brussels: European Commission. Available at http://ec.europa.eu/governance/white_paper/en.pdf (last accessed January 2007).

Eyerman, R. (2004) 'The past in the present – culture and the transmission of memory', *Acta Sociologica*, 47(2), 159–69.

Fine, R. and Chernilo, D. (2004) 'Between past and future: the equivocations of the new cosmopolitanism', *Studies in Law, Politics and Society*, 31, 25–44.

Freedland, J. (2005) 'European elites can't ignore the views of their peoples', *The Guardian*, 5 October.

Geertz, C. (1973) *The Interpretation of Cultures*, New York: Basic Books.

Giddens, A. (1991) *Modernity and Self-Identity: Self and Society in Contemporary Life*, Cambridge: Polity Press.

Habermas, J. (2001) *The Postnational Constellation: Political Essays*, Cambridge: Polity Press.

Halbwachs, M. (1992) *On Collective Memory*, Chicago, IL: University of Chicago Press.

Held, D. (2002) 'Culture and political community: national, global and cosmopolitan', in S. Vertovec and R. Cohen (eds), *Conceiving Cosmopolitanism: Theory, Context, and Practice*, Oxford: Oxford University Press, pp. 48–58.

Honneth, A. (1996) *The Struggle for Recognition: The Moral Grammar of Social Conflicts*, Cambridge, MA: MIT Press.

International Organization for Migration (2005) *World Migration 2005: Costs and Benefits of International Migration*, Geneva: IOM. Available at http://www.iom.int (last accessed January 2007).

Kearney, R. (2002) *Strangers, Gods and Monsters: Interpreting Otherness*, London: Routledge.

Kumar, K. (2003a) 'Britain, England and Europe – cultures in contraflow', *European Journal of Social Theory*, 6(1), 5–23.

Kumar, K. (2003b) 'The idea of Europe – cultural legacies, transnational imaginings, and the nation-state', in M. Berezin and M. Schain (eds), *Europe Without Borders: Remapping Territory, Citizenship and Identity in a Transnational Age*, Baltimore, MD: Johns Hopkins University Press, pp. 33–50.

Levy, D. and Sznaider, N. (2002) 'Memory unbound – the Holocaust and the formation of cosmopolitan memory', *European Journal of Social Theory*, 5(1), 87–106.

Llobera, J. (2003) 'The concept of Europe as an idée-force', *Critique of Anthropology*, 23(2), 155–74.

Luckman, T. (2003) 'Transformations of religion and morality in modern Europe', *Social Compass*, 50(3), 275–85.

Malmborg, M. and Stråth, B. (2001) 'Introduction: the national meanings of Europe', in M. Malmborg and B. Stråth (eds), *The Meaning of Europe*, Oxford: Berg, pp. 1–25.

Mayer, F. and Palmowski, J. (2004) 'European identities and the EU – the ties that bind the peoples of Europe', *Journal of Common Market Studies*, 42(3), 572–98.

Mazower, M. (2000) *The Balkans*, London: Phoenix Press.

Pagden, A. (2003) 'Human rights, natural rights and Europe's imperial legacy', *Political Theory*, 31(2), 171–99.

Rumford, C. (2005) 'Cosmopolitanism and Europe – towards a new EU studies agenda?', *Innovation*, 18(1), 1–9.

Sassatelli, M. (2002) 'Imagined Europe – the shaping of a European cultural identity through EU cultural policy', *European Journal of Social Theory*, 5(4), 435–51.

Shamir, R. (2005) 'Without borders? Notes on globalization as a mobility regime', *Sociological Theory*, 23(2), 197–217.

Somers, M. R. (1995) 'Narrating and naturalizing civil society and citizenship theory: the place of political culture and the public sphere', *Sociological Theory*, 13(3), 229–74.

Stevenson, N. (2002) 'Cosmopolitanism and the future of democracy: politics, culture and the self', *New Political Economy*, 7(2), 251–67.

Stjernø, S. (2005) *Solidarity in Europe: The History of an Idea*, Cambridge: Cambridge University Press.

Stolke, V. (1995) 'Talking culture – new boundaries, new rhetorics of exclusion in Europe', *Current Anthropology*, 36(1), 1–23.

Stråth, B. (2002) 'A European identity – to the historical limits of a concept', *European Journal of Social Theory*, 5(4), 397–401.

Strauss-Kahn, D. (2004) *Building a Political Europe: 50 Proposals for Tomorrow's Europe*, Brussels: European Commission.

Therborn, G. (2002) 'The world's trader, the world's lawyer – Europe and global processes', *European Journal of Social Theory*, 5(4), 403–17.

Turner, B. S. (2002a) 'Cosmopolitan virtue, globalization and patriotism', *Theory, Culture and Society*, 19(1–2), 45–63.

Turner, B. S. (2002b) 'Sovereignty and emergency: political theology, Islam and American conservantism', *Theory, Culture and Society*, 19(4), 103–19.

Vertovec, S. and Cohen, R. (2002) 'Introduction: conceiving cosmopolitanism', in S. Vertovec and R. Cohen (eds), *Conceiving Cosmopolitanism: Theory, Context, and Practice*, Oxford: Oxford University Press, pp. 1–22.

Wallace, W. (2001) 'As viewed from Europe: transatlantic sympathies, transatlantic fears', *International Relations*, 16(2), 281–86.

Zielonka, J. (2003) 'Borders in the enlarged EU: fixed and hard or soft and fuzzy?', in R. Lindahl (ed.), *Whither Europe? Borders, Boundaries, Frontiers in a Changing World*, Goteborg: CERGU, pp. 19–24.

CHAPTER 13

Security: Cosmopolitan and European

F. Peter Wagner

This chapter addresses the question of security in the context of the ongoing process of European identity formation. Cosmopolitanism, I argue, presents both an attractive and a necessary conceptual bracket for joining the reconstruction of the space called 'Europe', including the processes of integration and enlargement of the European Union (EU), and the vision of Europe (specifically the EU) as a 'civilian power' (*Zivilmacht*). The chapter is therefore both methodological and substantive. It links the analytical theme of security to the normative theme of cosmopolitanism. This linkage is achieved in the following via a critical reconstruction that interprets both concepts as – historically and phenomeno-logically – dynamic relationships between a 'self' and its 'other', and localizes those self–other relationships within the context of a European identity space (Neumann 1999; Paasi 1999; Wagner 2001, 2002). A few initial words are in order to place this argument in the context of what are, in effect, ongoing debates.

Critical scholars in the fields of international relations (international studies) and foreign policy analysis have long argued for a broader understanding and conception of 'security', an understanding and conception not defined by and as such not confined to the nation state, its vital interests and its military/defence needs and capacities (Agnew 2003; Ó Tuathail 1999; Wæver 1996). In this context, the notions of 'civilian power', used to characterize the EU, and 'human security', spawned by and akin to the United Nations' notion of 'human development', have made their appearance in the scholarly literature and in political public discourse (Glasius and Kaldor 2005). While this development towards a broader under-standing of security can and should be lauded, its definition remains rather vague and the connections between such a broader conception of security and Europe in general and the EU in particular remain rather controversial. In the first place, the central questions of actor (who) and means (what and how) continue to vex analysts and commentators with regard to European politics and policy-making in general because the nation state, *in the form of EU member states*, seemingly continues to keep itself alive *within* the European project (Wæver 2004: 211; Youngs 2004). Moreover, critical scholars wishing to advance the notions of civilian power and human security in connection to Europe have to confront the realist camp in international relations and security studies scholarship. For realists, the notions of civilian power and human security are but nice words that obfuscate the fact that Europeans today simply lack the strong military and defence capabilities to pursue traditional power politics (Kagan 2004; Sjursen 2004).

While the noted reinterpretation of the notion of security is debated by scholars in relation to European (Union) foreign policy, the relationship between the EU's professed democratic values and its avowed aim to create an area of freedom, security and justice (AFSJ) inside the EU, especially here the recent push for heightened police cooperation, data collection and data exchange (even with third parties) in the wake of the attacks on the US of 11 September 2001, has become a major scholarly and public concern (Lodge 2004). Spurred by the unfolding dynamic of justice and home affairs (JHA) policies, the AFSJ and the 'war on terror', scholars have begun to break down the traditional barrier separating external from internal security studies and to bring the concept 'home', so to speak (Mitsilegas *et al.* 2003; Henderson 2005). The defensive, traditional liberal stance against the state in the name of individual rights, which is how criticisms of security measures introduced since 11 September 2001, including within JHA and the AFSJ, have been framed regionally and internationally, appears increasingly helpless at a time when the need to curb civil liberties, to attain more security, is proudly proclaimed and openly adopted by political elites and even accepted, if not without misgivings and criticism, by general publics.

Thus, in addition to the need to clarify the connections between alternative conceptions of security and the European project (EU and otherwise), one notes a present need for a 'critical articulation' (Ryan 1982) that manages to give voice to normative concerns in the context of an observable dissolution of the traditional (i.e. modern) division separating 'external' from 'internal' security. For both those needs, I think, it is important to engage the philosophical presuppositions underlying our modern and contemporary thoughts about cosmopolitanism and security within the European context (arena, theatre).

The central thesis of this chapter is twofold. First, by forging a connection between the discourses of 'cosmopolitanism', 'Europe' and 'security', the notion of security can be grounded (localized, so to speak), that is, 'security' can be put into a specific historical normative context that allows the term to be interpreted beyond its traditional understanding of state-centred and military interventionist politics. Second, in confronting the issue of security, the vision of a cosmopolitan

Europe can be grounded within the process of European identity formation as a (conscious) choice *against* Europe's past.

In the following, this argument unfolds in three parts. The next section situates or localizes cosmopolitanism and security within a specific historical normative identity space: Europe. In the following section the relationship between cosmopolitanism and security within contemporary EU-Europe is presented. The last section then synthesizes the preceding discussions into a perspective on the meaning of cosmopolitan security for the European project.

Cosmopolitanism, security and the space called Europe

Cosmopolitanism, security, Europe: at first glance, the relation between those three terms appears nothing short of antithetical. Cosmopolitanism is generally defined as a philosophical perspective on human affairs (a *Weltanschauung*), a belief, an attitude, or even just a mere 'lifestyle' that deprivileges any particular, localized political and ethical/moral arrangements, for example territorial (national) societies or territorial (national) states, in favour of a reasoned, posited or simply felt community of all human beings, by way of a reasoned, posited or simply felt dignity and sanctity of each and every individual as a human being. Cosmopolitanism therefore takes the globe as the only meaningful political community, namely as the only one that encompasses the entire human race. As a consequence (or at least by implication), cosmopolitans do not easily belong to any particular, localizable community or political or societal arrangement, if they can be said to belong (and would identify themselves as belonging) to any concretely existing community at all (Kleingeld and Brown 2002). Given this – albeit highly general and pointed – definition of cosmopolitanism, any politically constructed *boundary* that sets a specific physical/geographical space apart from all other possible spaces, a boundary such as 'Europe', would appear to be at least questionable, if not illegitimate. Even flights of the imagination that did not centre on humanity and the world in the construction of their identity spaces, as is again the case with 'Europe' and the question of what it means to be 'European', would fail the litmus test of an essentially boundless space defined only in terms of a normative commitment to humanity as such and to the world that each individual inhabits as a member of the human race.

At best, cosmopolitanism could become the measuring rod for the creation of a political community. Yet while this provides the ground of critique and a measure of progress (and regress), in realizing a cosmopolitan commitment a political community basically would have defined itself out of existence, as it could not, at least not legitimately, maintain any concrete territorial presence in the form of (its) borders. At any rate and in any case, even in this regard

'Europe' is not a cosmopolitan category of thought and identification, *a place of belonging and allegiance*. Or, rather, it is not one that is readily apparent as such from within the cosmopolitan perspective or framework. But let me not get ahead of myself at this point.

This antithetical relation between the essentially borderless and the essentially bounded appears to be even more pronounced when considering the concept of security. By definition, security is always a term referring to a 'security for' and a 'security from/against' and is therefore based on a dynamic of identity formation that clearly separates the one from the other, for example something threatened from that which is threatening, the endangered from the danger, an 'us' from a 'them' (Campbell 1998). The act of 'securitization', namely 'dramatizing an issue as having absolute priority' (Wæver 1996: 106), presupposes this vital – indeed, existential and decisionist – differentiation. A borderless conception of 'security' therefore would be nonsensical, as it would prevent exactly this act of differentiation upon which the need for and definition of 'security' is built in the first place.

Cosmopolitanism actually is able to resolve this particular antithetical relation in its radicalization, in that it can represent a response to a threat that encompasses the globe and engulfs all of human kind. Given the threat of global ecological disaster and other dangers that do not respect national or societal borders, from terrorism to deadly diseases, such a radicalization has not only become conceivable, it has turned into a constitutive presence and major argument for cosmopolitanism itself (Held 2002). One needs to step back for a moment in order to appreciate this development in the context of the general debate surrounding cosmopolitanism. Ever since cosmopolitanism's earliest formulation, the extent to which 'the world' and its ethical/moral subject – 'human kind', 'humanity' or the 'individual' as a member of the human race – can and do represent a positive conception of *belonging* and *allegiance* that can both ground and mandate rights, responsibilities and obligations of some kind has been unclear and hence controversial. Thus, the stock motif of the debate on cosmopolitanism, at least since the Enlightenment, has been the contrast between, on the one hand, the image of the cosmopolitan as a rootless, ethically and morally relativistic individual who in the last instance cares but only for himself or herself, and, on the other, the cosmopolitan as the enlightened globalist who cares about and feels for humanity and therefore stands against all kinds of oppression – wherever it may occur. While this general debate motif (the Rousseauean negative image versus the Kantian positive one) has arguably been only slightly modified or refined since then (Mulhall and Swift 1996), one is able to observe since the mid-1990s a decided and decisive turn towards 'security' in the debate surrounding cosmopolitanism.

The question of military and humanitarian interventions in conflicts, in wars and in the aftermath of natural disasters of all kinds has become the central empirical and normative concern in the contemporary debate. Indeed, it is even fair to say that the very notion of a 'humanitarian intervention' would not be possible without the kind of moral reasoning and commitment associated with cosmopolitanism. Although contemporary mass media bring 'distant suffering' into our living rooms, whether or not (and to what degree) the viewing public responds depends on how the suffering in question is actually perceived (Boltanski 1999). While helping in order to keep suffering (and, arguably, the sufferers) at bay is one possible motif behind the impulse to intervene, there certainly is also an accepted responsibility for helping other, far away humans in need: a moral acceptance that would not be possible without rendering both physical distances and concrete (also political) circumstances meaningless by virtue of that larger community called humanity and the conviction that this (such and such a fate) should not be tolerated, for the sake and in the name of all of 'us', as equal members of one human race (Kaldor 2001: 130; Pogge 2002a).

However, as the exchange between Pogge (2002b) and Miller (2002) shows, the communitarian objections to cosmopolitanism cannot easily be assuaged. Pogge's formulation of an 'intermediate cosmopolitanism', situated between the poles of 'weak' and 'strong', recognizes that there exists a difference between 'us' and 'them' as far as stronger (*'increased'*) responsibilities and obligations are concerned; these responsibilities and obligations individuals can claim for themselves and may feel that they owe to each other as members of a lived community. Yet Pogge maintains that such stronger responsibilities and obligations do not *'decrease'* what is owed to strangers as fellow human beings and to other communities of fellow human beings. Thus, from the position of an intermediate cosmopolitanism, one can legitimately claim (or, rather, feel) that one should help one's starving compatriots more than the starving strangers one encounters on the evening news, but such an increased obligation arising from closeness – irrespective of how that closeness is defined or comes about (a point to which I will return shortly) – does not legitimize inaction in the face of tragedy or injustice, let alone serve to legitimize the creation, existence and maintenance of international arrangements that force and keep other human beings systematically in conditions that compromise, threaten and/or harm their existence. In this vision, then, the justice, or rather injustice, of the international system is a central concern, regardless of the question of whether or not an individual can be said to harbour stronger feelings of attachment and to have stronger obligations to what she or he regards as her or his 'own' community.

The explicated turn towards security in the recent debate about cosmopolitanism therefore has sharpened the fundamental problematic at the heart of cosmopolitanism itself: the debate about cosmopolitanism is fundamentally a debate about what constitutes a 'community', how human allegiances are formed and the extent and the limits, the rights and obligations, of those allegiances. And this leads us back to the antithetical relation between cosmopolitanism and Europe noted at the beginning of this section.

Seen from within the traditional cosmopolitan paradigm, as noted, the world presents the only accepted and acceptable community, namely, as the space of a common humanity.

For critics of cosmopolitanism (Miller 2002) 'closeness' or lived experience is the defining context/moment of rights, responsibilities and obligations, in turn. Humanity or human kind presents an abstract, empty universalism in comparison with the rights and obligations that appear to emanate quite naturally and logically from a particular, lived community: the family, the neighbourhood, the nation. Yet in the communitarian line of reasoning, distinct levels or modes of belonging are collapsed as if no critical distinction need be made, for example, between a family and a modern-day polity. In addition, 'closeness' itself is reduced to an automatism inherent in a posited lived experience that is defined as a continuum from the natural to the national – and *not* beyond.

Exactly this line of communitarian reasoning one encounters in recent and not-so-recent objections against the idea of a common European identity. As the German political theorist Graf Kielmansegg has formulated:

> collective identities are created, stabilized and reproduced by communities based on communication, experience and memory. Europe, even the more restricted Western Europe, is not a communication community, barely a community of shared memories and only in a limited sense a community of shared experiences. (Graf Kielmansegg 1996: 55)

While questioning the seamless natural logic of a lived experience and its seemingly natural compatriotism has been the hallmark and central concern of cosmopolitanism, the contemporary cosmopolitan response readily submits itself in the European case to the same logic: Europe remains neither close nor wide enough to warrant identification and concern. For the contemporary cosmopolitan position, the critical issue is the legitimate possibility of addressing oneself as an individual member of a specific, particular community to the problems that the international system poses. An *intermediate* community as an actual point of reference and concern simply does not enter the argumentative equation. Between a common humanity and the nation state, between the bonds of humanity and those of nation, kinship and neighbourhood, there exists – nothing.

It is, of course, possible to reconstruct cosmopolitanism as a powerful identity marker for a pluralization of 'Europe' (Rumford 2002). In this interpretation, the very absence of a European identity is the *result* of contemporary processes of societal differentiation and contestation. Thus, the absence turns out to be empowering. It precludes the imposition of any one identity while opening up the possibility of a genuine debate on tolerance and its limits, without precluding any voice from the start as not being European (enough). Yet while the diagnosis of another great transformation in European affairs, postmodernity, post-communism or globalization, provides necessary insights into the problematic of European identity formation today, the vision of 'Europes', plural and decidedly non-monolithic, remains in the end defined by what it opposes: the EU and the EU-centred and EU-defined process of European integration. Thus, this interpretation does not offer a satisfactory answer to the contemporary creation of 'Europe' and to the question of what it means to be European, as, in the final instance, the grounds for any *mediation* (resolution) of the depicted contending forces and movements remains unexplored (Rumford 2002: 237–66).

Instead of presenting the space called Europe *through* the prism of cosmopolitanism, it makes sense for historical, normative and analytical reasons to turn this conceptual relationship upside down. It is usually implied, if not explicitly maintained, that cosmopolitanism (at least in a normative sense) defines the space called Europe. Thus, the vision of a cosmopolitan Europe is primarily a vision of cosmopolitanism, an attempt to put the concept into practice. This, as noted, cannot be accomplished without brushing over the basic antithetical relationship between cosmopolitanism and a bounded space but it does, of course, work as a normative point of critique. However, the normative point of critique that cosmopolitanism presents vis-à-vis a bounded territory (a polity, political authority, etc.) historically has its foundation in the space called Europe itself. Cosmopolitanism *was* European, if at origin only because Europe presented a pastiche of political and societal formations that militated against the very idea of one superior identity or mode of belonging. For the same reason that Aristotle is always cited in political science textbooks as the first comparative political scientist, cosmopolitanism emerged as a possible stance towards the plain givenness of this or that particular order or community. Europe in this sense always was plural, always meant 'Europes' and as such provided the birthplace for cosmopolitanism as a *negative* stance against the kind of natural ontology presented by the communitarian conception of belonging and allegiance.

More importantly, the plural identity of the space called Europe also brought forth cosmopolitanism as a positive conception of rights, duties and obligations, as a critical conception of belonging and allegiance. This development came about in response to another aspect of Europe's historical identity as a pastiche of political and societal formations. For most of its history, the Europe people knew and inhabited was characterized by conflict, strife and war, poverty and disease. It was in reaction to this lived experience or, more concretely, in reaction to the devastation that the long sixteenth century had wrought, that the turn to and acceptance of a common humanity, of individual rights and the rule of law – the latter also at the level of relations between sovereign entities – was eventually accomplished. Indeed, from the earliest stirrings of republican thought in European antiquity to Kant's argument for a perpetual peace, and beyond to the Ventotene manifesto and the Schuman declaration of the twentieth century, the vision of a united and peaceful Europe was guided by a past one wanted to leave behind. The choice for Europe, *pace* Moravcsik (1998), *is* cosmopolitanism. It was a choice made – and made as such very explicitly after the Second World War – against a Europe defined and plagued by conflict and war, distrust and hatred. It is therefore also not accidental that the vision of security that has animated that choice is not – in the meaning of the term understood in international relations theory – realist. On the contrary, even the Kantian conception, tied as it is to conflict between states, is based on dialogue grounded in reason and rationality, and *not* in a sentiment arising from a communitarian sense of belonging.

It therefore also makes *analytic* sense to differentiate between an *adversarial conception of security* and a *cooperative conception of security* and to view the development and final implementation of the latter as *the* European civilizational accomplishment *par excellence*. If the aim was to prevent conflicts and wars of all kinds (international as well as intra-national), security within the European space could not be adversarial, but had to be seen as *cooperative*. This intricate historical relation between cosmopolitanism and a cooperative conception of security, in turn, provides one with a non-ontological conception of Europe, without having to resort to taking the parts, 'Europes', for the whole. In line with the historical point made above, Europe can be seen as a project – a *u-topos* derived from a concrete, lived experience: the positive against its own negative, the dream that was posited against the reality that was actually known. In this sense, the dynamic of self/other that has been noted, quite correctly in my view, in the discourse and practice of 'security' can and should be located *within* the notion of Europe itself.

The best historical moment for seeing this relationship between cosmopolitanism and security is provided by the official onset of European integration in the aftermath of the Second World War. As is widely known, the 'German question' posed the greatest challenge for the rebuilding of Europe, that is, in what quickly became the new Western Europe, after the Second World War. Yet instead of punishing Germany for the devastation it had wrought, the reconstruction of Germany became part of a general reconstruction of (Western) Europe. French–German reconciliation has, of course, become something like the founding myth of European integration, so I hasten to point out that the mundane was also at play: economic interests and necessities, the French interest in keeping Germany down and the German interest in becoming a respectable member of the (anti-communist) world community, and the new international context of the Cold War should not be overlooked when making sense of the forces that led to European integration. Yet what needs to be stressed is that at least some European leaders, and certainly the leading figures at the time, also had a conception of 'Europe' in mind. That conception, when reading between the lines, was based on a past that they wanted to avoid and the only way they saw that this past could be avoided was by something that had not quite been tried in a systematic manner in Europe, at least not on such a massive scale: cooperation. Security in cooperation with – and not against – Germany was therefore seen as an organic, necessary part of a larger vision. At issue was a Europe that would finally fulfil the promise of being a community of democratic norms and values, and a community that would thereby further peace and democracy in the rest of the world (Monnet 1962).

Now that cosmopolitanism and security have been put in (their) place, the European identity space, we need to turn to how cosmopolitanism and security are defining the European project today.

Security in and for Europe: between the traditional response and its cosmopolitan alternative

As argued above, a common problematic can be said to link cosmopolitanism, security and Europe: 'Europe' as both a specific historical context of normative development and a distinct metaphysical project of societal identity formation. This is still a far cry from presenting the relevance of this interrelation and co-determination for contemporary purposes. How – if indeed at all – does the above translate into European politics today? It might be surprising, but the clearest indication one finds today is exactly in the one policy area that, to many, represents the failure to find a European identity: the development of a common European foreign, security and defence policy.

Perhaps nothing has galvanized the debate about a common European foreign, security and defence policy as much as the debate that ensued between Europeans and US Americans and between an 'old Europe' and a 'new Europe' following the US-led military invasion of Saddam Hussein's Iraq in 2003. Most European (and even some US American) political commentators and scholars, if by no means all, pitted in a positive manner a European reliance on multilateralism, international law and discourse against a US American Manichaean world view and military interventionist politics. Yet the professed clear-cut stance – the Europeans from Venus versus the US Americans from Mars, *pace* Kagan (2004) – is, as such, rather misleading. As the war against the Taliban's Afghanistan, troop deployments and general security cooperation in the aftermath of '11 September' amply demonstrate, the 'war on terror' that US President George W. Bush proclaimed is fought even by those who did not agree to participate in Operation Iraqi Freedom. The emphatic response of the former German Foreign Minister Joschka Fischer, 'I am not convinced!', to US Defense Secretary Donald Rumsfeld here stands alongside the emphatic acknowledgement from the former German defence secretary, Peter Struck, that today 'Germany is also being defended at the Hindu Kush'. The actual outcome of the intra-European debate once more underlined that a common European foreign, security and defence policy still is hard to come by. In the end, as is well known, common ground was not reached, as several European states decided to join the US, while others decided quite openly (and loudly) not to participate.

Nevertheless, and here critics and supporters were correct, the intra-European debate did reveal the specific European constellation or problematic when it comes to the interpretation of security and the use of military force. Yet this European problematic, *pace* Kagan (2004), does not concern political and military alliances and the pragmatics of a new power politics (*Realpolitik*) in a post-communist world and, thus, cannot be grasped through the traditional language of power politics as an issue of how 'strong' states and 'weak' states view international relations. In the first place, what divided Europeans was not the question whether or not to use (military) force, but whether or not to stand with the US, a division the US government actually knew quite well how to exploit. Thus, at issue in the intra-European debate were historical memory and conceptions of a (national societal) self. The governments of the former Eastern Europe allied themselves to the US not just because they were convinced of the case against Saddam Hussein, but because of a deeply felt commitment to the one power that had stood for freedom and that had stood by them in their own struggles for freedom during the communist period. It should also be emphasized that the famous 'letter of the eight' (the UK, Spain, Portugal, Italy, Denmark, Poland, the Czech Republic and Hungary) in support of the US only appeared after France and Germany – the two 'heavies' on the continent – had vociferously positioned themselves against the US and – as usual – expected everyone else to fall in line behind them.[1] If both France and Germany, and here especially Germany, had actually played by the genuine European rules of cooperation (consultation and consensus-building) and furthermore if they had accepted the special condition of post-communist historical memory, the drama could have easily been avoided.

1   See 'Europe and America must stand united', *The Times*, 30 January 2003.

Thus, the debate among Europeans was and, indeed, continues to be a debate about the meaning of Europe itself. With the fall of communism ended the Cold War division of Europe into a West and an East, divided in terms of political/ societal organization and power politics, defined by the two opposing centres of Washington and Moscow. The *topos* of the 'integration of Europe' therefore presents itself today in a very different context. The choice for a united, peaceful, democratic and prosperous Europe that set in motion the process of European integration after the Second World War in reality took place within the context of a deep division of both the continent and the world. It is this choice, however, that in essence has to be made again: for a post-communist, united Europe within a post-communist, united world.

The area of foreign, security and defence policy has proven to be the one area in which, *despite and because of* the difficulties in its institutionalization within the EU framework, the experiment of a new, post-communist Europe is beginning to take shape.[2] In the first place, the continued reliance on a national voice (unanimity and the dreaded power of veto in the decision-making process) in foreign and security affairs commits all members to take each other seriously in negotiations and thereby breaks down the barrier that has separated West from East. This has already led to a marked difference in concerns when it comes to assessing partners, competitors and friends. Not only the insistence on the importance of a partnership with the US but also the insistence on a more critical stance towards Russia is here a case in point. The importance of the national in foreign, security and defence matters has also provided the newcomers with a ready and powerful stage on which to air their own visions of Europe and to launch initiatives in this regard, as happened when Poland became the driving force behind the EU's commitment to Ukraine's 'orange revolution'. This integration via a national voice finds its counterpoint in the possibility for so-called 'enhanced cooperation', which was introduced to the EU framework by the Treaty of Amsterdam and has since been revised by the Treaty of Nice (which is the treaty framework presently in operation). While not extending to any activities concerning military and defence matters, it does offer the space for sidestepping the strict rule of unanimity that otherwise defines foreign and security matters in the EU. It is interesting to note in this context that the possibility for member

---

2 To provide a discussion at this point of the institutional framework concerning foreign, security and defence matters, the so-called 'second pillar' of the Treaty on European Union, would be to stray too far from the central concerns of this chapter. The area continues to be intergovernmentally organized and thus handled by the Council of Ministers (depending in its portfolio representation on the exact issue involved), with the final and ultimate power, including for the principles and general guidelines, resting with the European Council (the meeting ground of the heads of state and government). For excellent discussions see Smith (2003), Archer (2004) and Eeckout (2004).

states to engage in any activity under enhanced cooperation, in the last instance, is defined by the tacit assent of all those member states that (at that particular moment) do not wish to participate in the activity. Such a tacit assent of course will be possible only in the event by virtue of the kind of consensus-driven dialogue and coordination that, as a genuine European necessity, characterizes (or as noted above should characterize) politics and policy-making in the EU.

Known institutional complications notwithstanding, at the time of writing (summer 2006), the EU has made great strides in the development of military capabilities and the commitment to a common foreign and security policy that includes military force. The European Council at its meeting in Cologne (June 1999) concluded that 'the Union must have the capacity for autonomous action, backed by credible military forces, the means to decide to use them, and the readiness to do so, in order to respond to international crises without prejudice to actions by NATO' (European Council 1999a: 33). Later that same year, at the European Council meeting at Helsinki (December 1999), the heads of state and government of the member states agreed to the so-called 'Helsinki Headline Goal', which asked member states to 'be able, by 2003, to deploy within less than 60 days and sustain for at least 1 year joint forces of up to 50–60000 persons with appropriate air and naval elements' (European Council 1999b: point 28). Although the Capability Improvement Chart of January 2006 still listed many tasks to be solved, even if projects were listed as under way, thirteen so-called 'battlegroups' (combined units in battalion size of 1500 with additional combat support elements) were scheduled to be ready by 2007 (European Union 2005). The military operation in the summer and autumn of 2006 to secure the democratic election process in the Democratic Republic of Congo (EUFOR RD Congo) underlined the EU's developing presence in military interventions. It also underlined the fact that the EU's military role remains embedded in multilateral and international decision-making procedures and commitments.

The multilateral international context of the Congo mission, including its goal to secure a democratic election process, also demonstrates clearly that the area of foreign, security and defence policy has turned into the area in which the European project itself has become most clearly articulated after the fall of communism. The 'European security strategy' launched by the Council in 2003 (Council of the European Union 2003) and the more recent vision of a 'human security doctrine for Europe' (Study Group on Europe's Security Capabilities 2004) can be seen as not so much advancing as actually presenting the core principles that have come to define the European project. In particular, the historical normative relationship between cosmopolitanism and security defines those formulations and a cooperative conception of security is clearly advanced. Granted, the specific term 'human security' has been modelled after the United Nations' own 'human development', but the vision behind the term is about and carries the distinctly European problematic of cosmopolitanism and security (as explicated above). At the same time, one is also able to note the crisis of identity and purpose that the European project is presently undergoing. For example, in both these key documents, 'Europe' and 'European Union' are used interchangeably. Furthermore, the blending of the two terms leads to an inability to present any spatial demarcations, which once again leaves the EU with the high ground when it comes to settling what is meant by Europe. This opaqueness in the use of terms raises exactly those questions that the current public debate is all about. Where do Europe's new borders lie? What does it mean to be European? Who is European and who is not? And who can legitimately ask and answer these questions? The identification of Europe with the EU, an identification made by members and non-members alike, is least common denominator and continuing question mark alike.

The vision of 'human security', however, makes it clear that the *need* for such an approach unites Europeans and unites Europeans with the rest of the world (Glasius and Kaldor 2005; Lerch 2004). In the traditional geopolitical sense of the term 'identity', namely the joining of political authority to a clearly demarcated physical territory, the answer to all those present questions about a European identity has to be: *it does not matter*. The very reasons for raising and answering these questions have become moot. In a world in which security is embedded in and defined by processes of deborderization, European security in the traditional, strict sense of the term cannot and does not exist. There is no 'Europe' that can claim the status of a unitary state actor; there never was and, indeed, there never will be. The term 'Europe' instead refers to an identity space characterized by a multitude of interrelations structured by practices that (historically) have come to situate themselves in cultures, peoples, political authorities – in multiple 'Europes', to use Rumford's felicitous term (Delanty 1995; Rumford 2002). What continues to exist, however, is the legacy of Europe, the European project itself: the choice made against the past and for a different future. The idea(l) of a united, peaceful, democratic and prosperous Europe continues to animate present concerns and thereby continues to provide the empirical backbone to the vision of cosmopolitanism. While the historical conditions for this choice, the choice for a cosmopolitan and against a national(istic) Europe, have changed and are changing, the choice preserves itself exactly in the area and within the dynamic that gave rise to it in the first place: *security*.

European security as an embedded concept

Some analysts, a great many more political commentators and most politicians claim that the world fundamentally changed on 11 September 2001. Certainly, when it comes to the ideas and ideals, the responses and the determination behind the EU's efforts to create a *common* foreign, *security and defence* policy, the terrorist attacks in the US and the train bombings in Madrid in March 2004 and the London bombings of July 2005 present something of a watershed. European nation states have become less reluctant to give up certain national prerogatives in internal security matters (Council of the European Union 2005a, 2005b). More importantly, they also have shown themselves less reluctant to cooperate with third parties, more specifically the US, if the introduction of cooperation measures could be deemed (or at least presented) as important for the prevention of terrorist acts and for identifying and catching (potential) terrorists (Priest 2005).

Yet for all the evidence of an increased *traditional* concern and cooperation in security and defence matters between member states of the EU and between the EU area and third parties, most notably the US, recent evidence also provides a different story line, for several such cooperation measures have elicited dismay and a rather critical response by publics and their democratic representatives at both national and EU levels. While the issue of the US using its bases in Europe for transporting suspects for interrogation purposes to states with questionable human rights records and the issue of secret US prison camps in EU member states have both somewhat disappeared from public debate, the more general issue of cooperating in practices that violate human rights standards continues to unsettle and occupy publics and elites across Europe (Gebauer 2005). If anything, the difficulties that the European executive elites are encountering in security matters – the resistance mounted by their own parliamentary assemblies (national and European), electorates and publics, as well as their own second thoughts – are ample testimony to the patterns of European identity formation explicated above. There exists at the very least an awareness that not only certain types of measures, but also certain idea(l)s of 'security' are not in line with the European project itself.

What we are therefore able to diagnose at the moment is a tension between state-centred, state-led security politics/policies and the idea(l) of Europe as a specific historical context of normative development and a distinct metaphysical project of societal identity formation. The concept of security as linked to norma-tive conceptions of human beings and their humanity – 'human security' – has in effect brought 'Europe' back home in this sense. The normative aspirations behind the historical process of European integration provide the context for the present EU European efforts to redefine security in and for Europe and Europeans, embedding the concept of security as it were, and thereby set the normative bar for security politics and policies inside and outside the EU European arena. As explicated, security in and for Europe has come to mean security in line with the promise of being a community of democratic norms and values, and a community that can be said to further processes of democratization, both internally and with regard to the outside world. This security, I have argued, can only be cooperative and not adversarial in design and nature: an embodiment of the civilizational and civilizing lesson learned from Europe's quite different past.

However, as US Americans would put it, there is no such thing as a free lunch. There is a price to be paid for adhering to the vision of a cosmopolitan Europe as both civil *and* civilizing. In the first place, politicians and publics need to accept that security, as a protective absolute, cannot be achieved. A cosmopolitan Europe will have to live with insecurity, both inside and outside its political boundaries, and the best Europeans can therefore hope for is the management of insecurity; again, cooperation is here key, but it will be a cooperation that refrains from attempting to destroy or even squelch 'threats'. This much, I would argue, is a small price to pay, as the alternative would be, at least in the last instance, a police or security state for which even its own population represents a potential threat.

The second point is a bit more uncomfortable. In recent discussions of the right or obligation to intervene when human lives are systematically endangered or severely threatened through either natural disaster or human (in)action, the problem of 'fatigue' has featured prominently. If 'eternal vigilance' was the price that freedom was supposed to demand during the Cold War, a commitment to intervene has to be the price that Europeans have to be willing to pay in a world without 'islands': islands of peace *and* islands of terror. While absolute security is impossible to achieve, the management of insecurity cannot stop at the gates of a sovereignty derived from the nation state.

This leads me to the third and most uncomfortable concluding point that needs to be made. Taking certain norms and values seriously as civilizational accomplishments means that one has to present and treat them not as accidental or bound to a specific place (or time), but as desirable in themselves and as desirable goals to achieve – for oneself *and* for others. This conclusion may trample upon the notion of a cultural exclusivity upon which the conception of multiculturalism has been founded: 'our' values, European values, need not be, nor should they be, 'their' values, the usual argument goes. The legacy of (European) imperialism and its civilizational and naturalized geopolitics, it is maintained, should serve as a lesson and warning here. What tends to be confused in those arguments are the values and the imperialist politics, and the plain fact that the former *did not* go well with the latter, even if the former provided the ideological smoke-screen and protection blanket for conquest and (mass) murder. There is, I am afraid, no choice here: one either takes on the responsibilities that come with the acceptance of democratic norms and values such as human rights, or one forfeits the validity of those norms and values themselves (as any dictator knows when pointing out the shortcomings, the hypocrisy, of the West in this regard).

In sum, Europe is a metaphysical project and in its present historical variant can be said to be *the* postmodern, post-industrial, post-national project *par excellence*. If it fails – that is, if disintegration, conflict and strife should become the norm again – then cosmopolitanism would have lost the only anchor point, the only existing example of how post-national and regional cooperation can and does work for the betterment of all involved. Again, cosmopolitanism, the choice for norms and values such as human dignity, did not come easily to Europeans. It is a choice (West) Europeans made for themselves in the aftermath of the Second World War because it essentially had been made for them by their past. It now presents a choice that all Europeans will have to make again and again for the sake of their future. And that future, it needs to be stressed, is global and, as such, universal – or will turn out to be an instant replay of a devastating past.

References

Agnew, J. (2003) *Geopolitics: Re-visioning World Politics* (2nd edition), London: Routledge.

Archer, C. (2004) 'The European Union as an international political actor', in N. Nugent (ed.), *European Union Enlargement*, Houndmills: Palgrave/Macmillan, pp. 226–41.

Boltanski, L. (1999) *Distant Suffering: Morality, Media and Politics*, Cambridge: Cambridge University Press.

Campbell, D. (1998) *Writing Security: United States Foreign Policy and the Politics of Identity*, Manchester: Manchester University Press.

Council of the European Union (2003) 'A secure Europe in a better world: European security strategy', 12 December. Available at http://www.europa.eu/scadplus/leg/en/lvb/r00004.htm (last accessed January 2007).

Council of the European Union (2005a) 'Draft conclusions of the representatives of the governments of the member states on common minimum security standards for member states' national identity cards', Brussels, 11 November, document number 14351/05.

Council of the European Union (2005b) 'The European Union counter-terrorism strategy', Brussels, 30 November, document number 14469/4/05.

Delanty, G. (1995) *Inventing Europe: Idea, Identity, Reality*, Houndmills: Macmillan.

Eeckout, P. (2004) *External Relations of the European Union: Legal and Constitutional Foundations*, Oxford: Oxford University Press.

European Council (1999a) 'Presidency conclusions. Annex III: European Council declaration on strengthening the common European policy on security and defence', Cologne, 3 and 4 June, document number 150/99 annexes.

European Council (1999b) 'Presidency conclusions', Helsinki, 11 December, document number 00300/1/99.

European Union (2005) 'Factsheet: the EU battlegroups and the EU civilian and military cell', Brussels, February.

Gebauer, M. (2005) 'Die dunkle Seite des Anti-Amerikaners', *Der Spiegel*, 5 December.

Available at http://www.spiegel.de/politik/deutschland/0,1518,388564,00.html (last accessed January 2007).

Glasius, M. and Kaldor, M. (2005) 'Individuals first: a human security strategy for the European Union', *Internationale Politik und Gesellschaft*, 1, 62–82.

Graf Kielmansegg, P. (1996) 'Integration und Demokratie', in M. Jachtenfuchs and B. Kohler-Koch (eds), *Europäische Integration*, Opladen: Leske und Budrich, pp. 46–71.

Held, D. (2002) 'Violence, law, and justice in a global age', *Constellations*, 9(1), 74–88.

Henderson, K. (ed.) (2005) *The Area of Freedom, Security and Justice in the Enlarged Europe*, Houndmills: Palgrave/Macmillan.

Kagan, R. (2004) *Of Paradise and Power: America and Europe in the New World Order*, New York: Vintage.

Kaldor, M. (2001) *New and Old Wars: Organized Violence in a Global Era*, Stanford, CA: Stanford University Press.

Kleingeld, P. and Brown, E. (2002) 'Cosmopolitanism', in E. N. Zalta (ed.), *The Stanford Encyclopedia of Philosophy*. Available at http://plato.stanford.edu/archives/fall2002/entries/cosmopolitanism (last accessed January 2007).

Lerch, M. (2004) *Menschenrechte und europäische Aussenpolitik: Eine konstruktivistische Analyse*, Wiesbaden: Verlag für Sozialwissenschaften.

Lodge, J. (2004) 'EU homeland security: citizens or suspects?', *Journal of European Integration*, 26(3), 253–79.

Miller, D. (2002) 'Cosmopolitanism: a critique', *Critical Review of International Social and Political Philosophy*, 5(3), 80–85.

Mitsilegas, V., Monar, J. and Rees, W. (2003) *The European Union and Internal Security: Guardian of the People?*, Houndmills: Palgrave/Macmillan.

Monar, J. (2004) 'The EU as an international actor in the domain of justice and home affairs', *European Foreign Affairs Review*, 9, 395–415.

Monnet, J. (1962) 'A ferment of change', in B. F. Nelsen and A. Stubb (eds) (2003), *The European Union: Readings on the Theory and Practice of European Integration* (3rd edition), Boulder, CO: Lynne Rienner, pp. 19–26.

Moravcsik, A. (1998) *The Choice for Europe: Social Purpose and State Power from Messina to Maastricht*, Ithaca, NY: Cornell University Press.

Mulhall, S. and Swift, A. (eds) (1996) *Liberals and Communitarians* (2nd edition), Oxford: Blackwell.

Neumann, I. B. (1999) *Uses of the Other: 'The East' in European Identity Formation*, Minneapolis, MN: University of Minnesota Press.

Ó Tuathail, G. (1999) 'De-territorialised threats and global dangers: geopolitics and risk society', in D. Newman (ed.), *Boundaries, Territory and Postmodernity*, London: Frank Cass, pp. 17–31.

Paasi, A. (1999) 'Boundaries as social processes: territoriality in the world of flows', in D. Newman (ed.), *Boundaries, Territory and Postmodernity*, London: Frank Cass, pp. 69–88.

Petley, J. (2003) 'War without death: responses to distant suffering', *Journal for Crime, Conflict and the Media*, 1(1), 72–85.

Pogge, Th. (2002a) *World Hunger and Human Rights: Cosmopolitan Responsibilities and Reforms*, Cambridge: Polity Press.

237

Pogge, Th. (2002b) 'Cosmopolitanism: a defence', *Critical Review of International Social and Political Philosophy*, 5(3), 86–91.

Priest, D. (2005) 'Foreign network at the front of CIA's terror fight: joint facilities in two dozen countries account for bulk of Agency's post-9/11 successes', *Washington Post*, 18 November, A01. Available at http://www.washingtonpost.com/wp-dyn/content/article/2005/11/17/AR2005111702070.html (last accessed January 2007).

Rumford, C. (2002) *The European Union: A Political Sociology*, Oxford: Blackwell.

Ryan, M. (1982) *Marxism and Deconstruction: A Critical Articulation*, Baltimore, MD: Johns Hopkins University Press.

Sjursen, H. (2004) 'Security and defence', in W. Carlsnaes, H. Sjursen and B. White (eds), *Contemporay European Foreign Policy*, London: Sage, pp. 59–74.

Smith, K. E. (2003) *European Union Foreign Policy in a Changing World*, Cambridge: Polity Press.

Study Group on Europe's Security Capabilities (2004) *A Human Security Doctrine for Europe: The Barcelona Report of the Study Group on Europe's Security Capabilities*, presented to the EU High Representative for Common Foreign and Security Policy, Javier Solana, Barcelona, 15 September. Available at http://ue.eu.int/uedocs/cms_data/docs/pressdata/solana/040915CapBar.pdf (last accessed January 2007).

Wæver, O. (1996) 'European security identities', *Journal of Common Market Studies*, 34(1), 103–32.

Wæver, O. (2004) 'Discursive approaches', in A. Wiener and Th. Diez (eds), *European Integration Theory*, Oxford: Oxford University Press, pp. 197–215.

Wagner, F. P. (2001) 'From monuments to human rights: redefining heritage in the work of the Council of Europe', in *Forward Planning: The Function of Cultural Heritage in a Changing Europe* (CC-PAT, 16), Strasbourg: Council of Europe, pp. 9–27. URL= http://www.coe.int/T/E/Cultural_Co-operation/Heritage/Resources/ECC-PAT%282001%29161.pdf.

Wagner, F. P. (2002) 'Beyond "East" and "West": on the European and global dimensions of the fall of communism', in G. Preyer and M. Bös (eds), *Borderlines in a Globalized World: New Perspectives in a Sociology of the World-System*, Dordrecht: Kluwer Academic, pp. 189–215.

Youngs, R. (2004) 'Normative dynamics and strategic interests in the EU's external identity', *Journal of Common Market Studies*, 42(2), 415–35.

CHAPTER 14

Figures of the Cosmopolitan: Privileged Nationals and National Outsiders

Eleonore Kofman

Cosmopolitanism has been revived during a period of seemingly greater possibilities for bridging worldwide differences following the demise of a bipolar world, the promise of more open and collaborative international initiatives, and the extension, deepening and intensification of economic and cultural globalization. A survey of the burgeoning literature shows that two broad strands of thought engage with cosmopolitanism. The first emanates from a socio-cultural and aesthetic understanding of the cosmopolitan figure, often associated, as we shall see, with the comfortable culture of middle-class travellers, intellectuals and business people. The present period is singular in the global freedom of movement, which facilitates the capacity to engage with cultural multiplicity and presents new ways of belonging, forms of identity and citizenship (Vertovec and Cohen 2002). One may be both at home and anywhere else, if not virtually, then within short periods of time.

The second, political strand has worked with the fissures and pressures of the state system, through arguments that contemporary problems require solutions at a political level that transcends states. A new global democratic order needs to complement the existing internationalism of states. Historically, the proponents of cosmopolitan democracy trace their lineage to the Stoics and especially the Kantian legacy of perpetual peace (Archibugi 2003; Archibugi and Held 1995). Some, however, have critiqued the possibility of an effective cosmopolitan citizenship (Arendt 1967; Bowden 2003) guaranteed by a human rights regime. Others (Calhoun 2003; Tarrow 2001) have counselled against downplaying the continuing salience of local solidarities and communitarian approaches in underpinning cosmopolitan democracies. They argue that cosmopolitanism needs an account of social solidarity and a 'thicker' conception of social life, commitment and belonging. Cosmopolitanism tends to dismiss the nation and, for the most part, to model political life on a fairly abstract liberal notion of the person as a bearer of rights and obligations (Calhoun 2003).

In bringing together the cultural and political strands (Scheffler 1999), we might note the often unexamined assumption (Favell 2004; Kennedy 2004) that the mobile individual has a disposition or proclivity to universalizing political thinking and activism.

As this very brief overview indicates, the current debates are wide-ranging and overlapping. My own intervention seeks to raise questions about the socio-cultural and aesthetic understandings of the cosmopolitan and to suggest that there is a darker dimension, which is too easily forgotten in the celebratory figures of the cosmopolitan based on unfettered movement and consumption of places. What I want to suggest in this chapter is that, although mobility and cross-border flows quintessentially define the *Zeitgeist* of the present epoch and are said to constitute the driving forces of our contemporary economy and society, mobility and multiple attachments can signify both positive and negative attributes, celebrated for some, demonized for others. Mobility also needs to be situated against and conjoined with notions of fixity and rootedness, from which it is too frequently divorced. This is the subject of the first section. In the second I examine a more ambiguous, if not hostile, attitude towards cosmopolitanism in earlier epochs, when populations were also on the move, especially in the urban centres of European empires and colonies. I suggest that, in the present period, an often unacknowledged ambiguity continues towards cosmopolitan dispositions, and especially against Muslims, in part reflecting the contradictions and tensions between national belonging and processes of globalization.

Cosmopolitan dispositions: detachment and mobility

In contemporary European social and political thought, cosmopolitanism is frequently closely linked with the cultural citizen, 'the modern person who is able to exercise rights and who conceives him or herself as the consumer of other cultures and places' (Urry 1995: 165). The cultural citizen is open to the variety of global cultures and can participate equally at all levels of society, from the local to the global. From a secure vantage point, the privileged national and entitled subject, bearing a valued passport from a member state of the Organization for Economic Cooperation and Development, moves freely and unfettered in space. And wherever cosmopolitans venture, they are at home. Being at home and not 'out of place', difference does not faze them; they are open to it. Although this may be true where cosmopolitans create a home and lifestyle similar to those left behind, it is not at all clear how they actually confront difference. It may be that they are indifferent to difference, where difference itself seems to have been flattened out through globalization (Simonsen 2004). Intellectual and business discourses privilege the transcending of local and national particularities and the possibility of embracing a multiplicity of identities.

Networks, flows and fluidity of goods and people have replaced the traditional bourgeois attachment to fixity, whether it be in the home or the nation (Skeggs 2004). Hence many social and cultural theorists celebrate mobility as the hallmark of the cultural citizen (for critiques see Favell 2003; Ray 2002). For some, mobilities as metaphors and processes should be at the heart of a reconstituted sociology (Urry 2000: 210), which focuses upon movement and contingent ordering, rather than upon stasis, structure and social order. The new sociology should investigate the uneven reach of diverse networks and flows as they move within and across societal borders, and of how they spatially and temporally interconnect.

It is not, of course, surprising that mobility, which encompasses a diversity of circulations, should be so central to the contemporary epoch. After all, globalization is frequently defined in terms of acceleration, time–space compression (Harvey 1989) and the withering of borders. The world of neo-liberal capitalism has given rise to trans-national functionaries of global capitalism. This class, with its globe trotting habitus, may be limited to a select group of specialists and professionals who work outside the 'cultures of the nation state'. Elites, as the vanguards of the new information economy and knowledge society (Castells 1996) and untrammelled by borders, treat the world as their oyster. Unlike the majority of the world's population, their lives are supposedly delocalized, denationalized, and deterritorialized;[1] they are the culturally detached new cosmopolitans (Stevenson 2002).

Privileged and urbane nationals generally have a secure home to return to, whether they be sojourning for work or education, or travelling and consuming cultures. This celebratory writing has certainly been criticized. Some have pointed out that to be in a position to claim to be a global citizen is a privilege that is reserved for the modern, affluent global bourgeoisie (Bowden 2003); it is the privilege of those who can take a secure nation state for granted. More specifically, the figure of the cosmopolitan has been critiqued for its emphasis on the 'frequent traveller' trope (Calhoun 2003), the failure to recognize everyday sociality and networks (Favell 2003, 2004; Kennedy 2004) or the ordinary cosmopolitanism of working-class (Lamont and Aksartova 2002) and migrant groups (Vertovec and Cohen 2002; Werbner 1999).

What these studies share, however, is attention to the everyday lives of migrants, and this enables one to dig beneath the globalization rhetoric and to transcend the facile dichotomy between provincial locals and sophisticated worldly

1 So much of the globalization literature confuses and conflates a number of distinct processes, and in particular trans-border or trans-national movements with not having any location or living virtually. It is the truly exceptional person who lives nowhere and without territoriality.

cosmopolitans. Closer scrutiny and more attention to everyday lives yield a different account of an individual's cyber or supposedly deterritorialized existence. For those who stay at home, such as the high-technology workers in Cambridge (UK), their mobile working lives and use of global communications are premised on a settled location (Massey 1991). Ethnographic research on expatriates (Hardill and MacDonald 1998) and trans-national business elites has similarly shown (Beaverstock 2002) that they have a home, underpinned by traditional gender relations of trailing wives, and/or they rely on the global redistribution of social reproduction (Agustin 2003; Parrenas 2001) provided by migrant labour.

For those who move, the local, national and global intersect and intertwine. Paul Kennedy (2004) has investigated the friendship networks of trans-national professionals (British and non-British) in building design. Their networks were largely multinational in composition and consisted of clusters of individuals known to each other, or were based on cohabitation or marriage. He asked to what extent their investment in work may have made it more difficult for them to devote time and effort to their local civil society or to participate in global social movements. Few had engaged seriously with their new national culture(s) and societies or developed a consciousness of world problems, as their mobility might suggest (Tomlinson 1999). This finding complements Sidney Tarrow's (2001) conclusion that it is more likely to be those rooted in domestic social networks and cultural frames who are able to engage in wider social transactions and therefore constitute actual cosmopolitans. And that is why it might be easier to configure oneself as a concerned cosmopolitan while at home, which, as Hannerz (1990) points out, is where most cosmopolitans reside. Adrian Favell's (2003, 2004) large study of intra-European mobilities and professionals in European cities should reveal more about the barriers that mobile European residents face in participating in everyday aspects of the city, and the interaction of the national, the European and the global.

Of course, mobility and migration are not just the privilege of elites and the professional middle classes. Working-class migrants, exiles and refugees, too, act and think beyond the local. For ordinary and working-class people, cosmopolitanism is not necessarily based on an abstract universalism but is locally and nationally derived, using 'cultural repertoires of universalism that are differentially available to individuals across race and national context' (Lamont and Aksartova 2002: 2).[2] For Pollock *et al.* (2000: 582) the 'cosmopolitans of today are

---

2 The men interviewed by Lamont and Aksartova (150 in the US and France) corresponded more to the 'old stable' working class and were in fact well educated (i.e. to high-school degree) and had worked continuously in 'proper jobs' for the previous five years. The sample therefore did not cover those who had been unemployed or working in flexible and part-time employment, a growing number in both the US and France, especially among racialized minorities.

often the victims of modernity, failed by capitalism's upward mobility and bereft of those comforts and customs of national belonging'. Yet this, too, is problematic, since such a view excludes the ordinary migrant, reserving cosmopolitanism for those being forced from the Third World. In contrast, Werbner (1999) traces the multiple global pathways[3] of working- and middle-class migrants within globally stratified communities, such as South Asian communities in the UK, in which the class dimension plays an important part in forging global links, not just through work and business but also through marriage strategies. Middle-class and elite Pakistanis form a small but exclusive diaspora, which extends beyond the large cities of the world. Although patterns of movement for them may not involve return to Pakistan, they are oriented towards other members of that diaspora and its centre in Pakistan. For Ong and Nonini (1997), class and trans-national subjectivity render wider relations more complex and, as with the Pakistani group, such differences pertain both to work practices and to marriage strategies. We always need, as Jan Pieterse (1995: 57) warns us, to 'investigate the terms of mixture, the conditions of mixing and melange'. There are thus multiple modalities of cosmopolitanism and ways of combining different forms of the universal and the particular (Baban 2003).

The ability to derive the benefits of mobility and to extend one's economic, social and cultural networks is, of course, variable. It cannot be read off from a simple North/South polarization but, rather, derives from global stratifications cutting across North and South (Kofman 2004). Bauman (1998: 2) has noted insightfully that 'mobility climbs to the rank of the uppermost among the coveted values – and the freedom to move, perpetually a scarce and unequally distributed commodity, fast becomes the main stratifying factor of our late-modern or post-modern times'. Staying immobile is not an option but the effects of this are radically unequal. Some of us become fully and truly global; some are fixed in their locality (Skeggs 2004) in a world in which the global sets the rules. Being local may become a sign of social deprivation. Some choose their mobility, while others have it imposed upon them, for example displaced persons, asylum seekers and those whom economic restructuring has forced into a search for other pastures (Massey 1994). And the types of people who become mobile, too, are multiple, from the strangers, primarily asylum seekers forced to seek hospitality from states (Derrida 1997; Dikeç 2002), the trafficked and the illegal, to transients, able to circulate and dependent on new geopolitical situations, to

---

3 The emphasis on the positive connotations of 'cosmopolitan' leads many writers to replace what is actually the more neutral and less charged concept of 'trans-national' with 'cosmopolitan'. Thus, Werbner (1999: 34) concludes that 'cosmopolitanism, in other words, does not necessarily imply an absence of belonging but the possibility of belonging to more than one ethnic and cultural localism simultaneously'.

official 'contract workers' or the contemporary version of the older 'guest worker', to the skilled worker, increasingly welcomed into many First World states.

What has clearly emerged since the late 1990s is that states are increasingly differentiating between those who are economically useful and performative, that is the skilled, and those who are supposedly not useful, the unskilled, who may be seen as problematic and dangerous for social order and stability. In terms of cosmopolitanism, the opening up of migratory routes has enabled the skilled and professional classes to move between countries and to create complex diasporic and familial networks, which facilitate continuing circulation and mobility, as is the case with the Chinese and Indians. There is no reason why diasporic migrants from the South could not fit Hannerz's (1990) definition of the 'true' cosmopolitan, whom he distinguishes from merely mobile people, such as trans-nationals,[4] tourists, exiles and labour migrants. His cosmopolitans exhibit a culturally open disposition and the 'willingness and the ability to engage with the cultural "Other"'. It entails an intellectual and aesthetic openness to divergent cultural experiences, a search for contrasts, rather than uniformity. It often involves the building up of competence and skill, and hence an active rather than passive engagement with other cultures. In fact, such migrants may have a greater propensity for cosmopolitanism when defined by indicators such as nationality, marriage and languages (Kaweh 2004). As individuals they may have more of the qualities which enable them to measure up to Beck's (2002) definition of cosmopolitanism as a 'dialogic imagination' of a clash of cultures and nationalities within one's own life, the *internalized* other, that is, in which the individual reflects upon, critiques and understands contradictory certainties and in which cultures are interpenetrated within an individual.[5]

On the other hand, for the less skilled, especially those from states equated with the 'axis of evil' and posing security risks, or with cultures resistant to Westernization, mobility has become far more difficult. Restrictions of entry for the less skilled and asylum seekers are closing off possibilities for work and settlement in First World states. Even more significantly for our discussion of

---

4 Trans-nationals, who simply transfer their cultural baggage to another country, exiles and frequent travellers (usually occupational) who share 'structures of meaning carried by social networks', may be only very marginally cosmopolitan.

5 For Beck (2002: 18), cosmopolitanization 'means internal globalization from within national societies in which interconnections not only are made across borders but more fundamentally transform the quality and nature of social and political life within national societies. It is thus a methodological concept which helps overcome methodological nationalism and build a frame within which to analyse the new social conflicts, dynamics and structures of Second Modernity.... It corresponds to rival ways of life and puts the negotiation of contradictory cultural experiences in the centre of activities'. Unfortunately, it seems to be waning with the revival of national understandings and prioritization of national or Western value systems being demanded of migrants.

cosmopolitanism, increasing stigmatization and racism push such migrants and refugees back into their own communities. Werbner (1999: 28) comments that even the better-educated and sophisticated Pakistanis 'remain a transnational rather than a cosmopolitan diaspora because they live in the knowledge that they are scorned and stigmatised by the wider society'. The important point that Wernber is making is that prejudice and discrimination by dominant groups can reduce interaction and wider relations in a way that restricts cosmopolitanism as an opening towards other groups. Thus, what is interpreted positively in the privileged national is deemed to be negative and problematic in the 'national outsider' and migrant. Cosmopolitanism, then, is not simply the attribute of the liberal unfettered subject but is also shaped by power relations in particular societies at particular times, as studies of colonial cosmopolitanism highlight.

Historical configurations of the cosmopolitan

The negative figure of the cosmopolitan draws upon an ambiguous historical figure of the rootless but flexible outsider, who was nevertheless treated with suspicion and hostility. This dark side of cosmopolitanism had less to do with Christopher Lasch (1995) lambasting elites for detaching themselves from national obligations and citizenship but more with the hostility of nationals to those migrants who had multiple origins and social and territorial allegiances, and hence whose cosmopolitanism was suspect. The negative configuration cannot be equated solely with the current age of mass migration and accrued global inequalities (Castles and Miller 2003). The tension between the national and the cosmopolitan, and mobility and fixity, is not new. Migrations and mobility have not suddenly erupted; they defined colonial modernity (van der Veer 2002). The emerging world system depended on migration and settlement, and the mass migrations of the nineteenth century, both to the Americas and within Europe, outstripped contemporary migrations. And even more significant for the historical tapestry of cosmopolitanism, the populations and cultures of cities and empires depended on the mixing of populations. Cosmopolitanism was at this time often associated with migrants, refugees and outcasts of various kinds (Harvey 2000). For George Bernard Shaw the typical English bigot rails against 'Germans, Jews, Yankees ... [and] cosmopolitan riffraff'. Richard Tawney spoke of Antwerp as a cosmopolitan city, which was a refuge for those outlawed elsewhere in Europe (cited in Brennan 1997: 20).

Cosmopolitan cities were created both at the outposts of empire, especially in trading enclaves such as Shanghai or Tangiers, and at metropolitan centres, where rural, peripheral and imperial populations settled. The city as opposed to the individual was said to be cosmopolitan, in its diversity and mingling of disparate populations. Difference, otherness, fragmentation, splintering, multiplicity, heterogeneity, diversity and plurality characterized some of the colonial trading enclaves well before the emergence of 'mongrel cities', a term used by Leonie Sandercock (2003) for the new urban condition in the twenty-first century.[6] Colonial cities were collective cosmopolitan formations in which different groups and systems of meanings of cultures cohabited, mingled to varying degrees and came into conflict. Individual and collective cosmopolitan milieux coexisted. In the nineteenth century in the Ottoman Empire, the opening up of formerly closed communities created new spaces of cosmopolitanism for intellectual and business populations, while excluding the mass of the indigenous population (Zubaida 2002). Colonialism provided both the basis for a reclassification of knowledge and the impetus for the homogenization and transformation of other cultures to produce a Eurocentric cosmopolitan culture (Venn 2002).

Such historical cosmopolitanisms existed in contexts where disparate populations of clerics, intellectuals, artists and merchants were not at the helm of government (Calhoun 2003). It was especially in the interwar period that the pinnacle of colonial cosmopolitanism was achieved in Egyptian cities and in the Far East. In Shanghai the international settlement (American/British) and French concession were established in the decades after the British victory in the second opium war, in 1842. This, together with the absence of any need for passports and visas for residence, attracted disparate European, Middle Eastern and Asian populations. Just before the outbreak of the Second World and up to 1941, over 20,000 European Jews escaping Nazi persecution added to the already diverse population of the city (Wagenstein 2004).

At the same time, in the metropolitan cores, national bourgeoisies consumed products and styles drawn from diverse ethnic, exotic and geographical origins. The 'world exhibitions' in France, England and the US in the second half of the nineteenth century not only crowned national and imperial global reach and successes but attracted vast crowds to view imported exotic peoples and traditions. Hence the entrenchment of the nation state occurred simultaneously with a vast extension of international trade and the incorporation of imperial subjects. Metropolitan centres, especially Paris, attracted intellectuals, artists and students. Berlin and Vienna performed similar functions. Cosmopolitanism could be the quintessential character of the nation. Thus, cosmopolitanism and nationalism coexisted and commingled in the nineteenth century, in what

6 As Sandercock rightly notes, much of the discussion of cosmopolitan rights and citizenship has been in terms of the nation state. However, there is a distinct literature on cosmopolitanism relating to the urban experience. She defines the cosmopolis as an acceptance of connection, with respect and space for the stranger, the possibility of working together on matters of common destiny and forging new hybrid cultures and urban projects and ways of living (Sandercock 2003: 127).

Eric Kaufman (2003) called a double consciousness. Hence the French saw themselves as enlightening mankind through the 'rights of man' and their language, both of which had universal applications.

Nationalism and cosmopolitanism, however, did not always peacefully coexist. As Sharon Marcus (2001) comments, philosophers would see themselves as cosmopolitans vaunting universal values as citizens of the world, but nationalism confronted cosmopolitanism most virulently in the break-up of the old order or in times of economic and political crisis. In European states, the rise of nationalism and attempts to carve out homogeneous nations made the outsider problematic. The outsider, and those previously marginal to society and the polity, who installed themselves in metropolitan and imperial capitals, found a generally hostile or at best ambiguous welcome.

With the spatial and social opening of empires in Europe, such as the Hapsburg, minorities settled in the cities. And this coincided with their emancipation, for example of the serfs, and the acquisition of citizenship by those previously excluded, such as religious minorities. In Vienna, for example, Jewish emancipation in the mid-nineteenth century brought an influx of immigrants and an acknowledgement of those who had been living there illegally. The move of people from the land as they took up opportunities in cities was, though, seen to be destabilizing. Cultural conservatives such as Thomas Carlyle and Oswald Spengler (cited in Brennan 1997) complained about the impure culture of cities, where 'traditional values' and loss of solidarity were on the wane. Nationalists described not themselves but others, especially internal others, as cosmopolitans. Jews in particular represented rootless and unstable ubiquity; they were perceived as a corrupting element, foreign to the people and the nation. Artists and intellectuals were associated with modernity, and liberalism was seen as the culture of the Jewish bourgeoisie (Traverso 1997). They had no homeland but had connections with Jews in other countries, which they used to build commercial trans-national ties; they were therefore international and presented a problematic universal element. As a group, Jews were less than national and thus insufficiently attached to the nation and the land; on the other hand, they were more than national and hence threatened the nation's transcendent, universal status. Later, in the twentieth century, the radical solution to cosmopolitanism and modernity in Nazi Germany resulted in the extermination of the 'outsider' within the nation (Fine and Cohen 2002).

Negativity towards cosmopolitanism and its coupling with rootlessness extended beyond Central and Western Europe, to, for example, Russia. The selective movement and ascension of Jews to the city had begun in the 1860s and 1870s with the abolition of serfdom in 1861. The pogroms instigated by Alexander III in the 1880s also led to mass emigration. During the Soviet period, large-scale urban movements accompanied the programme of heavy industrialization and led to the introduction of an internal passport system in 1932. Citing Buck-Morss, Humphrey (undated) notes that 'Stalinist culture abhorred uprootedness. Cosmopolitanism became synonymous with betraying the motherland.' In Soviet ideology minorities should have assimilated and, indeed, by the end of the Stalinist era many had adopted Russian language and culture. So while it espoused a policy of internationalism, that is between states, the term *kozmopolitizm* became a poisonous accusation (Humphrey undated). It implied superiority and breadth of culture, as in its Enlightenment sense, and was used against people whose rootlessness could be attributed to themselves (rather than their having been compulsorily uprooted). It also implied contact with other people and the possibility of moving between spheres and places. Only certain groups were attacked – primarily Jews but also Armenians, Poles and Greeks and those of mixed European ancestry. In colloquial speech 'rootless cosmopolitanism' became mainly associated with the Jews. Readers were informed that there was no social basis for cosmopolitanism, which was merely a legacy of pre-revolutionary capitalism and which amounted to admiring everything European and denigrating everything Russian (Humphrey undated, citing Zemtsov 1991). Mass arrests of prominent Jewish intellectuals and the suppression of Jewish culture began in 1948 under the banners of campaigns on 'rootless cosmopolitans' and anti-Zionism. The so-called 'doctors' plot' in 1953 was fabricated in an attempt to target corrupt Jewish bourgeois nationalists in a deliberately anti-Semitic policy, eschewing the usual code worlds like 'cosmopolitans'. Only Stalin's death prevented further waves of arrests and executions.

It might be argued that such hostility to external influences belongs to the past and to an ethnically divided and closed bipolar Europe, and that negative attitudes to cross-border networks have no meaning or place in an economically and culturally open and globalized world. However, the refrain of many far-right parties in recent decades has been similar to that of the past. They, too, have excluded from the national imaginary groups deemed not to belong to European cultures. The National Front in France has argued that Europeanness is derived from existing territorial attachments, more deeply and emotionally anchored in *patrie*, its rootedness and closeness to the land, and which alone confers membership of the common European home (Kofman 1997; Traverso 1997). In addition, groups such as the Roma, with their non-conforming mobilities and non-sedentary circulations, have also been excluded from national imaginaries and spaces (Kofman 1995; Sibley 1995).

One might want to counterbalance these closed attitudes with the vast scholarly writing on the virtues of diasporic and trans-national exchanges generated by migrants and the ways these have affected and disrupted national, ethnic and gender identities (Anthias 1998; Vertovec and Cohen 1999). Yet an analysis of recent political and policy discourses on migration and multicultural policies demonstrates a renewed questioning of who is capable and worthy of belonging to a national community and under what conditions, especially in the light of bombings and violence in the US (2001), the UK (2005) and France (2005). Issues of loyalty and allegiance have been placed more prominently on the social and political agenda. Today, desirous of benefiting from economic globalization, state policy seeks at the same time to control and orient cultural composition and reproduction (Home Office 2002). And at the same time, making higher immigration levels acceptable to the indigenous population means that multiculturalism as a normative principle must be scaled back (Joppke 2004: 252). Cultural diversity is beneficial as a commodity to the extent that it promotes economic growth.

In many European states, neo-assimilationist agendas have been revived through new social contracts between the state and migrants. Migrants are required to fulfil obligations, to demonstrate not only language competence but also a sense of commitment and belonging to the national society and even, in some cases, exclusive allegiance. This may apply not just to citizens but also to long-term residents. Migrants are often depicted as threats to national harmony and peace, and responsible for problems of unemployment, criminality and insecurity. There is a sense that they are disturbing a pre-existing national consensus and culture. Such demands for conformity to an unchanging and homogeneous cultural norm have probably been pushed furthest in Denmark. We hear echoes of the British rhetoric of the 1970s of the 'swamping' of the settled population by newcomers. A conservative Danish politician expounded the following view:

> Denmark is a country that is built around one people.... Danish Christianity, history, culture, view on democracy and our thoughts about freedom must continue to be the foundation that Denmark rests on.... We don't want a Denmark where the Danish become a temporary ethnic minority and where our freedom is pulled away. (Wirten 2002)

When a right-wing government took office in Denmark in 2002, it proceeded to promulgate a law that would restrict family reunification, primarily from two Muslim countries (Turkey and Morocco), to individuals aged over twenty-four years. In addition, those bringing in members of their family had to show they had more attachment or allegiance to Denmark than to their country of origin. Thus trans-national practices, let alone cosmopolitanism, had to conform to Danish specifications. In the Netherlands, similarly, the old multicultural policy was seen to be problematic because people did not feel attached to Dutch culture and society (Joppke 2004). Hence a new programme of civic integration requires ethnic minorities and new migrants to opt for Dutch society. In France, too, integration has been closely equated with loyalty to Republican values (Jospin 2002), especially the separation of church and state, which Muslims are presented as undermining.

Pressures to demonstrate loyalty are not new. Norman Tebbit, a former Conservative British minister, had argued in April 1990 that immigrants' loyalty needed to be demonstrated by support for the English cricket team rather than that of their country of origin (Carvel 2004). At that time, the sport that the UK had exported to its colonies was faring badly domestically. The mother country was being beaten at the game by its former colonies, especially the West Indies. After the terrorist attacks on the US of 11 September 2001, the loyalty debate took on a new momentum (Werbner 2002), directed particularly at Muslims.[7] One media commentator noted that 'Britain's Muslims resent being cast as a band of outsiders'.[8]

Others have noted that anti-Muslim racism now seems to be replacing anti-Semitism as the principal Western expression of bigotry (Dalrymple 2004). In the UK, the focus on Muslims was due not only to the events of 11 September but also to disturbances in the summer of 2001 in three northern English cities with large Muslim populations (Bradford, Burnley and Oldham). David Blunkett, the Home Secretary at the time, was to announce on the eve of the publication of the Cantle report on those disturbances, 'We have norms of acceptability and those who come into our home – for that is what it is – should accept these norms' (cited by Sandercock 2003: 91). As he stated in the white paper (Home Office 2002: 27), newcomers would have to 'develop a sense of belonging, an identity and shared mutual understanding which can be passed from one generation to another'. The Cantle report (Home Office 2001) identified the problems as: the lack of a strong civic identity; the lack of shared social values that could unite diverse communities; the fragmentation and polarization of those communities; excessive segregation; and the disengagement of young people. It also noted problematic practices, such as arranged marriages, especially where these involved bringing in partners from countries of origin. In the popular press Muslim communities were depicted as fanatical and a kind of fifth column. The dark side of diasporas – persecution and exclusion – have returned in force (Werbner 2002). The notion of belonging to the *ummah*, the Muslim world nation, and allegiance to Muslim law are seen as conflicting with national loyalty and the centrality of English law (Cesarani 2004).

---

7 Muslims form 2.5 per cent of the population in the UK, 3.7 per cent in Germany and 10 per cent in France.
8 Dina Shillah writing in the *San Francisco Chronicle*, 15 June 2003.

Thus, the much celebrated dispositions of the privileged national (detachment from local communities, mobility, being at home anywhere, having no fixed allegiance) are on the contrary treated with suspicion and hostility when demonstrated by minorities and migrants. Today, the fear of divided loyalties and trans-national political participation falls in particular upon Europe's Muslim populations, who must demonstrate that they are not truly cosmopolitan. In Europe the bombings in Madrid in March 2004, in London in July 2005 and the urban riots in France in October and November 2005, which have too frequently been simplistically analysed as a problem of disaffected Muslim youth (Roy 2005), focused attention on Muslim populations and their supposed inability to integrate and demonstrate loyalty to national values. As with Jews in the past, they are both insufficiently national and excessively international.

Conclusion

Drawing attention to the historical and contemporary negativities surrounding cosmopolitanism should lead us to question the all too prevalent celebratory tone reserved for the term. The right to develop a cultural cosmopolitan sensibility based on mobility, multiple identities and contact with other places enjoyed by the privileged national is certainly not universal. Many nationals themselves do not have the economic resources and cultural capital to pursue a cosmopolitan disposition, and in any case such a disposition may not translate into a cosmopolitan political vision.

It is not just the fact that cultural cosmopolitanism is not uniformly enjoyed but that, for some, cosmopolitanism may actually be denied. The economic insecurity generated by contemporary globalization and welfare restructuring as well as geopolitical conflicts and terrorist attacks have led to increasing demands for security and fixity against external and internal threats. The state is supposed to ensure that the nation be a safe haven, in the same way that a home is supposed to be. As the protector of the nation, the state has the right and the duty to keep out alien elements that may disturb and threaten its wellbeing. Only those guests willing to accept the conditions laid down by the host state are allowed to enter for more than a short period. Discussion increasingly focuses on the degree of diversity and multiple identities which a nation as a community can incorporate and manage if its sense of integrity is not to be disturbed and threatened. Allowing too much diversity therefore becomes a risk for the security of the nation.

Historically, as I have outlined, the tensions between cosmopolitanism and nationalism emerged at times of rapid population movements and socio-economic and political transformations. Bringing the outsider into the nation meant that the cosmopolitan, as a bearer of non-national practices and values, was depicted as a threat to its stability and homogeneity. Today, national outsiders, and especially those whose lives are actually trans-nationally grounded, must justify their multiple links and contacts. Suspicion of worldwide affiliations and support falls heavily on Muslim populations, now emblematic of the national outsider and increasingly accused of disloyalty to the state. Their worldwide contacts with and support for co-religionists undermine an unquestioning and singular loyalty.

One of the responses to problematically perceived universality and fluidity is to nationalize practices and institutions such as religion. Thus Nicolas Sarkozy, at the time the French minister of the interior, finally established in 2003 a French Council of Muslims (Conseil Français du Culte Musulman), which institutional-ized Islam and nationalized it into the French system of the separation of church and state. So, too, has it become much more difficult in many European states to import foreign-born and foreign-trained religious leaders. At the same time, attention is focused on the international aspect of practices that are portrayed as being inimical to prevailing national norms. Hence it is the importation of foreign spouses that prevails in the critique of arranged marriages, rather the nature of the marriage itself. What is most important is that the partnership is contained within national borders, rather than transcending it. Too often, legislation is justified on the basis of stereotypes of migrant groups, denying them any diversity. Thus the Muslim population is treated as if it were homogeneous, and stripped of national and class differences. Generalizations are derived from extreme practices. For example in the British case, it is Muslim women who come to represent the vulnerable migrant woman in general, a woman who is unable to speak English (Phillips in Blunkett *et al.* 2003) and is trapped within her patriarchal community (Yuval-Davis *et al.* 2005).

Unlike the long-standing national, those of more recent, migrant origin are called upon to proclaim their allegiance and their acceptance of the imagined community (Fortier 2005). In the UK, citizenship ceremonies were introduced in 2004 and citizenship tests in November 2005. In part this reflects an acknowl-edgement of the UK becoming a society of immigration, as in the traditional settler societies, and thus acquiring the symbolic accoutrements of this type of society. Just as significant an intervention in many European states has been the introduction of 'integration contracts', which lay down conditions to be fulfilled for residence, not just for those becoming citizens but also those wishing to settle. Citizenship and integration contracts indicate a shift towards migrants and ethnic minorities being expected to relate to the liberal core values, such as human rights and respect for the law, to know the national language(s), to affirm undivided loyalty to the nation state and to accept the separation of state and religion.

However, one of the other lessons we can draw from historical examples are the different repertoires and pathways of being simultaneously cosmopolitan, national and local. In the past, and especially in colonial and imperial formations, different degrees of individual and group cosmopolitanism coexisted within cities, which themselves constituted cosmopolitan collectivities. Insights into the functioning of these cosmopolitan dispositions and practices require an understanding both of the economic, social and political resources that enable individuals and groups to transcend particularistic boundaries, to interact with others who are different, and of the wider context within which cosmopolitan links are forged. This is an area in which there is much scope for further research. So, too, does the relationship between cultural and political cosmopolitanism warrant more attention. As more grounded studies have shown, cosmopolitanism often begins at home and in the locality. On the other hand, those who are on the move may find that the lack both of a dense network of contacts and of local embeddedness prevents them from actively engaging in more cosmopolitan political projects. Too much of the celebratory writing on cosmopolitanism is not substantiated by empirical evidence and is more concerned with generating a new orthodoxy of theorizing social life based on the entitled and privileged subject, who enjoys unfettered movement, who effortlessly consumes different cultures and places, and who is free to proclaim multiple identities.

References

Agustin, L. (2003) 'Sex, gender and migrations. Facing up to ambiguous realities', *Soundings*, 23, 84–98.

Anthias, F. (1998) 'Diasporas: beyond ethnicities?', *Sociology*, 32(3), 557–80.

Archibugi, D. (2003) *Debating Cosmopolitics*, London: Verso.

Archibugi, D. and Held, D. (eds) (1995) *Cosmopolitan Democracy: An Agenda for a New World Order*, Cambridge: Polity Press.

Arendt, H. (1967) *The Origins of Totalitarianism*, London: George Allen and Unwin.

Baban, F. (2003) 'Cosmopolitanism, modernity and political community', TIPEC working paper number 03/8, Peterborough, Ontario: Trent University, Trent International Political Economy Centre. Available at http://www.trentu.ca/org/tipec/3baban8.pdf (last accessed January 2007).

Bauman, Z. (1998) *Globalization: The Human Consequences*, Cambridge: Polity Press.

Beaverstock, J. (2002) 'Transnational elites in global cities: British expatriates in Singapore's financial district', *Geoforum*, 33(4), 525–38.

Beck, U. (2002) 'The cosmopolitan society and its enemies', *Theory, Culture and Society*, 19 (1–2), 17–44.

Blunkett, D., Rowthorn, B., Phillips, T. and Page, B. (2003) 'Managing Britain's people flow', *Open Democracy*, 23 October. Available at http://www.opendemocracy.net/debates/article.jsp?id=10&debateId=96&articleId=1554#15 (last accessed January 2007).

Bowden, B. (2003) 'The perils of global citizenship', *Citizenship Studies*, 7(3), 349–63.

Brennan, T. (1997) *At Home in the World: Cosmopolitanism Now*, Cambridge, MA: Harvard University Press.

Calhoun, C. (2003) 'The class consciousness of frequent travellers: towards a critique of actually existing cosmopolitanisms', in D. Archibugi (ed.), *Debating Cosmopolitics*, London: Verso, pp. 86–116.

Carvel, J. (2004) 'Tebbit's cricket test loyalty test hit for six', *The Guardian*, 8 June.

Castells, M. (1996) *The Rise of the Network Society*, Oxford: Blackwell.

Castles, S. and Miller, M. (2003) *Age of Migration* (3rd edition), London: Palgrave.

Cesarani, D. (2004) 'What the Muslims can learn from the Jew', *Times Higher Education Supplement*, 3 September, pp. 20–21.

Dalrymple, W. (2004) 'Islamophobia', *New Statesman*, 19 January.

Derrida, J. (1997) *De l'hospitalité: Anne Durfourmantelle invite Jacuqes Derrida à répondre*, Paris: Calmann-Lévy.

Dikeç, M. (2002) 'Pera peras poros. Longings for spaces of hospitality', *Theory, Culture and Society*, 19 (1–2), 227–47.

Favell, A. (2001) 'Migration, mobility and globaloney: metaphors and rhetoric in the sociology of globalisation', *Global Networks*, 1(4), 389–98.

Favell, A. (2003) 'Eurostars and Eurocities: towards a sociology of free moving professionals in Western Europe', Center for Comparative Immigration Studies, University of California–San Diego, working paper number 71. Available at http://www.ccis-ucsd. org/PUBLICATIONS/wrkg71.pdf (last accessed January 2007).

Favell, A. (2004) 'Eurostars and Eurocities: free moving professionals and the promise of European integration', *European Studies Newsletter*, 33(3/4), 1–11.

Fine, R. and Cohen, R. (2002) 'Four cosmopolitan moments', in S. Vertovec and R. Cohen (eds), *Conceiving Cosmopolitanism: Theory, Context and Practice*, Oxford: Oxford University Press, pp. 137–62.

Fortier, A-M. (2005) 'Pride politics and multicultural citizenship', *Ethnic and Racial Studies*, 28(3), 559–78.

Hannerz, U. (1990) 'Cosmopolitans and local in world culture', in M. Featherstone (ed.), *Global Culture: Nationalism, Globalization and Modernity*, London: Sage, pp. 237–52.

Hardill, I. and MacDonald, S. (1998) 'Choosing to relocate: an examination of the impact of expatriate work in dual-career households', *Women's Studies International Forum*, 21(1), 21–29.

Harvey, D. (1989) *Condition of Postmodernity*, Oxford: Blackwell.

Harvey, D. (2000) 'Cosmopolitanism and the banality of geographical evils', *Public Culture*, 12(2), pp. 529–64.

Home Office (2001) *Community Cohesion* (Cantle report), London: Her Majesty's Stationery Office.

Home Office (2002) *Secure Borders. Safe Haven: Integration and Diversity in a Modern Britain*, London: Her Majesty's Stationery Office.

Humphrey, C. (undated) 'Cosmopolitanism and Kozmopolitizm'. Available at http://www. innerasiaresearch.org/KOZMOPOLIT.pdf (last accessed January 2007).

Joppke, C. (2004) 'The retreat of multiculturalism in the liberal state: theory and policy', *British Journal of Sociology*, 55(2), 237–57.

Jospin, L. (2002) 'Lutter contre le 'deficit de citoyennété', interview, 5 May, *Magazine de la Médina*. Available at http://www.sezamemag.net/Lionel-Jospin-lutter-contre-le-8220;deficit-de-citoyennete-8221;-8230;_a53.html (last accessed January 2007).

Kaufman, E. (2003) 'The rise of cosmopolitanism in the twentieth century West: a comparative historical perspective in the United States and European Union', *Global Society*, 17(4), 359–83.

Kaweh, R. (2004) 'Living cosmopolitanism: exploring definitions of cosmopolitan individuals', presented to the conference 'Cosmopolitanism and Europe', Royal Holloway, 22–23 April.

Kennedy, P. (2004) 'Informal sociality, cosmopolitanism and gender among transnational professionals: unravelling some of the linkages between the global economy and civil society', *Global Networks*, 4(2), 157.

Kofman, E. (1995) 'Citizenship for some but not for others: spaces of citizenship in contemporary Europe', *Political Geography*, 14(2), 121–37.

Kofman, E. (1997) 'When society was simple: the far and new right on gender and ethnic divisions in France', in N. Charles and H. Hintjens (eds), *Gender, Ethnicity and Political Ideologies*, London: Routledge, pp. 91–106.

Kofman, E. (2004) 'Gendered global migrations: diversity and stratification', *International Feminist Journal of Politics*, 6(4), 642–64.

Lamont, M. and Aksartova, S. (2002) 'Ordinary cosmopolitanisms. Strategies for bridging racial boundaries among working-class men', *Theory, Culture and Society*, 19(4), 1–25.

Lasch, C. (1995) *The Revolt of the Elites and the Betrayal of Democracy*, New York: W. W. Norton.

Marcus, S. (2001) 'Anne Frank and Hannah Arendt, universalism and pathos', in V. Dharwadker (ed.), *Cosmopolitan Geographies: New Locations in Literature and Culture*, New York: Routledge, pp. 89–132.

Massey, D. (1991) 'Flexible sexism', *Environment and Planning D: Society and Space*, 9(1), 270–81.

Massey, D. (1994) *Space, Place and Gender*, Cambridge: Polity Press.

Ong, A. and Nonini, D. (1997) *Underground Empires: The Cultural Politics of Modern Chinese Transnationalism*, London: Routledge.

Parrenas, R. (2001) *Servants of Globalization*, Chicago, IL: University of Chicago Press.

Pieterse, J. N. (1995) 'Globalisation as hybridisation', in M. Featherstone, S. Lash and R. Robertson (eds), *Global Modernities*, London: Sage, pp. 45–68.

Pollock, S., Bhabha, H. K., Breckenridge, C. A. and Chakrabarty, D. (2000) 'Cosmopolitanisms', in C. A. Breckenridge, S. Pollock, H. K. Bhabha and D. Chakrabarty (eds), *Cosmopolitanism*, Durham, NC: Duke University Press, pp. 577–90 (special issue of *Public Culture*, 12(3)).

Ray, L. (2002) 'Crossing borders? Sociology, globalization and immobility', *Sociological Research Online*, 7(3). Available at http://www.socresonline.org.uk/7/3/ray.html (last accessed January 2007).

Roy, O. (2005) 'The nature of the French riots'. Available at http://riotsfrance.ssrc.org/Roy/ (last accessed January 2007).

Sandercock, L. (2003) *Cosmopolis II. Mongrel Cities in the 21st Century*, London: Continuum.

Scheffler, S. (1999) 'Conceptions of cosmopolitanism', *Utilitas*, 11(3), 255–76.

Sibley, D. (1995) *Geographies of Exclusion: Society and Difference in the West*, London: Routledge.

Simonsen, K. (2004) 'Networks, flows and fluids – reimagining spatial analysis?', *Environment and Planning A*, 36(8), 1333–37.

Skeggs, B. (2004) *Class, Culture, Self*, London: Routledge.

Stevenson, N. (2002) 'Cosmopolitanism, multiculturalism and citizenship', *Sociological Research Online*, 7(1). Available at http://www.socresonline.org.uk/7/1/stevenson.html (last accessed January 2007).

Tarrow, S. (2001) 'Rooted cosmopolitans and transnational activists'. Available at http://falcon.arts.cornell.edu/Govt/faculty/Tarrow%20docs/rooted%20cosmopolitans.pdf (last accessed January 2007).

Tomlinson, J. (1999) *Globalization and Culture*, Cambridge: Polity Press.

Traverso, E. (1997) 'Antisemitisme comme code culturel', in *Pour une critique de la barbarie moderne. Ecrits sur l'histoire des juifs et de l'antisemitisme* (revised edition), Paris: Editions Page.

Urry, J. (1995) *Consuming Places*, London: Routledge.

Urry, J. (2000) *Sociology Beyond Societies*, London: Routledge.

van der Veer, P. (2002) 'Colonial cosmopolitanism', in S. Vertovec and R. Cohen (eds), *Conceiving Cosmopolitanism: Theory, Context and Practice*, Oxford: Oxford University Press.

Venn, C. (2002) 'Altered states: post-Enlightenment cosmopolitanism and transmodern socialities', *Theory, Culture and Society*, 19(1–2), 65–80.

Vertovec, S. and Cohen, R. (eds) (1999) *Migration, Diasporas and Transnationalism*, Aldershot: Edward Elgar.

Vertovec, S. and Cohen, R. (eds) (2002) *Conceiving Cosmopolitanism: Theory, Context and Practice*, Oxford: Oxford University Press.

Wagenstein, A. (2004) *Adieu Shanghai*, Paris: L'Esprit des Peninsules.

Werbner, P. (1999) 'Global pathways. Working class cosmopolitans and the creation of transnational ethnic worlds', *Social Anthropology*, 7(1), 17–35.

Werbner, P. (2002) 'The predicament of diaspora and millennial Islam: reflections on the aftermath of September 11'. Available at http://www.ssrc.org/sept11/essays/werbner_text_only.htm (last accessed January 2007).

Wirten, P. (2002) 'Free the nation – cosmopolitanism now!', *Eurozine*. Available at http://www.eurozine.com/articles/2002-11-22-wirten-en.html (last accessed January 2007).

Yuval-Davis, N., Anthias, F. and Kofman, E. (2005) 'Secure borders and safe haven: the gendered politics of belonging beyond social cohesion', *Ethnic and Racial Studies*, 28(3), 513–35.

Zemtsov, I. (1991) *Encyclopedia of Soviet Life*, New Brunswick: Transaction Publishers.

Zubaida, S. (2002) 'Middle Eastern experiences of cosmopolitanism', in S. Vertovec and R. Cohen (eds), *Conceiving Cosmopolitanism. Theory, Context and Practice*, Oxford: Oxford University Press, pp. 32–42.

Index

Note: page numbers in *italics* refer to information contained in tables.